MORE PRAISE FOR ED BRODOW'S
BEATING THE SUCCESS TRAP

"Brodow's diagnosis of an all-too-common personal dissatisfaction is convincing, and his prescriptions are well grounded in both basic psychology and common sense."
—*Publishers Weekly*

"A wake-up call for all of us who are chasing an empty dream of success. Brodow clearly outlines the steps to defining—and achieving—success on our own terms."
—Laura Davis, author of *I Thought We'd Never Speak Again* and *The Courage to Heal*

"Ed Brodow offers a red alert to those who are running out of time to make their lives joyful and meaningful. He makes a strong case that true success is not related to achievement, but to aliveness. If you are feeling trapped by your 401(k), read this book before it's too late!"
—Susan Page, author of *If We're So In Love, Why Aren't We Happy?*

"*Beating the Success Trap* has the one thing people are looking for in their quest for success . . . Answers!"
—Jeffrey Gitomer, author of *The Sales Bible*

"Brodow tells the hard-hitting truth about the many ways that striving for 'career success' can lead to feelings of unhappiness, dissatisfaction, and failure. I urge everyone to read, use, and benefit from his wisdom and insights!"
—Al Siebert, Ph.D., author of *The Survivor Personality*

"In a world fixated on image, expectation, and external trappings, Ed Brodow brings a rare but welcome and refreshing message: Stop. Take Stock. Define success in your own terms and get a life—the life you truly want and deserve."
—C. Leslie Charles, author of *Why Is Everyone So Cranky?*

"*Beating the Success Trap* can create a rebirth. With clarity, humor, and self-revelation, Brodow helps us steer free of the danger signals of success not by focusing our light on the siren, but on ourselves."

—Warren Farrell, Ph.D., author of *Why Men Are the Way They Are*

"What a timely, provocative message. The perfect book for anyone who agrees with Maurice Sendak's classic line, 'There must be more to life than having everything.' Author Ed Brodow shares real-life suggestions and fascinating insights to help readers have the quality of life they've always wanted . . . now, not someday."

—Sam Horn, author of *Tongue Fu!* and *What's Holding You Back?*

"At last a book that helps people understand what is really important. Brodow has written a must read for everyone who feels like they are on a fast-moving treadmill and can't seem to get off."

—Marjorie Brody, author of *Help! Was That a Career Limiting Move?*

"*Beating the Success Trap* is a MUST READ for everyone, the earlier in their career the better. It shows people how to focus on what really makes them happy and fulfilled. RUN OUT NOW and invest in Ed Brodow's book so you can start immediately to live the rest of your life in happiness."

—Dr. Anthony Alessandra, author of *The Platinum Rule*

BEATING THE SUCCESS TRAP

Also by Ed Brodow

Negotiate with Confidence

BEATING THE SUCCESS TRAP

Negotiating for the Life You Really Want and the Rewards You Deserve

Ed Brodow

HarperResource

An Imprint of HarperCollins*Publishers*

HarperCollins books may be purchased for educational, business, or sales promotional use. For information please write: Special Markets Department, HarperCollins Publishers Inc., 10 East 53rd Street, New York, NY 10022.

First HarperResource paperback published 2004

Designed by Deborah Kerner

Printed on acid-free paper

Library of Congress Cataloging-in-Publication Data has been applied for.

ISBN 0-06-000882-2
ISBN 0-06-000883-0 (pbk.)

04 05 06 07 08 ❖/RRD 10 9 8 7 6 5 4 3 2 1

CONTENTS

INTRODUCTION

While on a recent business trip to New York, I was treated to a sumptuous dinner at the Plaza Hotel by my old college buddy, Alfie Hunt, who had started his own electronics company. After dinner, my generous host and I went for a walk to enjoy the beautiful fall weather. As we stopped outside his posh Fifth Avenue penthouse, Alfie looked at me wistfully. "You know," he said, "it would be nice to be really rich."

I was startled. Alfie was worth at least thirty million dollars at the time of this conversation. Call me crazy, but that seemed like plenty of pocket change to me, so I wasn't sure how to respond. "What do you mean, Alfie," I inquired tentatively, "when you say *really* rich?"

"Oh, you know," he replied, "like Warren Buffett."

Warren Buffett is a multibillionaire, one of the five richest people on the planet. Alfie Hunt is a multimillionaire, but that isn't enough for him and never will be. No matter how much he achieves, Alfie won't feel successful.

Alfie is not an isolated case. Millions of people have struggled and sacrificed for the happiness that is supposed to come with success, only to meet with disappointment. Too often they find themselves well into their careers with their creativity stifled and their dreams unfulfilled. Outwardly, they may look like Alfie—prosperous, seemingly content, on top of the world. Inwardly, however, they feel empty and unsatisfied. As the *Wall Street Journal* observes, "A growing number of the disenchanted are asking: 'Is this all there is to life?'" This phenomenon is not limited to those with graying hair. Many younger people feel they "bought into a dream, but the dream didn't give them what they thought," says Reverend Greg Cootsona of the Fifth Avenue Presbyterian Church in New York. Even movie stars are not exempt. "I thought that when I became a success, something would change," confessed Jamie Lee Curtis on a TV talk show. The star of *A Fish Called Wanda* and *True Lies* added, "Well, I made it, but nothing changed!" So if conventional success is not the Holy Grail, then what is?

In this culture, success means acquiring riches, fame, status, and power: money to buy, or have the option to buy, the most luxurious material trappings; mention on the evening news; recognition in one's chosen field; the ability to exercise power over others. These symbols of success are supposed to guarantee happiness and contentment. Instead, our narrow definition of success has trapped millions of unsuspecting people in lifestyles that do not satisfy their real needs and cravings. They have acquired the symbols of success, but rather than feeling successful they are burnt out and disillusioned. "The trouble with the rat race," observes Lily Tomlin, "is that even if you win, you're still a rat." The solution is to quit the race and focus your energy on leading the kind of lifestyle that reflects your needs. It is the quality of your life, not the size of your bank account, that ought to determine whether or not you have made it.

Each of us deserves the privilege of creating our own definition of success that is based on our personal values, not on those we have been brainwashed to accept. This book affirms that it is possible for you to be a success on your own terms, not only functioning as a part of society but actually making a greater contribution to that society as a direct result of having paid attention to your individual needs. Success and individuality are connected. Termites don't succeed, people do. You will feel successful in direct proportion to how much your life is in alignment with who you really are. To be truly successful is to be able to say, "I spend my time doing what is meaningful to me."

The proof that this is not just an American issue but a universal one is found in the reactions to Arthur Miller's *Death of a Salesman*, which has fascinated people all over the world since Miller wrote it back in the 1940s. Willy Loman, the play's tragic hero, spends his entire life trying to measure up to society's concept of success, only to lose himself in the process. Why are international audiences—whether in Madrid, Oslo, Rome, Athens, or Tokyo—so transfixed by this quintessential American story? The answer is that there are no national boundaries on the issue of personal fulfillment in the modern postindustrial world.

Instead of offering relief, most books on success aggravate the problem by perpetuating society's myopic definition of what it means to "make it." Like Willy Loman, we have been brainwashed to accept the party line: fame, fortune, status, power. For some reason, I've never been able to do it. I made a decision early in my life that unless I risked doing things my own way, I would never be content. I have refused to settle for less. If something wasn't working in my life, I changed it. I have transitioned through four careers: sales executive, actor, negotiation expert/motivational speaker, and author. Each of the lifestyle choices that are discussed and encouraged throughout this book have been informed by my own experience and shared with thousands of business executives in my Negotiation Boot Camp™ and Success Seminars.

Don't get me wrong—this life of risk-taking and change hasn't been easy. For years, my friends and family thought I had lost my marbles. I admit there have been times when even I thought so. But in the end, I have no regrets. My life today is what I have carved out for myself in response to my needs and temperament and worldview. Unlike Alfie, my success is not measured in terms of money, fame, status, or power. I am a success on my own terms, which means this: My day-to-day existence brings me joy and satisfaction. I look forward to getting up in the morning. As the philosopher Joseph Campbell would have put it, I am "following my bliss."

It is with infinite sadness that I see millions of people around me for whom getting out of bed every day is pure drudgery. My purpose in writing this book is to bring the real causes of their disenchantment and deep suffering out into the open and, in so doing, to encourage readers to follow their own paths to a meaningful lifestyle. The tragic events of September 11, 2001, serve to underscore that life is a gift. This is not a dress rehearsal; you are somewhere between the first and third acts of the real play, which is entitled "Your Life." To those who were unable to finish the play, the rest of us have a responsibility to live our lives to the fullest. Are you doing that? Do any of the following statements grab you?

- *I have all this stuff, but deep down I don't feel successful.*
- *Other people seem to have more satisfying, inspiring, and adventurous lives.*
- *I am in a continual state of wanting and not getting.*
- *The world appears overwhelming and powerful while I feel small and clueless.*
- *My life is devoid of joy.*
- *My life is boring.*
- *If only I had _____, I'd feel successful.*

If any of these statements pushes your buttons, don't despair. The good news is that in today's world—where there is more personal freedom than at any time in history, where there is more mobility so that you can live wherever you want, where there is more surplus income so you can satisfy more than just your survival needs—everything you have dreamed about and hoped for is possible. This book will help you to understand why it is so difficult to live the life you really want, and it will offer concrete prescriptive advice on how to overcome the obstacles.

Part One describes how we are caught up in the success trap; it will help you to escape the trap by creating your own personal definition of success; and it will show you how to tap into your intuitive knowledge about what your life ought to be. Part Two exposes the "abuse-based thinking" that forms an invisible barrier between you and the lifestyle you would love to be living; it also prescribes a formula for replacing the abuse in your life with an affection-based support system. Part

Three explains how we often give away our power to succeed, and offers practical techniques for reclaiming that power. Part Four will show you how to visualize the lifestyle you've always wanted; how to create and implement a business plan to make that lifestyle a reality; and, finally, where to find the courage to act on your convictions.

The new paradigm for success offered in these pages has changed my life, and I hope it will change yours. I believe that if we view success as an individual decision, not as a conditioned reflex, we will live longer, healthier, more fulfilling lives. After reading this book, you may be lucky enough to conclude that the life you are already living is the life you really want to live. If, on the other hand, you are one of the millions who are not so fortunate, you will be armed with the tools to make the necessary changes.

Which brings me to one final point. I believe we must take responsibility for our behavior and the outcome of our lives. Unfortunately, in this culture we seem to be moving away from the acceptance of individual responsibility and moving toward placing the blame on external causes. One example is the idea that personal issues can be resolved by a visit to the drugstore. Instead of dealing with depression—the new epidemic of our affluent age—by attempting to understand and deal with its origins, we are encouraged by the medical establishment and the drug companies to take Prozac, Celexa, Zoloft, Paxil, and their successors. These drugs may be appropriate for some people, but for others they treat the symptoms instead of addressing the underlying causes. By swallowing a pill, we avoid dealing with the real question: *If I feel so discontented with my life, why don't I do something about it?*

ED BRODOW
MONTEREY, CALIFORNIA

BEATING THE SUCCESS TRAP

A MODERN SUCCESS FABLE

*The following is a story that has been passed down through
the national grapevine of jokes and anecdotes:*

A businessman is vacationing in a sleepy fishing village in Maine. He meets a local fisherman who is docking his small boat, which contains a few fat fish. The businessman admires the man's haul of the day and asks how long it took to catch.

"Oh, a couple of hours," is the reply.

"Why didn't you stay out longer and catch more fish?"

"Because I already have enough to feed my family."

"Well," the businessman continues, "what do you do with the rest of your time?"

"I sleep late, play with my kids, make love to my wife, walk into town every night where I have a glass of wine and play cards with my buddies."

The businessman hands him his card. "I'm a business consultant. I can help you out. You need to spend more time fishing. Then you could sell off the extra fish and buy a bigger boat with the money. With the income from the bigger boat, you could buy several more boats. If you play your cards right, eventually you could have a fleet of fishing boats and your own cannery. You could then move to New York where you would be able to oversee your growing operation."

"How long will all this take?" the fisherman asks.

"Twenty years."

"Then what?"

"Then you would go public and sell your stock for millions."

"Then what?"

"Then you would be able to retire. You could move to a small fishing village where you could afford to sleep late, fish a little, play with your kids, make love to your wife, and play cards with your buddies every night."

Part One

BRAINWASHED

Chapter 1

IF I'M SO SUCCESSFUL,
WHY AM I TAKING PROZAC?

[The law of success] says that a failure in society and in business has no right to live. Unlike the law against incest, the law of success is not administered by statute or church, but it is very nearly as powerful in its grip upon men.

ARTHUR MILLER

America is obsessed with success. Through numerous sources, the concept is imposed on us practically from birth. The educational system shames children who don't measure up and injects them with the notion that the worst label that can be pasted on them is that of *failure*. In study after study, when young people are asked what they want to be when they grow up, it is not the type of work they stress as important; the salient point for them is that whatever field they go into, they have to be successful at it.

And what do they mean by that? What is the yardstick for measuring success? More often than not it amounts to how rich and famous we are. It translates into a big house in an opulent neighborhood, a magazine-cover spouse, a couple of luxury sedans in the driveway, exotic travel cruises. How many teenagers think the image of success is a person sitting cross-legged on a mountaintop, someone with few possessions but in a magnificent state of serenity? Or a fire-fighter with a modest home in a middle-class community with a happy family and a dog? Or a single writer living in a small Manhattan apartment who loves the perks of the big city?

Webster's *New World Dictionary* confirms the conventional meaning of the word. It defines success as "the favorable outcome of an undertaking or career, or the attainment of a desired goal—especially the gaining of wealth, fame, and rank." One famous book on success is *Think and Grow Rich* by Napoleon Hill. It implies that success can only be equated with riches. Everywhere you turn, the media and the culture bombard you with this view by idolizing Bill Gates, Madonna, and Michael Jordan, and by downplaying anyone whose net worth adds up to less than seven figures. I don't buy it.

The purpose of this book is to help you evaluate whether *you* buy it. Do you know what it really means to be a success, or have you been brainwashed? If you truly want an answer, here is the question to ask yourself: "What is really important to me?" You may come up with a page full of answers to that, but if you pull them all together and distill the common factor, what you will probably arrive at is this: The one thing that is truly important to us all is *quality of life*. How do you spend your short time on this planet? My theory is that life is just one long weekend and nothing more. It isn't a decade. It isn't a year, or even a week. You're born on a Thursday afternoon, you hit some rush hour traffic trying to get out of town, you have a few good times with sun and ski, and then you die on Monday morning. How much time can you afford to lose between Thursday and Monday? What's the point of being alive if you don't make the most of your weekend?

It doesn't matter how much you earn, or how much you possess, or how many trophies you have won. Life is really about how you spend your time from day to day to day. None of us knows if we'll run out of money, but we know with absolute certainty that we will all run out of time.

Time is our most important commodity. *You sense that you are truly successful when you experience the deep satisfaction and happiness of knowing that right here, right now, you spend your time doing what is meaningful to you.* You are able to be yourself in an authentic way and go after what your *self* wants. If you have reached this point, you can declare with equanimity that you are not wasting your time.

Few people in America can look into their hearts and say that. The more money we make, the more disillusioned we seem to be. A good indicator that this is true is the rise in the number of depressed people. Depression, which is often caused by stress, is characterized by mood swings, reduced energy level, loss of appetite and sex drive, and feelings of guilt or worthlessness. The percentage of Americans experiencing serious depression at some point in their lives is believed to have increased from one percent in 1900 to more than 15 percent today. Some medical sources believe that one in five Americans, including 25 percent of women and 10 percent of men, will face some form of depression during their lifetime. A third of all cases are serious enough to justify medical intervention.

The *U.S. News & World Report* has suggested that as many as twenty-eight million Americans have taken some form of antidepressant medication. There are twenty-three different antidepressant medications currently available in the United States, including Prozac, Zoloft, Paxil, Luvox, Celexa, Effexor, Adapin, Aventyl, Wellbutrin, and Marplan. They are approved to treat a hair-raising list of disorders including major depressive episode (MDE), obsessive-compulsive disorder (OCD), panic disorder, post-traumatic stress disorder (PTSD), social phobia/social anxiety disorder, and generalized anxiety disorder (GAD). The most famous antidepressant, Prozac, has been used to treat forty million people in one hundred countries. "Prozac has catapulted depression from an embarrassing illness to a socially acceptable side-effect of increasingly stressful lifestyles," says the Internet publication *Country Doctor* (www.countrydoctor.co.uk).

In fact, according to the Harvard School of Public Health, depression is expected to be the second leading cause of death, after heart disease, in the twenty-first century. And because of job-related stress, say the folks at Harvard, we are facing an epidemic of heart attacks, strokes, ulcers, mental breakdowns, back problems, and severe gastrointestinal disorders.

What this means is that in the middle of the longest period of affluence in history, people are sick and depressed. Or they're headed in that direction. They are disillusioned by the conventional definition of success. Instead of making them feel successful, society's vision has left them alienated, unfulfilled, empty, and betrayed. People know that their general malaise not only involves the jobs they don't love, but also an array of situations—from mediocre relationships to undesirable living environments—which they fell into without really choosing and from which they can't escape. If this is a nation of happily successful people, how can this be explained?

THE SUCCESS TRAP ▼

One of the major reasons the American mood is headed in a downward spiral is what I call the "success trap." People are lured into putting all their resources—their hearts, souls, efforts, and time—into achieving a particular goal by being promised a kind of enduring happiness when they reach it, only to find themselves abjectly miserable years down the line. They work hard to accumulate all the symbols of success, but discover that they are still dealing with the same old feelings of frustration and inadequacy.

How do we get sucked into this trap? I have to admit that when you start out in life, you are outgunned and outnumbered. The culture shepherds people into standard careers before they've had a chance to taste life and decide for themselves what they want to do. Consequently, they are denied permission to explore their own routes to satisfaction through work and lifestyle. Society discourages people from exploring in a personal way the paths they truly want to follow. Instead, they are often guided down a path that is completely unsuitable to their heart's desire. They are spoon-fed a definition of success that is alien to their core being, and they are too young to understand what is happening to them. This is called *social brainwashing*.

Family Values

It all starts here. "Make sure you always have a day job." Acting out of the best of motives, parents often let their own fears get translated into what they teach their children about life: that people can't do what they really want and survive. Joseph Campbell was a professor of comparative mythology at Sarah Lawrence College and the author of many seminal works linking mythology to modern life. His ideas, popularized by his book *The Hero with a Thousand Faces* and the PBS miniseries featuring Campbell's discussions with journalist Bill Moyers, influenced a generation of thinkers. Campbell's refreshing thoughts on the meaning of success are exemplified by a compelling story he used to tell. While eating dinner in a restaurant one evening, Campbell overheard a conversation between two parents and their twelve-year-old boy. The father told the boy to drink his tomato juice. The boy refused, saying, "I don't like tomato juice." At this point, the mother joined in: "Don't tell him to do something he doesn't want to do." The father snapped back with, "He can't go through life doing what he wants to do. If he only does what he wants, he'll be dead. Look at me. I've never done a thing I wanted in my whole life!"

In a more subtle way, children pick up the generic values of the family system by recognizing and living up to what is expected of them. One important idea that is communicated is that it would be unforgivable for the children to slip down a peg on society's economic scale when they grow up. However much money your parents make, it is a foregone conclusion that what you make should exceed that amount.

Educational System

The push continues with the educational system. Schools tend to operate like personal training seminars for the business world. Teachers act as functionaries of society; either overtly or covertly, they end up espousing its ideals, promoting its values, and promulgating its definition of success. From early childhood you are driven to get good grades so you can get into a good college. Why? So you can get a high-paying job. If your grades fall a little, the threat that hangs over you is: "When you grow up, do you want to flip burgers for a living?" The old carrot-and-stick routine is widely used: "If you do well, you'll get to buy all the adult toys Mommy and Daddy have. If you don't, everyone will look down on you."

Media

Few movies or television programs show people genuinely being happy with less. Movie stars and sports stars themselves are walking advertisements for the message that you'll get all you ever wanted out of life if you make oodles of money and get your picture in the paper. Rich and famous people positively glow with success. They radiate the message: "Wouldn't you like to be like me?" These values are raised to an almost messianic level when they appear as flickering images on a huge screen in a dark movie theater.

Advertising

The whole idea behind Madison Avenue is to get you to buy more stuff, to spend more money on products, so that you too can project the American Dream. Advertising campaigns suck you in when you're young and keep you on a string your whole life if they can. Children and teenagers are particularly susceptible to their guile, their skill at convincing us that we need to spend money to have a good life. One classic example of selling the public a bill of goods is the campaign that convinced millions of American teens that they had to wear hundred-dollar sneakers. Another is the one selling them on carrying beepers so they won't miss a phone call. If you want to see cultural pressures at work promoting the importance of image, just watch teenagers in malls. Their behavior is not subtle.

Peer Pressure

Once again, this trap is especially effective with young people. As early as the ninth grade, teenagers are sent to career counselors to decide what they want to do with the rest of their lives. They are presented with a range of acceptable choices. In many high schools there is a great deal of competition over getting into the best colleges. I cringe at the recollection of the peer pressure I experienced when competing for high scores on my college boards and the Law School Admission Test. America is not alone in this. In Japan, students go through the worst Exam Hell in the world in order to get into an acceptable university. Some Japanese students commit suicide if they don't make it.

The Culture at Large

In the Industrial Age, the work ethic glorifies work for its own sake, not necessarily for the joy or satisfaction it brings. As a male, I had it drummed into me that my identity was based on the work I did; this is a common problem in our culture. It took me years to overcome this confusion. Most of my older friends still suffer from it. Even feminist Susan Faludi acknowledged this in an interview for her book, *Stiffed*: "These days every young man is supposed to be an Internet billionaire by the time he's twenty-two or he's a failure." In the past twenty years or so, women have become caught up in the same dilemma. In my grandmother's time, the source of a woman's disillusionment was being stuck in the home. Today she has the same opportunity as a man to be disillusioned and frustrated in her career.

And don't be fooled into thinking that the youth of today are any smarter than their parents. The workforce of tomorrow is following in our footsteps. According to a study reported in *The Los Angeles Times*, 270,000 college freshmen polled in the autumn of 2000 listed making money as their chief goal in life. High on the list were also status and recognition. Nobody listed finding their heart's desire or pursuing goals that were personally fulfilling but would make very little money.

▼   As a young person, you fell into the success trap because you didn't know any better. You lacked a wide enough perspective to process the input coming your way and then make a conscious decision about whether or not to go along with the program. You had no independent experience of the world and your mind was still forming. Most people go through their entire young adult years caught up in the success trap. They don't wake up to the snare until they spot their first gray hairs in the mirror. In my opinion, you are not even an adult in this culture until you reach the wise age of forty. Until then, you lack the life experience to know who you are and what you want.

THE NOOSE TIGHTENS ▼

Once you've been sucked into the trap, however, it is hard to get out. For one thing, brainwashing is very effective at hiding its existence. The conditioned mind doesn't tend to recognize that it is conditioned without some prompting. You may know that your life is a disappointment to you, but you probably think it's your own fault. You don't realize that you made the decisions you did because you were conned. You pass the problem off as your own inability to get the most out of life, or you pass it on to some incidental cause: "If only I had moved to Phoenix where they have better job opportunities." "If only I had become an orthodontist instead of an aerobics instructor."

Let's say you make it over the first obstacle: You wake up and smell the roses. Something isn't right here. What are you going to do about it? Not many people jump out of bed one morning and say, "Oh boy! I think I'll overturn everything I've done in my life up till now. Start all over. This will be fun." Change is regarded as highly stressful and not something you willingly take on. Psychologists have found that when people want to change even the tiniest habit, they encounter great resistance in themselves. Imagine the resistance you will be up against if you want to change something on a grand scale. For some people, it is excruciatingly painful just to admit they've been wrong. They cannot bear to say, "Gee, I've just wasted the last twenty-five years of my life because I made a wrong turn when I was seventeen." They cannot come to grips with the admission that they've made such a mistake. It is easier for them to justify how they've spent their lives than it is to face their errors head on and admit to them. It can take tremendous courage to do this. Of course, the culture makes it even more difficult to change because of a little trick called "golden handcuffs."

Golden handcuffs is a nickname for a trap that people don't, unfortunately, seem to mind being stuck in. Many people cannot be creative and risk even talking about a new lifestyle that would be an authentic match for them because they are so attached to the rich trappings of the lives they are in now. The way they are living may be all wrong for them, but they do love those perks. While it may be difficult to feel sorry for such individuals, they are truly deserving of our pity because they are spending their lives merely fulfilling a destiny they were never meant for, living out dreams they were brainwashed and seduced into believing in. In fact, such a dream is nothing but a silken spider web.

Not everyone wearing the golden handcuffs is rich. For many, there are simply comforts or perks attached to their present lives that they feel they cannot give up. Everyone knows people who could make lengthy lists of what they dislike about their jobs but who stay because the paychecks are satisfactory and they have their own parking spaces right under their office windows. Perhaps the next job won't pay as well and perhaps they'll have to park three blocks away. Yet how much of a sacrifice is it to give that up for work that is far more satisfying when the day is ended? We've all heard people who live on one coast complain that they wish they lived on the opposite coast. Why don't they move? It's the job market "which is so much more reliable here," or "my house is almost paid off." One of the most common complaints is "I have got to get out of this relationship." I've known people who have been with the same mate for years, and for at least half that time they have repeated this tired, hackneyed refrain. The older they get, the harder it is to make a decision because "I don't want to be alone at my age." I've even heard "I don't want to break up the CD collection." They seem not to have heard the chorus of people who find themselves unattached at age fifty or sixty and it feels like freedom. For the first time in their lives, these people feel that being single is perfectly agreeable.

Focusing on such minor reasons for refusing to opt for change is a result of not seeing the forest for the trees. The person with the expensive toys has so distracted himself that he fails to see that his overall sense of well-being is suffering. The person trapped in a lusterless relationship forgets that being with another person is supposed to bring warmth and love, not just stability. The love is gone, yet they stay anyway.

FACING THE ENEMY ▼

Let's say you've overcome even this hurdle. You have endured your dark night of the soul and come out fresh and alive in the morning. You have exposed the success trap and you've decided to take action. Now you have to face your family. Don't assume for a minute that they are going to be supportive of your newfound awareness. Their rejection, in fact, may knock you off your feet because you thought they loved you and wanted only the best for you; now it appears they are just holding you back from following your bliss. Don't despair too much. They really mean well. It's just that they are threatened by change as much as you are, and they didn't initiate this one. You did. They aren't in control. It would be so much more comfortable for them if you would just stop all this nonsense and stay the same old person to whom they are accustomed.

And if the change you are proposing involves a drop in income, you can expect a reaction that is even more charged. Just imagine how delighted your spouse and kids will be if you tell them that they have to move to a smaller house and sell off a few major appliances so you can become self-actualized.

Outright fear is often the primary factor behind their obstinacy. You are announcing that you want to alter the status quo and they feel threatened by it. "What will this mean to me? If she turns this part of her life—and mine—on its head, what else could be overturned? Think of all the things that can go wrong when you fool around with the way things are. Why mess with a good thing?" Being faced with the unknown is highly unsettling for them. For instance, you may want to pick up and move a thousand miles away, and your mother, who has never had one of her children move out of state, starts pulling her hair out: "I did not give birth to you and spend two years changing your diapers just so you could move away!"

And finally, there are your friends. The people with whom you play racquetball, have power lunches, meet down at the bowling alley on Friday night—they will act as if you've lost your mind. "You're going half-time on your job so you can take acting lessons? Are you nuts?" Once again, these people might not have malevolent intentions. They may just be frightened for you. It is inconceivable to them that this harebrained scheme of yours is going to lead to anything but disaster. Then too, it may be threatening *to them* in an entirely different way. It's possible that they too have wanted to escape the rat race for years and have been feeding themselves excuses for not doing so. The excuses let them out of having to take risks. If you take the risk and it pays off, their old excuses won't work anymore, and they will have to face up to a few truths of their own. Your friends and co-workers may end up becoming unwitting collaborators with the forces that are keeping you from being fully alive. When I quit my high-paying corporate job to become an actor, a close friend said to me, "This is just temporary insanity. You'll get over it."

THE PRICE YOU PAY ▼

Given all these obstacles, how many of us fall by the wayside and don't put up a genuine fight for our own souls? We label our malady "middle-age depression," and after that it's just business as usual.

When we do this, we pay a price. The price is burnout, disillusionment, and all too often addiction to some substance that helps numb the pain. Dr. Herbert Freudenberger, author of the book *Burn Out*, asks, "Why, with all these goals and visible rewards which we as Americans have accepted so unquestioningly, has the result been a singular lack of satisfaction?" His explanation is that we are simply burning out. According to him, a person who has burned out is "someone in a state of fatigue or frustration brought about by devotion to a cause, way of life, or relationship that failed to produce the expected reward." What he is saying, then, is that people are not at their wits' end because they work too hard or worry too much about money or care too much about their jobs. Burnout results when any of these situations exist along with *no payoff*. The great con is that we expect a payoff for all our troubles. People don't mind doing something difficult for a living if they love it. They don't mind sacrifice if there is a spiritual reward for it. They can handle trial and tribulation if the result is personal satisfaction. The problem in our society is that whatever the magic goal of all this prosperity is supposed to be, it is proving extremely elusive.

So the most affluent society in history is plagued with rampant discontent. When people are cut off from a personal connection to what they do in life, from being in alignment with who they really are, they become disenchanted, sometimes even bitter, and they end up seeking solace in drugs, alcohol, food, and sex. In extreme cases of mental anguish, they may often resort to violence.

INTOXICATED WITH SUCCESS ▼

Consider a friend of mine who I'll call Jim. He was raised in a dismal section of the Bronx. While growing up, all he could think of was keeping up with his brainy older brother who later became a physician. Jim took on responsibility early, marrying right out of college and hiring on immediately with a large conglomerate. He was able to buy a house in an affluent Connecticut suburb and support four children by working long hours. Eventually he moved up to expensive cars, fancy restaurants, the works. Even his teenagers drove BMWs. No doubt about it, Jim had reached a pinnacle.

What was wrong with this picture? The fact that Jim hated his job went largely ignored by him and everyone else. By the time I met him, Jim was having his first drink of the day before noon. Any occasion was an excuse for a drink. "It's Tuesday. Let's have a bourbon sour." He managed to get by at home and at work because he was high-functioning, and he was an entertaining drunk. Nobody could tell a joke like Jim. People liked him, so they let him get away with it. As time went on, however, his drinking took on dark overtones. One day, I noticed that his wife, Julie, was limping. I found out they'd had a fight the night before and Jim had hit her in the spine with a golf club. Good old Jim had a problem, and it was spilling over onto his entire family. Shortly after Julie's injury, their adorable five-year-old daughter began to stutter. I think the real low point for Jim was the time he was so drunk that he missed the last train home, and spent the night sleeping it off like a derelict on a bench in Grand Central Station.

Even Jim couldn't hide from his predicament forever. Eventually he was driven to go into Alcoholics Anonymous and get sober. But by then, the long hours and the spent liver had worn him out. He was never quite the same. I would see him on the commuter train looking as if the life had been drained out of him. It seemed that without the crutch of the bottle he could not maintain the facade that all was well.

He was still going through the motions, but all of the old liquor-infused enthusiasm had disappeared.

One day in a parking lot, he sadly admitted to me that the two things he had missed out on in life were becoming a stand-up comedian and taking up fly fishing. Alas, he had been too much of a "success" to get around to either one.

BREAKING AWAY AND
FOLLOWING YOUR BLISS ▼

Some people do manage to break away from the cultural consciousness. They are the ones who epitomize a personalized version of success that translates into true happiness and satisfaction. One such person was my Uncle Maury. He worked as a motion picture operator and never made a lot of money. Yet I would count him as one of the true success stories I have come across because he enjoyed his lifestyle. He had plenty of free time to go fishing, which was what he enjoyed the most. He would drive home from work, give his paycheck to my aunt, and grab his fishing gear. It was glaringly obvious to me as a boy that Uncle Maury had something special going for him that the traditionally successful members of my family lacked. While the other men were irritable and moody, Uncle Maury always had a smile on his face, an easygoing manner, and a joke to tell. At the age of eighty-five, he still walked with a noticeable bounce in his step.

Another hero of mine was a man whose name I did not even know. I met him when I was twenty-one. My buddy and I were on leave from the Quantico, Virginia, Marine Corps Base where we were stationed. As we headed to New York on the Pennsylvania Railroad, the conductor came by to check our tickets. At first sight, he was a rather ordinary-looking man, under average height but solidly built. His entire job consisted of asking passengers for their tickets and then punching holes in them. That was it. Nothing terribly complicated. Yet this plain man had an air of self-assured competence about him that captured my attention. It caused me to remark to my friend, "That conductor could be a bank president, the way he carries himself." He was not high up on the totem pole, but he was completely comfortable with his job and with himself.

Many times in the ensuing quarter of a century I have thought about that railroad conductor. For me, he was a living demonstration that success has little to do with fame and fortune. This was a man who felt himself to be successful. He judged it from the inside, not according to outside influences. "You may have a success in life," Joseph Campbell says in *The Power of Myth*, "but then just think of it—what kind of life was it? You've never done the thing you wanted to do." If you are following somebody else's plan, living by their definitions and rules, what kind of life are you having? Can you really call it your own? Are you following your bliss or going along with something you saw in a television commercial?

When you do have the feeling that you have found your bliss, Campbell urges you to "stay with it, and don't let anyone throw you off." This is where tenacity comes in. To follow your bliss you don't have to fight the system, but you do have to negotiate with it. It will place obstacles in your path, and you have to get pretty nimble at sidestepping them. If you don't, your beautiful long weekend between birth and death will be over before you know it.

CONFUSING IDENTITY AND WORK ▼

One thing that holds a lot of people back from making the changes necessary to break away from the unsatisfying lifestyle they've created is a little number called *identity*. Identity, according to Webster's *New World Dictionary*, is the "condition of being a specific thing or person; individuality."

Identity is one of those things we usually take for granted because it is like the air we breathe. We don't think about air because it is invisible and it is always there surrounding us. You will find yourself supremely aware of air, however, if you are ever cut off from it. The same is true of having an identity. We take it for granted every minute of the day. We look in the mirror and we see "me." "Me" is the object—with all its memories, associations, and history—that you take yourself to be. It's the tag you go by. It is all important. People live and die for it: "I am a Muslim. I hate Jews and I will die to prove it." What is that if not identity?

When people introduce themselves to others, primarily they are introducing their identity to the other person's identity. "Hi, I'm Madeleine. I'm a commodities broker." "I'm Tom. I'm an accountant." Unfortunately, men especially and women increasingly wed their identity to what they do in the marketplace. It plays a very large part in how we tag ourselves, and there are a multitude of associations that dictate whether that tag makes us proud of ourselves or ashamed of ourselves. The reason failure in the workplace has such a huge charge is that it affects our entire identity. If we perceive ourselves as failures professionally, for both men and women nowadays, that strikes at the foundation of our sense of worth. As Paul Terhorst, in *Cashing In on the American Dream*, observes: "The American Way often amounts to masochism rather than pleasure. When we fail at something we're told to tough it out rather than stop, reevaluate, then switch to something we're good at." In our society, we can't switch that easily. We can't simply break away from a job where we've been sleepwalking for ten years to one that lights a fire inside us. Before we can leave a job we have to find a way to do it in which we don't feel like we're going out in failure, our tail between our legs. This pressure makes it extremely difficult to change when change is necessary.

Terhorst made an interesting discovery for himself. As a consultant working for a Big Six accounting firm, he decided that the central issue was not what he *thought* he did at work but what he actually did. He posed the question, "What do I do at work all day that is so goddamn important?" When he took a good, honest look at his workday, he found that what he actually did from nine to five was talk on the telephone. Once he stripped away everything else and got down to this one essential activity, he was able to take some of the weight off his shoulders about the importance of succeeding. He could separate himself from his work and weigh other things of value in his life.

Some lip service is paid, in this country, to family values—religion, responsibility to children and community, morality, and so on. But for the most part, the American Dream embraces one value: Become a financial success. To make a free choice to leave the situation you are in, your entire personality structure—that is, all of who you take yourself to be—cannot be threatened by the idea that you will be a failure if you "step down in the world." It requires courage to take the risk of changing an entire lifestyle, but that courage must stand on a firm ground of self-confidence. You must find an identity that is based upon real substance, not on where you punch your time clock. You are made up of many more parts than your career. Your identity should reflect all of those parts: your likes and dislikes, value system, relationships, sexuality, hobbies, and so on.

THE SUCCESS TOTEM POLE ▼

In our culture, there are five positions a person can occupy on the success totem pole. These positions indicate not only how much money the person makes, but his attitude about where he is and his level of satisfaction. Success is a state of mind. If you don't *feel* successful, you're not—no matter what your income may be or how famous you are.

CATEGORY ONE · The Rich and Famous

"I'm rich and famous, and I like it!"

Donald Trump is the perfect role model for this category. He grew up in a family that lionized success, and he made his parents' values his own. It is the old-fashioned, American capitalist definition of success, and it works for him. I'm sure it has never occurred to the man to redefine his values and take a critical look at what being successful has brought him and what it has cost him. In this book, I do not place any judgment on people in this category because their hopes and aspirations are congruent with their goals. There is nothing wrong with being a business executive living in a penthouse overlooking Central Park, and being chauffeured around in a Rolls Royce. However, people who are able to find complete fulfillment through these attainments are in an increasingly dwindling group in this country.

CATEGORY TWO · The Disillusioned

"I have acquired all the conventional accoutrements of a person who has made it, but I don't feel successful."

A classic example is Elvis Presley, arguably one of the most famous and successful people of the last half of the twentieth century. By all accounts, he was also one of the most disappointed in life. He had Graceland, pink-and-gold Cadillacs, closets full of rhinestone-studded outfits, loyal and adoring fans, and then—death by overdose. He arose from poverty and built a brilliant career so he could acquire all the perks that had been denied to him as a youngster. But whatever meaning and satisfaction he had been looking for, he never found it in the lifestyle he chose. One night as he was ready to go onstage in Las Vegas, someone reportedly said to him, "You look tired." With an exhausted sigh he responded, "I'm tired of being Elvis." He had spent his entire life constructing this creature, and in the end he was stuck with it.

How many people fall into the same trap? They spend their lives constructing something they never wanted in the first place. After such a huge investment of time and money, they don't feel that they can afford to get rid of the monster. A conventional example is the person who suffered through medical school only to find that she hates the smell of hospitals. She would rather open a primitive art gallery and settle for less money. She is a successful surgeon, but she feels empty inside.

Unlike Category One, Category Two is a growing group. Look around. Millions of new people join this club every day. "Gee, I've got a swimming pool shaped like a piano, four Mercedes, and a backyard you could play professional football in, but this just isn't doing it for me."

CATEGORY THREE • The Maverick

"I haven't made it in society's eyes, but I experience my life as completely fulfilling."

Everyone's favorite example of a person in this category is Mother Teresa. There are thousands of anonymous Mother Teresas out there, people who devote their lives to the service of others but haven't won a Nobel Prize for it. People like Uncle Maury and the train conductor who find personal satisfaction in arenas not applauded by the culture. They may have few possessions and even less security. Because their values fly in the face of the traditional, materialistic values of modern industrialist societies, they need a strong sense of self to stay on track.

Unfortunately, I don't know many people who fit into Category Three. My yoga teacher does. I know some actors who do. Perhaps this is the category you belong in and you don't know it. Many people have nontraditional goals hidden inside themselves that they have never acknowledged or considered acting on. Sometimes that unrecognized side is just waiting to show itself.

CATEGORY FOUR • The Unseduced

"I have all the outer accoutrements of success, but my sense of accomplishment lies elsewhere."

A good example is Joseph Campbell. His work was so brilliant that it brought him money, respect, and fame, but the true compensation for his efforts came from his deep love of philosophy and mythic concepts. People like this have a strong internal value system that withstands the winds of outside influence and transcends the conventional ego needs of riches and adulation. Like those in Category Three, people in Category Four also need a strong sense of self, but in this case it helps them avoid being seduced by the perks of their success.

CATEGORY FIVE • The Dissatisfied

"If only I could attain everything I dream about, then I would finally feel successful."

It is a fictional character who best exemplifies this category: Willy Loman in Arthur Miller's *Death of a Salesman*. Willy's tragedy is that he misses out on every single day of his life by longing for what he will never have. His lifelong mantra starts with "If only . . ." You can fill in the rest. The "if only" picture is comprised of all those things the culture dangles in front of us that make us feel neglected and left out if we don't have them. Willy Loman never looks at what he has, only at what others have who are better off, and in his eyes the comparison always diminishes his own value. This is a sure recipe for poisoning one's life.

Category Five is another growing group in America. In the driveway, they have a perfectly good Nissan Stanza—slightly dented, yet in perfect working order—but it's not a BMW, and their least favorite in-laws have a BMW so it's eating them up inside. Like Willy, they are condemned to a life of perpetual waiting. They go to sleep at night thinking, "If only . . ."

One way of looking at Category Fives is that they are simply Category One wanna-be's. They have all the aspirations of the Rich and Famous, but they never made it.

▼ It is quite problematic to be in some of these categories, whereas in others, life is more harmonious. People in Category Three (Mavericks), for example, generally report high levels of satisfaction and happiness, even though they often spend their time in the midst of human suffering. People in Categories One (The Rich and Famous) and Four (The Unseduced) seem to be mostly satisfied with their lifestyles and content with the paths they have chosen. The most suffering occurs in Categories Two and Five—the Disillusioned and the Dissatisfied. These are the people who torment themselves because their perceptions of happiness do not match up with the lives they have created for themselves. If you want to avoid these categories, instead of taking Prozac, the solution is to re-engineer your lifestyle so that it does reflect your personal desires. But first you would do well to understand the images of success that are promulgated by our culture. The next chapter will help you to appreciate how you may have been taken in by those images.

Chapter 2

THE IMAGES OF SUCCESS

Each of us tends to think we see things as they are, that we are objective. But this is not the case. We see the world, not as it is, but as we are—or, as we are conditioned to see it.

STEPHEN COVEY

Lives of quiet desperation." What does that mean and why does it seem to apply only to the modern world when the struggle for survival is not as desperate for most people today as it has been throughout history? In other words, if life isn't that hard, what do we have to be desperate about?

More than ever, our modern middle-class-plus lifestyle has led us to the expectation of a rather constant state of happiness. And we are happy—sort of. It is a particular kind of happiness, one that's been sculpted by cultural mores and then sold to us one image at a time. Fundamentally, the sales pitch goes like this: "Make sure you look good. If you look good enough, feeling good will follow."

I call this image-based thinking. The pressure is to create the image of a life that commands respect and envy and causes others to want to emulate you. Much of our activity is directed toward this end. The promise is that if you do this, you will achieve a kind of permanent satisfaction. In advertisements, they don't tell you that the satisfaction you will receive from buying an Armani leather belt will only last a few hours, and then wear off. The suggestion is that the benefits will go on and on. Not only will you feel luxurious when you wear the belt, but it will convince others to see you as a prosperous, vital, and valuable person, and you can take their word for it that you have improved as a human being.

But it doesn't work. On a very deep level, we are missing the satisfaction that was promised. We have been handed a series of manufactured images of success and essentially been told, "Just attain this image and all your needs will be met." Ultimately, however, we must learn to distinguish the ways in which we have misled ourselves to believe that we are meeting our own needs, when in reality we are simply acting out our conditioning.

The reason we pursue these images is that they are a blind attempt to satisfy our needs and act out our values. But because the image is a false one, the pleasure that results from chasing it can only be superficial. This accounts for the millions of seemingly successful people who do not feel successful. Yet the needs themselves are entirely legitimate and should be pursued. What, then, is the answer? The answer is to sort out the real from the false, to discover what the real need is that we are pursuing and to understand what, in that image, is fooling us.

SUCCESS IMAGE NUMBER ONE: *I want to be successful.*

What the image really represents: When someone says he wants to be successful, what he really means is that he wants to feel good about himself, and, to do that, he must go after some major achievement. As long as he isn't successful, he is condemned to some form of self-loathing because his inner world is filled with disapproval and reproach. Hence, he becomes the classic overachiever—a driven, ruthless pit bull. He is compelled to do whatever is necessary to be a success because the alternative is so unacceptable. A person with high self-esteem, in contrast, is far more relaxed. Because he possesses the basic trust that he is intrinsically worthy, he does not have to do anything to gain that worth. It doesn't mean he thinks he is perfect and that's why he is worthy. He has strengths and he has weaknesses, which he acknowledges, but he is able to take himself as he is.

Aligning the image with reality: The confusion that arises from this image comes from the fact that people who appear successful according to all the outward trappings seem, for all intents and purposes, to possess an abundance of self-esteem. They flash big toothy smiles on the golf course, they are well groomed, and they kind of strut about as if they think the world of themselves. Don't let it fool you. In the absence of true self-esteem, take away the outer trappings and the person's sense of worth collapses. It was a house of cards all along. External success can never take the place of true self-esteem because the feelings of well-being depend on outward sources to prop them up. The person only likes himself for what he has done, not for what he is. The guy on the golf course with the set of gold-plated clubs may actually be lonely, dissatisfied, and depressed, and in a continual battle with himself to fight off those feelings. How does he do it? Bring in another new account or buy a new Mercedes. Ironically, the only way he can really combat those feelings is to cease his compulsive drive for success and find his intrinsic excellence. Once a person accomplishes this truly worthwhile goal, it is amazing how few of the old trappings he still needs.

SUCCESS IMAGE NUMBER TWO: *I want to be rich.*

What the image really represents: The desire to be rich often represents a deeply felt need for security and safety. Many people who are obsessed with making money fear that disaster is right around the corner. They perceive the world as an unsafe place where misfortune can fall upon them at any moment. Somewhere along the way, they formed the idea that money will protect them from destruction—or at least buy them out of it. This kind of fear is carried straight out of childhood. For a child to develop into a strong and confident adult, he needs parents who provide a certain amount of predictability, safety, tranquility, and orderliness. If, however, the early environment is hostile or chaotic, the child's entire nervous system is on edge; his defenses are on constant alert, scanning the horizon for danger. When parents are cruel, neglectful, or unfair, they foster the perception that the world is the same way. Hence their children's need for guarantees, for enough money to protect them from all the unforeseen threats lurking behind every bush.

Aligning the image with reality: When asked what he thought people really wanted to know about the universe, Albert Einstein answered that they wanted to know if it was benevolent. It appears that he believed it was. That does not mean it is a perfectly safe place. What we can come to see, though, is that it is usually *safe enough*, and that is a reality that we must, and can, live with. No amount of money can insulate us from misfortune, for many events are outside our control. What we can do is acquire the confidence in our own ability to muster our inner resources in the face of uncertainty so that we can deal with whatever occurs. The following is a very big idea, but many self-realized people have come to embrace it: The universe is unfolding exactly as it should. People who acquire this attitude have more equanimity and strength than those who try desperately to hold onto the myth that their money will somehow make them safe. And with that equanimity, they are freer to perceive and pursue the abundance that is all around them rather than fret about scarcity.

SUCCESS IMAGE NUMBER THREE: *I want to be famous.*

What the image really represents: This person really wants attention, recognition, acceptance, appreciation, admiration, and prestige. Her idealization of fame is that these prizes are all in the golden package that fame will bring her. She must have the adoring attention of others because without it she feels an empty pit inside her the size of a canyon. This canyon is a hole in her sense of self. Where there should be a sense of self, there is a feeling of emptiness instead, a feeling that seems intolerable to most people. They must cover it up. The only thing that seems to blanket it is the continual mirroring from others telling them they really are "somebody." That hackneyed old phrase, "I wanna be somebody," can be taken literally in the case of people with a wound to the sense of self. Inside, no one is there. Psychologically, all real inner growth is based on the perception of a self, and without it there is no inner worth or strength. Whatever strength this person possesses, whatever acceptance she feels for herself, comes only from other people. She, herself, is helpless and impoverished. When this person was a child, she was either ignored completely or she was "seen" only for how well she performed ("They only applauded when I tap-danced"), or she was appreciated only for how well she paid attention to her parents' needs. Her own needs went largely unacknowledged. The deeper the feeling of invisibility to oneself, the greater the need for the grandiose attention that only fame can bring.

Aligning the image with reality: Unfortunately, what most famous people find out is that no amount of attention fills such emptiness. The more they get, the more they need. They are just as attention-hungry when they are on top as when they were on the bottom. In fact, the dependency often grows, for the more the person depends on external support, the emptier she feels inside. When she is alone in her room after the applause stops, she still feels "there is no me." We cannot change the childhood that made us who we are, but we can change the inner child we have now. We can re-parent ourselves and find the inner essence that seems to have been lost so long ago. In fact, it never went away, it only went into hiding. The good news is that we live in an age when we are not stuck with our inadequate childhoods. There are therapists who can help us heal, even from the deepest wounds. The only real solution to the need to escape the merry-go-round of emptiness and dependency is to dig deep within ourselves and address the original wound. It takes courage, but it helps to remember that you're not a helpless child anymore. You are an adult with strength, wisdom, and resources.

SUCCESS IMAGE NUMBER FOUR: *I want to be powerful.*

What the image really represents: This is a person who actually feels quite helpless and has to offset the feeling with brute force, either physical or emotional. He seeks to cover up his weakness with an appearance of invulnerability. He seeks to remedy feeling paralyzed by being in absolute control. Clearly, then, acting out the need for excessive power is compensatory behavior. The telltale sign that behavior is compensatory is that there is no finish line. Whatever new tier of power the person rises to, he already has his sights set on the next tier. He is always moving on to the next battle because he cannot settle his inner fear that he is, in reality, an invalid, and that if he stops concealing it, everyone will know. Then he will feel truly vulnerable.

Aligning the image with reality: For the power-hungry adult, disappointment sets in when he discovers that exercising power over others does not really compensate for the vulnerability he experienced growing up. What he really craves is not to be impregnable or to possess superhuman strength, but simply to feel that his life is not running away with him, that he has some control over it. Often, the things he feels he has the least control over are his own emotions, impulses, and behavior. When a person doesn't call the shots in these areas, he really will feel impotent. If you are someone whose sense of powerlessness is a remnant from an abused childhood, it will help to recognize that you are not a child anymore. You may think you know that, but do you know it deep down inside yourself? The unconscious mind, where secrets and memories are locked away, is not aware of the passage of time. To that vast part of our minds, we are still children—helpless and choiceless. But now we've grown up, and now we do have the power to make our own choices. If, however, you are someone who is intoxicated by the feeling of power you have over others, you will probably not be highly motivated to face your hidden weakness. In fact, if you are using your superficial power over others expressly to avoid confronting your own vulnerability, it is your way of propping up a false sense of impregnability. The problem is that in the process of kidding yourself, you are ignoring your own real needs. Your focus is always outward—"Who can I control now?"—but needs are internal. After a while, you will go dead inside. You live in a penthouse with all this wealth and power, but you don't know who you are. If you are not living from inside yourself, you are living as a shell, and if you quietly tune in to your experience, that is exactly how you will feel—like a thin, brittle shell and nothing else.

If you are steeped in compensatory behavior of any kind, it means you are trapped into filling false needs, and that can only mean that you are ignoring your real needs. Because you aren't facing the real needs squarely, you simply cannot fill them. Clearly there can never be any sense of fulfillment in such a life. There is definitely something wrong, but you're not fixing it because you're not facing it. A person who has cancer and goes about saying, "No I don't, it's just normal aches and pains," does not take the steps he needs to cure himself. In effect, he fools himself until he dies, and he ends up being a victim of his own avoidance techniques. The comparison is an apt one because if you don't fill your emotional needs, you die in another way.

SUCCESS IMAGE NUMBER FIVE: *I want to live in my dream house.*

What the image really represents: Many people use their home as a form of inner support, a place of comfort and respite from a cold world. Their home, in effect, is like a large womb. The subconscious association is like the primal, merged state of an infant with its mother, a place where all the infant's needs will be met automatically, where she will be nurtured and loved unconditionally. It is the proverbial Garden of Eden, a state to which, secretly, we would all like to return because it was filled with comfort and bliss. For those who were fulfilled as infants and children, this desire does not take over their lives. But for anyone with cold, uncaring parents, anyone who felt utterly adrift and unloved, finding a substitute for this merged state can become a mission later in life. Without realizing what she is really after, she endlessly searches for a dream house or some other substitute because it holds the hidden promise of all those yearned-for qualities.

Aligning the image with reality: A house is a physical structure without any innate warmth or feelings. It cannot substitute for the mother we didn't have, yet desperately wanted. It can never meet those deep internal needs to be loved, protected, and accepted. If you take an honest look at the type of needs and associations you have with a dream house, you will find out what your actual expectations are from four walls and a roof. But how can a house meet these needs? Needs are internal. You cannot compensate for being out of touch with who you really are and what you really need by creating an external reality, no matter how perfect or charming it looks, no matter how elegant the architecture or how beautiful the decor. Until you can accept yourself, until you learn to find a genuine place within yourself where you feel loved, you will never feel settled or truly comforted by a home. Once you do find that inner peace, you will perceive the world in general as a more loving place. When that happens, the whole world is your dream house.

SUCCESS IMAGE NUMBER SIX: *I want a large family.*

What the image really represents: The person is seeking a sense of belonging, of human warmth, of social connection with people, all of which were probably missing in her upbringing. Perhaps she was an only child, or the people in her family were disconnected from their feelings and unable to reach out to each other. She grew up feeling isolated and without any sense of where she really belonged in life. She is not able to tolerate being alone, even for short periods; she must always be surrounded by people, and longs for a family of her own so she can find her place in the world. A person with an excessive need for social contact often reflects the fact that she feels fragmented and disconnected on the inside. Her mind is not connected with her heart or body, and she uses social contacts to keep herself feeling intact. Whenever she is alone she feels isolated, but it is because she does not have a relationship with herself. As a substitute, she is trying to have a relationship with everyone else.

Aligning the image with reality: A brood of kids running around the house will not banish genuine feelings of isolation. The noise may deflect your attention from those feelings, but they're still there. Because you haven't faced them, you do not know how to deal with what you don't like about yourself, with your insecurities, or with your perceived shortcomings. You continually use being with others as a way to avoid solitude and the dawning sense of reality that usually comes with it. Instead of having a loving, peaceful family, many in this category find themselves at odds with their loved ones, bickering constantly and feeling that they are always attending to everyone else's needs but never getting their own met. Friends of mine sought to end the fighting in their marriage by having a child, as though its presence would bond them together. It only drove them further apart because they were two people who felt fragmented and needy and were looking for someone else to patch them up. A child is not a fixer or a mediator between two people who are at war. Children have demands of their own, and this usually exacerbates the existing problems in a marriage instead of solving them. If you are trying to use others to avoid the feeling that you don't belong anywhere, it will never work. It is just another avoidance technique. You must go through a process of reconnecting with yourself, and find the courage to deal with your real issues. You cannot continue to use others as an excuse to avoid this essential task. Before you can ever really feel that you belong with other people, you have to belong to yourself. Creating a large family is no guarantee of love, warmth, and belonging. Belonging is a state of mind.

SUCCESS IMAGE NUMBER SEVEN: *I want to retire.*

What the image really represents: The individual is simply seeking the freedom to live her own life—right now. In her mind she is saying, "Life doesn't begin until I stop working. When is there ever time for me?" This person is highly cognizant of how much time she is spending in the workplace and feels it is a drain on her life's energy and creativity. She has a plan, in her head if not on paper, to do all the things that she believes would leave her more fulfilled, and it eats away at her that they must continually be put on hold. She receives stray faxes from travel agencies offering her time-shares in Hawaii, and she cannot accept. She watches people who have made savvy investments who have stopped working nine to five and can take off on adventures whenever they want. Every morning when the alarm goes off, she feels she is about to waste another day. Short of winning the lottery, the only way she can visualize beginning her "real" life is to retire early. Only then can she relax.

Aligning the image with reality: This person is looking for freedom; to her, work is the antithesis of that. Work has such a negative connotation for her that it is held up as the one thing depriving her of freedom, relaxation, and ease. Instead, it is consigning her to a life of drudgery. This is an excellent example of how fantasy conflicts with reality. Most people who long for retirement have no idea of the trap that is awaiting them. The freedom they crave, once they have all the time in the world to pursue it, can seem like a vast empty space that needs to be filled. Without something meaningful to do, the person can undergo a profound period of alienation and emptiness. Depression is not far behind. What is a person supposed to do when she is not engaged, when she has nothing left to be passionate about? If you want to have a real life, you have to start now. You have to stop idealizing retirement as an idyllic condition, and seek fulfillment in such a way that it can be realized in the present moment and on a daily basis. Remember, life is just a long weekend. Do you really want to wait until Sunday night before you start to enjoy it? If you feel your job is depriving you of this, it's time to take a look at the job itself, not at escaping from it. People who love what they do will tell you that what they do is not work.

SUCCESS IMAGE NUMBER EIGHT: *I want to be a jet-setter.*

What the image really represents: This person is looking for excitement and stimulation. He feels that his potential is being underutilized, that his creativity is being stifled, and as a result he is, frankly, bored. The lack of an engagement that occupies his attention in a meaningful way leaves him fidgety and anxious. "What's next?" he continually asks himself. Some misguided people of this type turn to drugs or drink, or seek out thrills. Often this kind of heightened need for excitement hides a deeper problem. The person cannot sit still in a chair with nothing to do because there are too many issues he would have to face in himself, and there would be nothing to distract him from them. He does not know it, but his worst fear is that if he does face them, he will be devastated by the experience. This means he has no faith in his own inner strength and resources. He may think of himself as a big risk-taker, but bungee jumping off a skyscraper is a walk in the park compared to facing one's own inner demons. All the while the person is proving to the world how brave he is, how unafraid in the face of danger, the one thing he is most afraid of is inside himself, and he will do anything rather than turn his attention inward and deal with it. External stimulation or the sedation of drugs provides a distraction from his real fears. It is his way of turning away from reality and losing himself in meaningless pastimes.

Aligning the image with reality: According to psychologist Abraham Maslow, as long as human beings are able to satisfy basic needs for food, sleep, sex, safety, love, and self-esteem, they will move in the direction of growth and self-actualization. In Maslow's famous "hierarchy of needs," the most important human need is the need to be self-actualized; all others are subsumed by it. A person's real drive is to grow and explore his own potential. But he cannot do this unless he uses all of himself. If he cuts himself off from the parts he doesn't like, if he turns a blind eye to the side of himself he doesn't approve of or is afraid of, he is operating like a person with one arm and one leg. It's hard to run a race that way. And yet people try to do it all the time and then wonder why they feel so thwarted. These are the people who feel a constant need for superficial stimulation. They are bored because nothing they do seems to use all of themselves. Even those who march excitedly off into the wilds of Africa to "find themselves" are off track, and they return vaguely unfulfilled. My experience of people who are always trying to find themselves is that they do not really want the "self" that they are. They want the self they think they should be. Instead of searching for thrills in distant places and searching for a self that doesn't exist, try staying home—in every sense of the word. Who you really are is right here and right now. You don't have to go anywhere to find it. The hunt for excitement, when it is nothing but a diversionary tactic, can only turn to disillusionment. The thrill always fizzles out because it was an illusion in the first place.

THE POWER OF SEDUCTION ▼

If you accept the validity of these images, every time you feel unsatisfied your interpretation will be that it is because you haven't pursued the image *enough*. Since the answer lies in the image, if the plan isn't working (as evidenced by the fact that you aren't happy yet), it must mean that the image has more to offer than you have so far gained. If you aren't successful, for example, it must mean that you should endeavor to achieve more.

There was a magazine cartoon of a penguin trying, unsuccessfully, to fly. It was flapping its tiny, inadequate wings and getting nowhere. His companion said he knew what the problem was: His friend just wasn't flapping hard enough. Of course, the truth is that penguins simply can't fly; it doesn't matter how hard they flap. But if a penguin believes that his attempt to fly really should work, he will spend half his life "trying a little harder." If he pursued his real life in the water, he'd be catching fish and he would be a happy, satisfied bird with a full stomach. How many rich people are desperately unhappy, yet stubbornly go on and on and on trying to make more money?

I am not saying there is anything intrinsically wrong with having a guiding image to aim for in life, but it is valid and useful only if it is not a compensation for something lacking—if it is, in fact, in alignment with your real needs. To be successful, you must bring the qualities that your inner self needs into your external life without becoming enmeshed in an image that distorts your original intention. This only underscores the saying, "Be careful what you wish for. You might get it." (Chapters Four and Five will tell you how to identify those real needs.)

The fallacy inherent in each of the above images is that they are fantasies. They don't reflect reality at all, but either a familial or cultural idea of what a human being should aim for. In spite of this, these images are seductive because they play right into a person's deepest needs for security, acceptance, recognition, a sense of belonging, personal power, support and comfort, relaxation, and stimulation. You experience unrequited longings inside yourself, and then: Bingo! Along comes this glittering image that promises to satisfy these longings. So you grab onto this image for dear life. To avoid being seduced by an image that can only satisfy your needs in the most superficial of ways, you must acknowledge and understand the real need that is calling out to be recognized. And then you must be creative, original, and true to yourself in how you choose to fill it.

The world makes it easy for us to be pulled by the nose in dozens of different directions, all the while missing out on what we are really searching for. We don't even realize that we are looking in the wrong corners for life's prizes, and we fail to recognize how much precious time we are wasting in pursuit of false goals while our real goals go unnoticed. Once we do see through our delusions, once we stop being pulled in all the wrong directions and decide to face the issues that stand between us and our real needs, we are finally in a position to look at what the elements of a successful lifestyle are. Only then can we evaluate where we are on track and where changes need to be made. In the next chapter, I will reveal some of the changes I've experienced and the lessons they have taught me.

Chapter 3

LESSONS FROM AN UNSEDUCED MAVERICK

If you say, "This is what I really want to do and I am going to pursue it," then you will find that something miraculous takes place. You may have to go hungry, struggle to get through, but you will be a worthwhile human being, not a mere copy, and that is the miracle of it.

J. KRISHNAMURTI

I could easily have ended up like my friend Jim, the alcoholic. I too was brainwashed to believe that success meant marrying a beautiful woman, having so much money you'd need an armored truck to carry it all, and owning a majestic house with a wide expanse of grass out front. Professionally, I wanted to become a trial lawyer and win a series of exciting legal battles. This image was exemplified for me by the television lawyer Perry Mason, who never lost a case.

As I reflect back on my formative years, the one word that pops up is "Dickensian." I grew up on the mean streets of Brooklyn in a neighborhood known as Bedford-Stuyvesant. It was the largest black community in the country, and we were white. The black kids were always ganging up on me. "Hey, white boy" became my nickname. The constant threat of violence was terrifying. Visually, it was a depressing landscape of rundown brownstones and tenements that reflected the poverty and despair of the inhabitants. Not a day went by when I did not think about how I was going to escape from this squalor by becoming rich and famous.

We didn't know it back then, but today my family would be referred to as dysfunctional; in our case this was typified by self-destructive, passive-aggressive behavior and a lack of communication. My parents were divorced when I was two, remarried each other when I was six (I was the best man at my parents' wedding), then split up again when I was seven. After that, I only saw my father six or seven times until he died thirty-two years later. My mother and I moved in with my grandparents. We had very little money coming in and we never knew whether next month's rent would be paid. We lived on the edge. A feeling of imminent doom hung in the air.

There was love in our family, but there was also a great deal of emotional abuse. My father was so uncomfortable and gruff during our few interactions that I was afraid of him. I have two clear memories of my father. When I was six, we went to a restaurant for dinner. Afterward, as we went for a walk, I tried to hold his hand but he refused, claiming that it was not a masculine thing to do. On another occasion, he bought me a bicycle. After only a few minutes of instruction in how to ride, I didn't pick it up immediately, so he walked away—leaving me feeling totally inadequate. To this day, I do not know how to ride a bicycle.

In my grandparents' home, major arguments were a daily occurrence. My grandmother would berate my grandfather, who would return the favor. My mother was manipulated by her mother and would attempt to manipulate me in return. Years later my mother confessed that her mother had never loved her. In that moment I realized that everyone in the family hated everyone else.

Although I received constant praise and affection whenever I achieved good grades, on most other occasions I was on the receiving end of sarcasm and ridicule. I would be praised for an "A" in math, but ridiculed because I couldn't repair a broken light switch. It seemed I had all sorts of shortcomings that were patently obvious to my mother and grandmother, but the nature of these shortcomings I could only guess at. My family mostly projected their own failings onto me. The only thing I knew for sure was that if I continued to achieve, I would be loved.

My family subscribed without reservation to the classic definition of success. Even though they weren't rich and famous, they unloaded that expectation onto me. As an only child, I found the pressure to achieve and succeed overwhelming. One of my family's values was education, so I focused on academic achievement as the way to satisfy their expectations. It was taken for granted that I would live up to my high I.Q. by distinguishing myself at school. Fortunately, I usually made good grades, so I was touted in the family as the up-and-coming Messiah of Success. But I always had the sense that the affection coming my way was strictly contingent on performance.

LAYING DOWN THE LAW ▼

With this strong motivation for achievement, I worked my way through college as a toilet cleaner, waiter, construction worker, and elevator operator. The highlight of those four years was being on the debating team. This was an activity at which I excelled; my partner and I came in sixth in a national debating competition. My success as a debater spawned my ambition to become the greatest trial lawyer since Clarence Darrow. In this endeavor, the men in my family were a great influence on me. Although my father was never around, the two strong father figures in my life were my grandfather and my Uncle Teddy. One was a prominent politician and the other a Harvard-trained attorney. I tried to follow in their footsteps and obtain a law degree, but the truth was that I hated law school. I remember going to see Uncle Teddy one day. He was sitting in his office with his law partner when I told him that law school was worse than boring, and I just wanted to blow my brains out.

"You're bored," Uncle Teddy said. "So what?"

"I can't spend my life doing something I don't like."

The two men exchanged a look, and my uncle's partner said, "Do you think we like what we do?"

I couldn't believe my ears. In spite of their criticism of my so-called youthful obstinacy, I swore that I wasn't going to repeat their self-sacrifice. But my decision wasn't going to be easy. The pressure from my family and friends to finish law school was intimidating. I found that I was critical of my own dislike for law school. "Not finish? There must be something seriously flawed in my personality," I suspected. The love my family had doled out to me was conditional upon my continuing to achieve. I had succeeded in internalizing this emotional abuse, and was now directing it at myself. Life is what we perceive it to be, and I perceived myself as a failure.

It was tough breaking away from the need to achieve, with which I had been brainwashed. I managed to extricate myself from law school only because I had no choice; something inside me was stronger than the brainwashing, and it refused to act on what it intuitively knew was wrong for me. Yet the stigma of being a dropout clung to me for years. The feeling of shame was so great that I remember thinking, "I would like to leave the planet." That was not feasible at the time, so I did the next-best thing. I joined the Marines.

My crime was not achieving according to expectations. The sentence was no less harsh for being self-imposed. It was 1967, the height of the Vietnam War. The average lifespan in Vietnam for a Marine lieutenant was about twenty-one seconds. Many of the young men with whom I trained at Officers Candidate School in Quantico, Virginia, lost their lives that year. The Marine Corps earmarked me for duty as a forward observer; of all the jobs in the Corps, forward observer is arguably the most dangerous. The F.O. commands a small unit that goes ahead of the infantry, locates the enemy, and radios back the map coordinates so the artillery and air support know where to direct their fire. If the enemy doesn't finish you off, friendly fire is likely to do the trick. My family evidently was correct—my failure to achieve had landed me in a world of hurt!

Well, as you probably have guessed, I survived. Ironically, my childhood allergies surfaced at a most opportune moment. Before they could ship me to Vietnam, I landed at Bethesda Naval Hospital where they found I was allergic to grass, trees, dust, pollen, and air-mold. I was given a medical discharge.

At this point in my young life, three lessons had surfaced. First, I had come face to face with one of my best traits: I refuse to settle for being miserable; I am compelled to be proactive. Second, I realized for the first time that life doesn't always follow a safe, predictable path; one has to improvise. Success, if it occurs at all, must be pursued through trial and error. Third, my flirtation with death in the Marine Corps gave rise to the image of life as just a long weekend, which has served as a constant reminder that each day should be lived to the fullest.

Now that I was a civilian again, I was able to accept that the legal profession and I were not good marriage material. However, that did not deter me from seeking the hen that would lay the golden egg. I went right on with the program, only venturing down a different road. I decided to make my fortune selling computers. By the age of thirty, I had an office on the sixtieth floor of 30 Rockefeller Plaza, one of the most distinguished buildings in New York City. While working my way through college cleaning toilets at night in Rockefeller Center, I had sworn that someday I would have an office in 30 Rock. And so I had done it. My view was dazzling. From the window I could see all of New York as far as the Verrazano Bridge. My desk was huge, the surroundings plush. The high-speed elevator to my floor positively hummed the sound of success.

What was wrong with this picture? I had money, but no time to spend it. I had a home with a lawn, but I was allergic to grass. I had an office with a view, but found I was afraid of heights. The problem with the great dream I had fulfilled was that it had never been my own. It had been Uncle Teddy's all along, in spite of the different spin I had put on it.

One day while having lunch with the executive vice president of the conglomerate for which I worked, a scene from the movie *Man in the Gray Flannel Suit* flashed before my eyes. Sitting across the table from me was a man who occupied the kind of position to which I still aspired. Yet he was a gray little man in a gray little suit telling gray little jokes while nursing a gray little ulcer. I remember thinking that day, "Don't let this happen to you." I returned to my eagle's nest office, locked the door, and turned the chair around to face my rarified view of a world that was supposedly at my feet.

THE DEFINING MOMENT ▼

We must all have a pocket of wisdom within us, for at that moment from the depths of my mind there arose a defining question: "What if your doctor told you that you have only six months to live? How would you want to spend that time?" The very first thing that occurred to me was that I would not want to spend it working in the computer business. Surely my destiny lay elsewhere. The natural question to follow was: "Well then, what would you like to do?" This one was not as easy to answer, and some time would pass before I could. What I did know then was that this was a major moment in my life.

I often wonder if my buddy Jim ever had such a defining moment. Did it hit him in the face at a specific time and place that what he had was not what he truly wanted for himself? If that moment did come to him, did he let it pass him by? Did he then start drinking to numb his pain and to avoid answering the mega-question: "What is my life for?"

It is easy enough to walk away from difficult questions like this. The Dalai Lama, in his book *The Art of Happiness*, says that avoiding things only provides temporary relief. However, he says on pages 136–137, if you can confront your suffering directly:

> You will be in a better position to appreciate the depth and nature of the problem. If you are in a battle, as long as you remain ignorant of the status and combat capability of your enemy, you will be totally unprepared and paralyzed by fear. However, if you know the fighting capability of your opponent . . . then you're in a much better position when you engage in the war. In the same way, if you confront your prob-

lems rather than avoid them, you will be in a better position to deal with them.

FARTING AROUND ▼

On some level I must have understood the Dalai Lama's message, because I was unrelenting in my pursuit of an answer to the crucial question I had asked myself. I spent a great deal of time alone contemplating it. In the end, I had my reward. Instead of letting my uncle or grandfather or the rest of the world be the author of the rules I would live by, I wrote my own rules. I became my own inner authority, defining for myself what success meant for me, and, more importantly, what it did *not* mean. Kurt Vonnegut wrote in *Timequake*: "We are here on earth to fart around. Don't let anybody tell you any different!" It is a seemingly simple statement that has had profound meaning for me. The rules I wanted to live by allowed for more free, open, and creative time. I had served in the Marine Corps and knew all about days that were so structured it felt like I had a steel rod up my backside. I could not see conducting the rest of my life that way.

I also began to find that I was not limited to one career or one approach to life. It was all an adventure—*if* I had the courage to walk through the doors of opportunity as they opened to me. By asking myself the question, "What if you had only six months to live?" I had opened the first door on my own, and had loosened my consciousness to embrace a more expansive view of life.

We can all ask ourselves one pertinent question that opens our consciousness. Perhaps the one I posed for myself will not be the right one for every person, but the one we all have to answer sooner or later is: "What am I living for?" Is it for a bowl of cornflakes in the morning? Payday? Fridays? Getting through an upcoming tax audit? A sale at Bloomingdales? Joseph Campbell said that instead of worrying about why we are here, we need to focus our energy on the simple experience of being alive. He called this "following your bliss," which by now is a rather famous phrase. But how many of us know what it means? Bliss is not merely garden-variety happiness. It is a kind of spiritually tinged joy, and it is inner directed. When you are able to act on your own definition of success, you can experience bliss. When you have a healthy balance between work and free time, you open yourself up to bliss. When you do the work you were meant to do, you invite bliss in.

We are distracted by so much clutter in contemporary America that it's hard to remember the joys of simplicity. In a way, it's all very simple: There is one moment, then there is another, then there is another. And so on. That's all life really is—a series of moments. But the culture says "There are goals to attain, new frontiers to conquer, money to be made. For God's sake, don't get left behind!" People burden themselves with a 60-hour-a-week job and a mortgage that keeps them awake at night. If they do think about "farting around," they have to pencil it in on their calendar between 10:15 and 10:30 on Saturday morning.

By the way, I am not preaching anarchy. In the interest of being true to yourself or leading a simple life, you cannot ignore the demands of society. You need to be responsible for yourself. As Joseph Campbell points out, the trick isn't just to satisfy your own desires, but to achieve a "harmonious relationship" between your needs and those of society. This is the fundamental ethical dilemma for all of us: Where does compassionate and sensible compromise end and martyr-like self-sacrifice begin? When does the need to be a functioning member of society stop before you turn into a drone? To some degree you must operate within the mores of the society in which you live; but to experience yourself in an alive way you need to create a lifestyle that is based upon your own values. As Campbell says, "It's ridiculous not to live in terms of this society because, unless I do, I'm not living. But I mustn't allow this society to dictate to me how I should live."

I would also like to clarify that I would not argue with the American Dream if it genuinely agrees with you. If you are an insurance executive living on a ten-acre estate in Greenwich, and you can look around and honestly say: "I love my life. I'm good at what I do, and I'm in a field that makes sense to me. I've always wanted an estate like this, and now that I've got it I can see why I always wanted it"—then you *are* following your bliss. You don't need to give it all up to go surfing in Bali, because you've created the world you truly want for yourself. You chose it consciously. Good for you! But as business consultant Dr. Robert Luthardt pointed out to me: "There is a big difference between having the perks of a life that you dislike versus having the life you would love to live if you made the time."

When I broke away from my corporate life, I found that for me, following my bliss had to do with balance. I have spent the last twenty-five years seeking a healthy balance between work and free time.

I COULD DO THAT ▼

In confronting my impatience with the corporate lifestyle, I eventually found my answer to the question "What other kind of work would you like to do?" It actually came as a huge surprise. From somewhere in my psyche, a voice said, "I've always thought it would be exciting to be an actor." I had never acted before, even in school. I knew no one in show business. I knew nothing about show business. Undaunted, I took the subway down to Greenwich Village where I signed up for an acting class with Lee Strasberg and his son, John. From the very first night, I was smitten with the acting bug.

Try to imagine the peculiar position I was in. My evolving career as a corporate executive brought with it coveted social and economic status. To suddenly give it all up to become an actor? My family and friends were dumbfounded. My mother-in-law practically accused me of being a bum. To many acquaintances, I was a nonperson, a lunatic. Most of them avoided me like the plague. I no longer fulfilled the role they were accustomed to. And the cardinal rule had been broken—I had rejected the holy dollar. But it was what I had to do. The remarkable quality about each of my major life transitions has been that in each situation, in spite of the fear and pain, I felt as though I had no choice. My vision was clear—this was what I had to do in order to maintain my integrity.

The rapid success I experienced as an actor was a surprise to everyone, including me. Within a year, I was cast in the leading role in a European movie called *Jackpot*, based upon a story by Harlan Ellison and produced by Wieland Schulz-Keil, who also produced John Huston's last two films. In no time at all, I had successfully transitioned from the button-down atmosphere of the corporate boardroom to the glamorous world of show biz. I discovered that, indeed, life is an adventure requiring only my willingness to go along for the ride.

I lived out my fantasies about show business and moved to Hollywood, working with famous celebrities like Jessica Lange, Ron Howard, Patrick Swayze, and Christopher Reeve. I did movies, television, plays, commercials, and industrial films. Work had never been so much fun, but it was not a dependable profession. Most of the Screen Actors Guild members are out of work at any given time, and I was no exception. Actors are treated as the lowest members of the Hollywood hierarchy, so when I wasn't working it was a tough challenge for my self-esteem. After a twelve-year rollercoaster ride of ups and downs, my career seemed to be in limbo. Someone once asked Al Pacino, "To what do you attribute your success as an actor?" Pacino is supposed to have replied, "I stuck it out for the second ten years." I eventually decided that, for the sake of my sanity, it would be prudent not to emulate Al's decision.

In some ways, leaving show business was more difficult than the transition out of the computer business. I had sacrificed the perceived safety of the corporate world and devoted twelve years of my life to an activity that gave me immense creative satisfaction. I thought my heart would break if I gave it up. It seemed that I was being a quitter. This is an excellent example of the kind of masochism referred to by Paul Terhorst in *Cashing In on the American Dream*: We are taught to remain in a painful job situation rather than search for a better alternative. Instead of making a change, I hit bottom. Depression set in and, for the first time in my adult life, I felt incapable of making a decision. Fortunately, I found a terrific therapist who helped me reconnect with my power—without taking Prozac.

At this fortuitous time, a seemingly insignificant event catapulted my life in an unexpected direction. My cousin Howard, a photographer, casually mentioned one day that he was about to take a seminar in photography. A light went on in my head. "Seminars," I thought. "I could do that." My thought process went something like this: I have a business background, plus I'm a trained performer, so giving seminars on business subjects ought to be a natural for me. And I would be able to use the acting skills I had enjoyed so much. On a practical level, I would have the control over my career that I had missed as an actor. Once I opened my consciousness to this possibility, opportunities fell into my lap. Within six months I was giving seminars on the art of negotiation to corporate clients such as American Express, Eastman Kodak, The Hartford, Microsoft, Mobil Oil, and Sun Microsystems. At no time did I stop and say, "Wait a minute, I've never done this before. No one will accept me." My renewed self-confidence led to the creation of the Negotiation Boot Camp™ seminars, a PBS special, and a book, *Negotiate with Confidence*. I have become a leading authority in my field, a sought-after speaker and expert.

Although I have acquired the symbols of success, the focus of my life has shifted from career to lifestyle, from achievement to experience, from living in the future to living in the present. It occurred to me a few years ago that for most of my life I was obsessed with the future and what I intended to achieve once I arrived there. With gratitude, I recognized that I had finally overcome the compulsion to achieve. Today, my energy is devoted to living in the moment, with a focus on quality of life in the here-and-now. Some of the lifestyle issues I care about are: working for myself and calling the shots; free time (to fart around); traveling; my home and friends; staying in good physical condition; eating well; access to creative outlets. What I do to earn a living is secondary to maintaining these lifestyle choices. In my eyes, they constitute success.

My path to success is ongoing, a process more than an end result. Each step along the way has been a reflection of who I happened to be, and what my priorities were, at the time. By defining success as doing what is meaningful to me, I have given myself permission to make career and lifestyle changes in accordance with my evolving needs. In the past, my brainwashing guaranteed that each transition was accompanied by varying amounts of fear and emotional pain; but as time goes by the memory of the suffering fades and what remains is the satisfaction of having done it my way.

▼ What is your pathway going to be? Are you going to limit yourself to a narrow scope, or are you going to take charge and experience your personal adventure? The first thing you must do is get in touch with who you really are.

Chapter 4

DISCOVERING THE *YOU* IN YOU

If the person insists on a certain program, and doesn't listen to the demands of his own heart, he's going to risk a schizophrenic crackup. Such a person has put himself off center. He has aligned himself with a program for life, and it's not the one the body's interested in at all. The world is full of people who have stopped listening to themselves.

JOSEPH CAMPBELL

WHAT DO YOU WANT FROM LIFE? ▼

Having a background as an actor has made me aware of the parallels between the craft of acting and the craft of living, which perhaps are not so different. One lesson I learned in my acting training, for instance, was that when creating a character, *your choices must be specific.* The richness of the characterization stems from the specificity of the images you can recall. In one scene that required my character to discover the solution to a difficult problem, I mentally substituted a real-life situation in which a sudden inspiration had enabled me to finish a screenplay I'd been working on. If I had thought about this situation in just a general way, my character would have lacked vividness, distinction, and a real personality of its own. Instead, I focused on the details of writing the last pages of my screenplay: the uncomfortable chair I was sitting in, the intense lamplight, the acrid smell of the typewriter ribbon, the coldness of the room, and the sense that I was finally reaching the end of a difficult project. The richness of my characterization derived from the specificity of my memories.

And so it is in life. The richness and originality of one's life derives from the specificity of the choices we make. Ironically, most of us rarely make pointed or well-defined choices. We meander our way through life never quite getting what we want, in part because we have neither identified it nor asked for it. When I ask people in my seminars, "What do you want out of life?" most of the answers are vague: "I want to be successful." If I push them further with "What do you mean by 'success'?" most of them cannot articulate what they want in specific terms. Is it becoming financially independent by age fifty? Is it a trip on the Orient Express? Is it being promoted to Vice President of Marketing? I suspect that, in many cases, people are afraid to admit that they really have no idea what they want, so they attempt to avoid the question. As a result, they go with the default option of "rich and famous," which is society's standard definition of success and its description of the Promised Land. As we saw in Chapter One, people who fall for this myth become prime candidates for the success trap. Many turn into the Disillusioned—*I have acquired all the conventional accoutrements of a person who has made it, but I don't feel successful.* Or they end up as the Dissatisfied—*If only I could attain everything I dream about, then I would finally feel successful.*

One sure way to avoid either trap is to be precise about what you expect from life. What is that one goal you must meet to consider yourself a success? Remember what my definition of success is: Right here, right now, you are spending your time doing what is meaningful to you. So—what do you want to be doing right this minute? Your goal should not be a prize on a piece of fishline dangling out in front of you sometime in the future. If you're having trouble zeroing in on your goal, try asking yourself the question: "What are the things that are really meaningful to me?" I suspect you will notice your rational mind taking charge immediately and feeding back to you the values you were brain-washed to embrace. So how can you move away from that kind of constriction and discover what the real "you" wants? The answer lies in your mind, but not exactly where you think.

LEARNING TO FEEL ▼

There is a tendency to use the words *brain* and *mind* interchangeably. In fact, they are not the same. The brain is an organ of the body, a mass of nerve tissue that conducts thinking processes, perceives sensory impulses, and regulates bodily functions. The mind, on the other hand, is much more than just a piece of meat sitting in our cranium. It is, in fact, the very seat of consciousness. It encompasses the consciousness not just of the brain and its processes, but of the entire body.

If we recognize the brain as the only source of information, we will effectively cut off a much richer and broader source of information that we could be using to guide our decision-making toward a successful life. Part of what this book is designed to do is to help you find your personal definition of success, and then live it. But you cannot do that if you are partitioned off from a significant part of yourself, the part that knows, that feels, that intuits.

All too often, we who live in the industrial world base most of our life decisions on what the brain tells us, not on what the body tells us. This has two disastrous consequences. One, we fail to pay attention to our bodies—literally, like not realizing when we are eating too much, when we are in stress or even in pain, or when we are poisoning ourselves with toxins. Two, we are severed from our emotions, which are also sent from the body. Without explicitly thinking about emotions, we unconsciously use them for survival all the time. We use fear to warn us about danger. The appearance of this emotion sets off a spurt of adrenaline, which makes us edgy and ready to react if need be. Sadness slows us down to force us to take the time to grieve over life's losses. Anger is there to protect both the body from assault and the mind from diminishment. Disgust warns us to avoid what is toxic or repulsive. On the other hand, positive emotions also contribute to our survival. Happiness tells us that whatever we're doing is healthy and we should do more of it. Love encourages cooperation, acts of caring, and bonding. Serenity allows us to conserve energy.

Emotions make up a language that is meant to communicate to a person what his needs are. Unlike children, who are in touch with their emotions, adults will sometimes literally die before they acknowledge their needs, and this is partly the result of the fact that they are only selectively aware of their emotions. Cultures vary in what emotions they will and won't permit men and women to be in touch with and express. In this culture, for example, men are encouraged to be in touch with anger, but not sadness.

So what happened to us that made us shut ourselves down? If we were so in contact with ourselves as kids and we expressed ourselves so naturally, how and why did we learn to sever off from part of ourselves and repress our emotions? The answer: All those influences you read about in Chapter One—family values, the media, advertising, peer pressure, and the educational system—taught you to give far more weight to the feelings of others than to your own. It is not that we should grow up self-absorbed, excluding all others. The problem occurs when a healthy balance is not struck, when we're taught to devalue our own needs and overvalue those of others. Children are given the especially strong message that they should respect Mom and Dad's needs because they are more mature and therefore their needs more "legitimate." Children are often conditioned to sit on any expression of emotions that is displeasing to their parents. What happens when the child grows up is that he has an emotion that signifies a need, but—believing (sometimes subconsciously) that the emotion is unacceptable or in conflict with those of others—he automatically represses the "disagreeable" feeling and goes along with the majority.

To put it bluntly, *we have been convinced to distrust and avoid our own emotions.* Do you understand what this means? It means that if we don't know what we need and what we feel, we don't know who we are. If you are not listening to your emotions, what kind of behavior are you acting out? Isn't it more than likely that your behavior does not represent who you are? Somewhere inside you is a "you," the real you. If you were to ask this "you" what you felt and what you needed, it would have no trouble telling you.

Unfortunately, most of us are stuck listening to someone else tell us what is important; we are clueless about the real person hiding inside. Before we can identify our personal path to success, we have to figure out what our needs are, who we are, and what is really important to us. Without the emotional component, the task of identifying our ideal lifestyle—one that will satisfy our real needs—takes on Herculean proportions. The dilemma is this: How can we depend on our emotions to guide us to a personal meaning of success if we are clueless about those very emotions. The good news is that your body has a built-in mechanism that can help you.

WHAT IS THIS THING CALLED GUT? ▼

The first really powerful desire I can remember having as a young adult was over the choice of college. During my senior year in high school, my room was littered with brochures from faraway colleges that I dreamed of attending. I bathed in fantasies of escaping from home and Brooklyn, and having the time of my life at Somewhere Else University. Alas, my family had no money to contribute to my dream, so Brooklyn College—highly rated, inexpensive, and a subway ride away—had to be my choice after all. If I was forced to go to a local school, however, I was determined to make it a home away from home by joining a fraternity and being a part of the frat house. After rushing several fraternities, I was accepted by the top house on campus. My newest dream had come true—I would be a bona fide fraternity man!

Before I was able to enjoy my prestige, though, a strange phenomenon occurred, one that would reappear at crucial times in my life. About halfway through the eight-week fraternity pledge period, I was plagued by powerful feelings of discontent. Raw anxiety kept me awake at night. Apprehension disturbed my studies. Something was very wrong and it was stopping me in my tracks, but I didn't know what it was. The clearest symptom I was aware of was a kind of fluttering sensation and tightness in my stomach. It was a gut feeling; my body was telling me that something was rotten.

One evening, I went into my room and lay down on the bed, feeling absolutely paralyzed. I didn't know where to turn. My stomach was in enough pain that it caused me to say to myself, "I have got to figure out what's wrong. There's nothing else I can do." Instinctively I knew that somehow this was all connected to joining the fraternity since pledging had marked the onslaught of the problem. My body was trying to tell me that if I wanted to get rid of the pain, I would have to confront whatever was wrong. This had been bothering me throughout the weeks I had been attending fraternity parties and events; for whatever reason, that evening it came to a head.

Clearly, there was a struggle going on inside me between two sides of myself. One side wanted the trappings of fraternity life: the prestige, the camaraderie, the sense of belonging, and the home away from home. The other part of me recognized the fact that I never did well in group situations in which I was being asked to conform. What I also saw as a problem was that all the assumptions I was complicitly making by joining a fraternity house were lies. Supposedly, we were all "brothers" and crazy about each other. The truth was that I couldn't stand a lot of the guys. If I joined this new "family," for four years of college I would have to put on a false face of congeniality, which would take a great deal of energy and ultimately break my spirit.

And there it was—the source of my stomachache. The reason I had so easily been able to access these deep realizations was that my body already knew the answers, and all I had to do was get out of the way and let my body reveal them. Its inevitable message was "Fraternity life is not for you, pal."

Scott Peck describes his version of my fraternity story in his book *The Road Less Traveled*. He was in an exclusive prep school only because his parents wanted him to attend. Immediately after starting, he became "miserably unhappy." He admits that "the reasons for my unhappiness were totally obscure to me then and are still quite profoundly mysterious to me today. I just did not seem to fit." And yet there was a truth to be known in regard to his predicament, not a linear, logical explanation but a deeper kind of understanding, one that could only come from his unconscious. "If I returned to Exeter," he realized, "I would be returning to all that was safe, secure, right, proper, constructive, proven, and known. Yet it was not for me. In the depths of my being I knew it was not my path." He was just a boy, and heaven only knows the forces pressing on him to do the "right and proper" thing, but he listened to his gut anyway. It was a less secure position for him, but he knew he had to do it. "I had taken the leap into the unknown," he says. "I had taken my destiny in my own hands."

I'm recalling these stories because they describe what I believe is the most important nugget of wisdom I have acquired in my lifetime. Whenever I have turned to my gut and followed its advice, I have prospered. Whenever I have turned my back on it and allowed my rational mind to override my gut feeling, I have lived to regret it.

So just exactly what is this thing called gut? Gut feeling is not an out-on-the-edge, New Age concept that appeals only to people who believe in past life regression and the healing power of crystals. In fact, it is something real and tangible that has been acknowledged by great modern thinkers from Freud to Einstein. *Gut feeling or intuition is knowledge acquired without the use of reasoning.* Or as Gavin De Becker writes in *The Gift of Fear*, "It is knowing without knowing why." Albert Einstein agreed when he said: "I believe in intuition and inspiration. I sometimes think that I am right without knowing the reason." De Becker goes on to say that "it isn't just a feeling. It is a process more extraordinary and ultimately more logical in the natural order than the most fantastic computer calculation. It is our most complex cognitive process and at the same time the simplest."

Using intuition is the only way to discover one's true path in life, and it is not a function of the rational mind we are so wedded to, but of the emotional mind. As I said in the first chapter, people are being brainwashed as a matter of course in this culture: "You've gotta do this when you grow up. You've gotta do that or you're a loser." But this mentality does not respect the needs of the individual, so the individual wakes up one morning in midlife and finds himself in a terrible crisis of meaning. "I feel like I've wasted my life," he says, not sure how he got there or what to do about it. So far he has made a series of disastrous decisions based on his rational mind's reasoning, which has encouraged him to go along with the herd, to take the safe, beaten path instead of following his own inner voice that leads to the "road less traveled."

An alternative to brainwashing is to listen to the gut instead of the rational mind. And gut feelings come from the emotional mind. In his book *Emotional Intelligence*, Daniel Goleman explains the source of this kind of knowing in this way: "In a very real sense we have two minds, one that thinks and one that feels." One is the seat of rational intelligence, the other of emotional intelligence. It is surprising, however, the number of people who are afraid of their emotions, believing they should be kept out of the decision-making process. In fact, they are a crucial part of it. Says Goleman, "While strong feelings can create havoc in reasoning, the *lack* of awareness of feeling can also be ruinous, especially in weighing the decisions on which our destiny largely depends: what career to pursue, whether to stay with a secure job or switch to one that is riskier but more interesting, whom to date or marry, where to live, which apartment to rent or house to buy—and on and on through life."

In other words, the bigger the decision the less you should leave it to the inferior capacities of the rational mind. "Such decisions," Goleman says, "cannot be made well through sheer rationality; they require gut feeling, and the emotional wisdom garnered through past experiences. . . . [All of the above] are realms where reason without feeling is blind."

The brain stem, from which this alternative intelligence comes, is a very primitive part of the brain, and "acts as a storehouse of emotional memory," in Goleman's words. Intuitive signals come not from the more recently formed (from an evolutionary point of view) cerebral cortex area of the brain, but from the limbic system. They are "surges from the viscera that Damasio [a neurologist] calls 'somatic markers'— literally gut feelings." What Goleman is saying is that our body is giving us the very signals we need to pay attention to in order to make intelligent and wise decisions. When I was in college lying in bed in intense pain, all the facts were in front of me. I just didn't know what to do with them. Yet I did not resort to Tums or Alka-Seltzer to quell the gnawing sensation in my stomach so I could ignore the signals it was presenting to me. Instead, I let myself feel the sensations and dropped down into a deeper part of myself. I was lost in my misery, but not without hope because this older part of my brain, one that knew how to ensure survival with a fight-or-flight response, was also able to act with a certain assuredness; it simply knew that something was wrong with the course I was on.

This innate intelligence is a gift, and insanely, most of us don't use it. The brain is not the only source of one's intelligence. Our heart, liver, pancreas, and so on all have their own form of intelligence. And not only does each organ of the body have intelligence, so does each cell. As we go along in life and gather experiences, our cells store up the wisdom of those experiences. The accumulation of our experiences is then available to us in the form of intuitive responses, signals from the body offering us invaluable information about the world and what we need from it. Because they are feelings, though, they cannot be accessed directly via the rational mind. Unfortunately, most people in the industrialized world are so identified with their rational mind that they take it to be who they are. It is not who you are. "You" are the accumulation of all the consciousness, information, and experience in your cells.

When it is aligned with the rational mind, intuition points you in the direction of your bliss. Bliss is an experience of great joy, rapture even, that occurs when you are in alignment with who you really are. If our rational mind were in alignment with our emotional mind, we would be able to experience bliss on a regular basis. Our conditioning, however, prevents that. In place of that bliss there is often pain and emptiness, which, of course, we try to avoid feeling at all costs. In order to get through life, to function, and to avoid the pain of "no self," we develop what Swiss psychologist Alice Miller, in her book *The Drama of the Gifted Child*, calls the "false self." With the false self, the person reveals only what is expected of her by her parents or society. Such a person is unable to live as her true self, and so experiences a lifelong sense of emptiness and futility, a "partial killing" of her potential, a killing that "took place when all that was alive and spontaneous . . . was cut off." This is my definition of hell.

To free the true self from the conditioning and brainwashing that has kept it buried, we have to allow our intuition to guide us, to take precedence over the rational mind in making life decisions. Our true self is hiding, but we must access it so it can tell us how to be truly successful in life. The rational mind provides very little help in this endeavor. In fact, it is frequently working for the other side, for the society that brainwashed us in the first place.

THE OBSTACLE COURSE ▼

Wouldn't it be nice if this were a simple task? I have just told you that you possess the innate quality of intuition that will lead you in the direction of bliss. If only I could follow that with "All you have to do now is use it to guide you in the right direction. No problem." However, the complexity of modern life is such that a series of obstacles exist that make it difficult to get in touch with our gut feelings.

The Rational Mind

Again, we find ourselves discussing this same little devil. The rational mind has risen to power believing that it is an all-purpose tool, ready to take on any challenge. It believes it is a more competent judge of what is fundamentally best for us than our gut feelings. "Americans worship logic, even when it's wrong," says Gavin De Becker, "and deny intuition, even when it's right." We have been taught in subtle ways that reason is more powerful than animal instincts and therefore should supplant them. After all, isn't the rational mind what makes our species superior to the apes and everything on down the food chain?

Most people feel more comfortable depending on cold reason than on emotion or gut reactions. When they're in a situation that demands they make a life decision, a gut feeling will always be there to guide them. Unfortunately for them, it will feel wild, untamable, and unpredictable. It won't lend itself to the quick, linear logic they've come to depend on. It will come from a place in them that they are unfamiliar with and therefore distrust. Most likely it will challenge their worldview and strongly held beliefs. They won't feel articulate if they try to explain it to others. All these "threats" and discomforts will inexorably turn a person's attention away from his gut feeling and toward the easier, more traveled path of rational thinking. "We much prefer logic," says De Becker, "the grounded, explainable, unemotional thought process that ends in a supportable conclusion." The alternative, one shared by Einstein, Australian Aborigines, and yours truly, is learning to trust those feelings for which there *is* no rational explanation.

On *Star Trek*, in both the movie and the TV series, the embodiment of cold logic was in the person (or should I say Vulcan) of Mr. Spock. He was from an alien planet where the inhabitants functioned on reason alone; they were devoid of the feelings that interfered with a human's rather messy decision-making processes. To the credit of the series, in many episodes it was shown that Spock's inability to tap into the emotional mind prevented him from making the wiser decisions that his human counterparts were able to render. Yet in spite of all the times his rational mind failed him, he was always willing to defend it and scoff at the "weakness" of human beings.

We all have a little of Mr. Spock in us, a side that harbors a deep distrust for that which is not quantifiable and linear in our consciousness. If we are to counter that distrust, we must stand up for the part of ourselves that will prove to be a most trusted ally.

External Influence

Society depends upon conformity. It believes that stability lies in people behaving in predictable ways. The spontaneous nature of intuitive thinking represents a threat to that kind of conformity and is therefore discouraged. Instead, the rational mind is reinforced by a constant stream of subliminal and not-so-subliminal messages we receive telling us not to trust our natural instincts. In fact, all of our primary influences discourage paying attention to intuition. We are constantly being told how we "should" behave instead of being encouraged to follow our gut feelings.

When I dragged myself into Uncle Teddy's office and told him how dissatisfied I was in law school, his message was that my unhappiness was largely irrelevant. What was relevant to a mind like his was long-term stability. "If you get a law degree, you will always be able to get a job." It seemed at the time to be a sedate, mature response that made more sense than the unformed, chaotic feelings I was experiencing. Since I respected my uncle in many ways and since he was older and wiser than me, I decided to go with his advice. After all, he went to Harvard. How could a Harvard man be wrong? My choice to acquiesce and stay in law school led to nothing but another year of misery, at which point I "conspired" (as I will explain later) to find a way to escape my prison. If I had continued to ignore the deep emotional messages from my unconscious, I would be sitting in the corner of a dusty law library today instead of writing this book.

Joseph Campbell must have been thinking of me when he said, "The thing in our own experience is the person who in youth has the sense of a life to live, and then Daddy says, 'No, you'd better study law. Because there's money in law.' And you meet these people later on, and they are the ones who have climbed to the top of the ladder and found it's against the wrong wall. They have not lived their lives."

The media also is a major collaborator in influencing people to ignore their intuition. I'm always fascinated by television commercials about stomach upset and heartburn. The stereotypical commercial shows someone who has eaten too much pizza—yet again this month. "Are you plagued by stomach upset? Take Crapitola-X and feel better." Instead of cutting pizza from his diet, the viewer is deliberately being told to ignore the wisdom of his body and instead to keep right on with a destructive habit, get gas as a result, and then artificially avoid feeling it. I get gas just thinking about it.

Education and Prior Conditioning

Conditioning starts from birth, and it's hard to shake off because those first messages make such an indelible impression. When I reflect on my own upbringing and education, I find it striking that I was never offered any teaching about intuitive thinking. On the contrary, in school I was overwhelmed with classes that stressed the primacy of reason: mathematics, economics, grammar, science, and even philosophy (which often disintegrates into a nonsensical babble of logic and semantics). No wonder we worship the rational mind—our entire educational system supports it. Children who gravitate to creative, right-brain activities often have to seek instruction outside the school system, and adults who look for those types of jobs are regarded as less legitimate, labeled as flighty or lightweight, and castigated as misfits or failures in some way, precisely because they're not afraid to honor the intuitive process. If you are one of those people who as children thought in a nonlinear, intuitive way, your parents probably humored your "little hobbies," but in the final analysis they would rather you became an accountant than a flute player.

Prior conditioning can cause us to make the most costly of mistakes because we're thinking mechanically, and then to blame these mistakes on the casualties of life. When my friend Janet was growing up, she was conditioned to believe that she wouldn't be complete until she was married. No matter what other goals she met, without a husband she was merely a fraction of a person. So at thirty-four when Phil asked her to marry him, she was ecstatic that she was finally going to enter the world of respectability. But on her wedding day, she had a sneaking feeling that she'd be better off leaving town than heading up the aisle. What to do? The invitations had been sent out, the church reserved, and the guests were all climbing into their cars and heading over. How could she let everybody down? Twenty-five years of rotten marriage later she finally let in what her gut feelings had been trying to tell her on that day. She knew Phil was an alcoholic, but so had her father been, and she had been trained to put up with it. The conditioning to settle for a man who wanted her rather than to stay single was so strong that it overrode the giant NO that told her she was making a mistake before she ever took her vows.

Intuition could have saved Janet from wasting many precious years because on the day of her wedding, her intuitive mind possessed the wisdom of the ages even though she was still young and immature in many other ways. She had a wise old sage inside her that could have saved her years of "hard labor," and she didn't know it. Instead, she let her conditioning force her hand.

The Fast Pace of Life

So much to do, so little time to do it. In her book *Why Is Everyone So Cranky?* C. Leslie Charles writes: "People say it feels as if they're living on a fast-moving treadmill that gains momentum with each new day." This is not all in their minds, she explains, because we really have "fallen prey to the promise of *bigger, better, faster, more, now.* . . . It's hard thinking straight when your body is whipping along at warp speed." And when your life is nothing more than a high-speed chase, it's also difficult to tune in to subtler things like the changing color of the trees by the side of the road. While we're rushing around from one appointment to the next, one meeting to the next, it's easy to miss messages from our body. There is no time for such discriminating attention. To use another metaphor, suppose the headlights of a car are beaming, and alongside them is a single lit candle. How well can you see the candle light? It is virtually drowned out by the blinding headlights. That is life today.

When I lived in New York, I was constantly on the move. Rush here, zip off to there, get this done, cross that off my list. Hurry, hurry, hurry. I didn't know who I was. I was a verb, not a noun. There is now actually a book by Allan Ishac entitled *New York's 50 Best Places to Find Peace & Quiet.* When you need a book to tell you where you can go to be quiet, you know you're in trouble. In retrospect, I now see that I had no time to reflect and allow the emotional processes of the mind to come to the forefront of my consciousness.

The world is designed to draw your attention outward. If you want it to head inward, you must make a concerted effort to turn it around. But it takes time and the right atmosphere to get to know yourself, and that atmosphere won't be found at Moomba, Lotus, the Sky Bar, or the current reincarnation of Studio 54. You need the time to sit on a pillow with your eyes closed or walk on the beach and listen to the seagulls call to each other across the open sky. We all need quality time to explore ourselves.

Unless your life slows down to a manageable pace, you will find it impossible to listen to your gut feelings. They will simply be drowned out like a fragile candle flame in the light from a pair of high beams.

Fear of Facing the Truth

Sometimes a gut feeling, which can only represent the truth, flies straight in the face of our self-image. If you thought the other obstacles were big, this one is Mt. Kilimanjaro. We all put an extraordinary amount of energy into maintaining a self-image. It is the neon sign we wear through life that broadcasts how we want to appear to the world. The trouble is, we forget that it's just a neon sign and take it to be who we really are. So when a crack appears in it, we feel as if there is a crack in our entire sense of self. You can see why it can be truly terrifying to let in a gut feeling that dents our self-image by revealing the truth about ourselves.

An example of this that saddens me is the life story of my Uncle Teddy, the one who tried to pressure me into finishing law school. Some years later I realized the irony of my longstanding argument with him, for he himself hadn't been so sure about attending law school. He had really wanted to be a writer. But his father would hear none of it and bullied him into finishing at Harvard and going into private practice. Instead of standing up for himself, he succumbed. From time to time, I am sure it crossed his mind that his life would have been richer and more satisfying if he had followed the course he wanted to follow. But over time Uncle Teddy came to enjoy his prestige in the world, his image of himself as a Harvard-trained attorney. He could not let himself acknowledge his real desire because to him, being a writer was a second-class occupation, unworthy of his skills. To overcompensate for abandoning his true calling, he worked compulsively practicing law. To my regret, I don't believe he ever enjoyed a moment of it. I saw him drink too much, and I almost let him convince me to follow in his sorry footsteps. As Willy Loman's son says at the end of Miller's *Death of a Salesman,* "He never knew who he was."

▼ These obstacles may seem forbidding, but don't lose hope. I will show you how to overcome them and get in touch with your intuitive side.

Chapter 5

TAPPING INTO YOUR GUT

Contrary to what people believe about the intuition of dogs, your intuitive abilities are vastly superior.

GAVIN DE BECKER

We've established that you need to follow your gut if you're going to have a life that's worth living. We've also established that you haven't been raised to do it and that a multitude of obstacles will stand in your way. The major challenge is in discovering how to overcome the insistent influence of the rational mind, those external sources that are (so to speak) anti-gut, and the prior conditioning of our body's innate intelligence. If we want to get in touch with the deeper and wiser part of ourselves, we have to dodge the mindless brain activity and outside distractions so we can focus on the intuitive process. I have identified the following nine techniques for tapping into the intelligence of the gut.

1. Living in the Moment

We spend the lion's share of our time in the past and in the future. What about now? The following is a technique I discovered in acting class involving one of the most useful concepts that actors work with. It is called "working moment to moment" or "being in the moment." Without it, the actor's performance does not come across as real. When two actors are working together, they must maintain their spontaneity. This means listening to and reacting to the other actor's line as if they never heard it before. The opposite of this is called "anticipating." This means the actor's mind is leaping ahead to what he knows the other actor is going to say next and how the scene is going to end. He knows that after the argument, on page 39 of the script, the other actor will slap him across the face. If he is anticipating the slap, all of the dialogue that precedes it will be colored by that knowledge, and he will either flinch just before the slap or he'll fake a response. If the actor can be in the moment, though, he "forgets" page 39 of the script. In the beginning of the argument he is saying his lines, *being* his lines, right then and there.

Of course, this is not easy to do. The major challenge for an actor is keeping his performance fresh night after night. He has to be able to respond to the slap when it occurs and not a second before. And because the slap will be different every night, so too will his response. Being in the moment keeps his performance alive and real every time he steps on stage. And it also makes it more interesting to him as well as to the audience.

For a life to be called successful in the truest sense of the word, it must be lived in the moment. Otherwise, you're not actually steeped in the experience of your success, whatever form it takes. Success is "out there" somewhere, one step removed from you. Ironically, the whole American Dream admonishes you to live at some unspecified point in the future. You are trained to work eighty-hour weeks in the office and delay gratification until the weekend, when you will spend hours playing with expensive toys and thinking about the better expensive toys you will buy when you put in a ninety-hour week. But after you've bought the newest best toy, it often fails to deliver the gratification you've been waiting for. This dissatisfaction and staleness can be prevented by living right in the moment. By acknowledging your emotional needs and seeking to meet those needs in the present time with all your awareness brought to bear, you can chart the course that will provide satisfaction, not in some soon-to-be-determined point in the future, but in the here and now. Your moment-to-moment activities, your lifestyle, will then conform to your true needs. In other words, you'll be able to enjoy your life.

I used to work for a millionaire named Jerry. The company he owns is such a cash cow that it continues to reap handsome profits in spite of its poor management. Since Jerry grew up during the Depression and knew what poverty felt like, he was hellbent on accumulating wealth. The trouble is, he has never learned how to enjoy it. He is not in the moment with the pleasures his money can bring. Instead, he's always on the phone making deals for reaping the next bundle of money.

But although Jerry doesn't realize it, he also lives heavily in the past. One evening he called me to announce that he was going to London on business and wanted to "catch a few shows." He knew I traveled and asked me if I could recommend an inexpensive hotel. "He wants a hotel that won't cost much?" I thought. "This guy could buy and sell any hotel he stays in." Jerry's travel agent, who is a friend of mine, told me that he always books hotel rooms without a private bath to keep the price down. Without too much difficulty, I figured out why a guy like Jerry is stuck in this habit of mind. Like many in his generation, he experienced a great deal of deprivation growing up in the Great Depression. Because the experience made such an indelible impression on the way he views life, he is always anticipating another economic crash. If he knew how to bring his consciousness into the present, he would realize that he's living in economic boom times, and even though we still go through recessions (which he is in a position to weather painlessly), conditions are not likely to produce the same kind of all-out depression that occurred in the 1930s. Even after the recession that followed the Internet boom, dot.com fallout, and the attacks of 9/11, the economy rebounded in fairly short order. For Jerry, it is as if he received a slap in the face when he was ten years old, and still thinks another one is coming.

What good is all his wealth if he doesn't know how to enjoy it? What good is twenty million dollars if he's stuck in a hotel room with a bath all the way down the hall? People like Jerry are so far removed from their experience of success that they wouldn't recognize it if it jumped up and bit them.

And here's the bad news: Jerry is an old man. He doesn't have much time to reform his attitude and squeeze the most juice he can out of life because he'll be dead in a few years. Make no mistake about it— life is very short. Remember my theory that it is a long weekend, nothing more. It isn't a decade. It isn't a year. It isn't even a week. And if you're not following your bliss, if you're creating unnecessary stress for yourself, your body will send you a bill and the weekend will be even shorter. If you live in the moment, however, you can hear the messages from your body before the rational, conditioned mind has a chance to get in the way. So listen to your body and make the most of your weekend. Otherwise, what's the point of being alive?

2. Spontaneous Thinking

Living in the moment isn't merely a way of thinking, it is a way of *being*, and it is one of the most effective ways of living in the here and now. It describes a method of thinking that is responsive to the present situation and flexible to changing circumstances. In other words, it is spontaneous. This contrasts with our usual thinking behavior, which is preprogrammed and robot-like.

People sometimes fail to understand why their strategies don't produce the desired results: "I don't get it. I thought I was doing what I was supposed to with my life. Why don't I feel like I'm flourishing? Where did everything go wrong?" Quite often, the problem is that the kind of intelligence operating within us is comparable to that of a computerized robot; we are producing only a command/response type of thought. A robot is preprogrammed to react to a certain set of circumstances in a laboratory. Life is not as predictable as a lab test. If we behave in the real world the way a robot does in the lab, it means we continue to do what we were preprogrammed for, which necessarily means we are not monitoring the demands of the real world and not attending to the real needs of a complex life. The one thing robots distinctly lack is spontaneity.

A spontaneous person, on the other hand, is able to slow down her thinking mind and get in touch with the truth of her emotions and her body's intelligence, enabling her to respond to the truth of the moment. If you wake up at the age of forty and suddenly realize that you don't feel that you're alive and thriving, you probably haven't been dealing with the truths your body and emotions have attempted to communicate. You have not been listening to your instinctual needs and fixing problems as they occurred.

One of the reasons I enjoy traveling abroad is that I have to do exactly that; I am forced to deal with events as they present themselves whether I am prepared for them or not. All the tasks I perform here in the United States cannot be taken for granted in France where I don't speak the language and where I'm not familiar with the customs. Every day I have to exchange unfamiliar money for goods and services, figure out where I'm going in cities I've never been to, make telephone calls through a strange communications system, and order a meal in a restaurant from a menu I can't really read. Of course, the waiter won't stand there forever with his pen poised, so I have to offer a fairly immediate response, which for me carries with it a strong feeling of being alive. If I'm wrong, I could get a plate of octopus eyeballs instead of chicken in white wine sauce. Ironically, people are often afraid of spontaneity because they think it makes them more subject to doing something wrong. The truth is the opposite. Spontaneity allows you to respond appropriately to what is being asked of you because you are actually "there" to perceive what it is.

You are also more aware of your true needs. When Janet, for example, was at her wedding, she behaved like a robot. She walked down the aisle with the wrong man because she was listening to her programming instead of to her gut. She had been the good daughter all her life, the proper sort of person, and she had had no experience of spontaneity since she played in the sandbox in kindergarten. Had she known how, she would have stopped the programmed thinking and fixed her problem by halting the wedding ceremony.

An excellent way to gauge what your body wants at any given time is to pay attention to the first thing that comes into your mind; this is the uncensored intelligence of the body surging up into conscious awareness before the rational mind has had a chance to interfere. Ironically, people's inclination is to dismiss the first spontaneous thought. They want to rake it over the coals before they are ready to settle for an answer. The freshness, vibrance, and truth of first thoughts are thus usually lost. But these are probably the very thoughts you can trust the most.

3. Do the Right-Brain Thing

One important theme throughout this chapter is the virtue of right-brain thinking. Fortunately, in recent years we are becoming more enlightened about the left-brain/right-brain paradox. We have long recognized the need for left-brain activity, which is used by engineers, mathematicians, and nuclear physicists. But we are now beginning to recognize the value of right-brain thinking, which is associated with writers, artists, musicians, and others who must rely more upon inspiration than pure linear intellect. Intuition, a distinctly right-brain activity, is woefully underused.

As we have seen, our culture maintains a clear bias in favor of the logical activities of the brain. And as I have said, the rational side of the brain is more suitable for brainwashing. Society has the most access to the left side, making it better suited to the demands of conformity. Society believes it can thrive only by maintaining a system of conduct, standards, and activities to which everyone subscribes. If too many people reject these standards and deviate from what is considered socially acceptable conduct, then the status quo will be threatened. We can see, then, why society makes ample use of left-brain thinking to reinforce and maintain itself. The right-brain, in contrast, is the brain of revolution. It continually seeks the path of individuation, of making the distinction between society's needs and the person's own needs.

If society is to succeed in shunting you into an "acceptable" occupation and lifestyle, it must press upon you a literal, black-and-white approach to life. It must convince you to believe the simplistic adage, "Do this because this is the way things are done," without you demanding further explanation. When your gut sends you the message that the mainstream culture's way is not your way, society will encourage you to ignore it. If, however, you haven't been completely convinced to accept this formula, you are bound to say to yourself, "Wait a minute. Maybe life isn't that black and white. Perhaps I should start paying attention to my own inner voice."

Any attempt on your part to think individually and to overcome society's brainwashing must rely heavily upon your right-brain. Your creative faculties, and your intuition in particular, will guide you to the path that is properly aligned with the truth of who you are.

4. Nourishing the Inner Child

Because children are freer than adults in their ability to acknowledge and express their emotions, adults who want to develop their intuition are well advised to get in touch with their inner child. Although you may have lost much of your childhood spontaneity, you haven't lost it all. If you did, you'd be dead. The essence of the child we used to be exists in each of us, and we can access it. Some people are naturally better at this than others; they have retained the ability to be childlike. Notice that I did not say *childish*, which is a synonym for *immature*. To be *childlike* is to be able to view the world with innocence and awe and to have the capacity to express yourself in a more spontaneous way.

Because in children the rational mind is less evolved, it doesn't have the same power to get in the way as it does for adults. It doesn't waylay all the natural impulses and redirect the child's attention toward what she "should" want. Instead, children pretty much know what they *do* want.

Children are more primitive because they rely a great deal on an older part of the brain rather than on the cerebral cortex, which is still developing into adulthood. This is why they are able to believe in Santa Claus; the rational mind doesn't step in and rationalize it away. In fact, it is good that they do believe in Santa Claus because this is the part of the mind that can always be trusted to seek out the true heart's desire. Children are far more connected with their heart's desire than adults. However, when growing up, the heart's desire isn't always delivered. If the disappointment is too steady and too intense, it leads to disillusionment and a hard heart. The person doesn't want to feel her needs anymore because of the expectation that they will only lead to further disappointment, so she grows up deaf to the voice inside that simply says "I need." But feeling our needs is central to a full life because it leads us to understand ourselves on a deep level, and eventually it leads to our heart's desire. The reason for connecting with our inner child is that this is the part of us that is directly connected with knowing what our real needs are.

The very activity of being an actor, either onstage or on camera, involves doing what children do: expressing emotions using imagination and releasing repressed impulses, although in an imaginatively constrained way. An acting class, then, will bring people in touch with their inner child. In acting class, you are required to act out, to make explicit, all your emotions. Some adults, within their daily lives, are lucky if they have the opportunity to make one honest emotion explicit in a month. I believe all adults should be required to take an acting class so they can at least pretend, in an artificial situation, to do what they should be doing in real life.

5. Taking Time to Be Still

A significant reason for our difficulty in listening to the gut is that we are moving so fast, we cannot hear what is going on. People who don't slow down and commune with themselves on a regular basis are eventually headed for a crash. Leslie Charles, in *Why Is Everyone So Cranky?* advises us to periodically stop and ask, "What am I thinking? How am I feeling right now?" This is a good technique for putting the brakes on our 70-mph minds and coming to a full stop. Once you ask this question, it makes you conscious of the fact that you are thinking and feeling something at this very moment. And this makes you conscious of the fact that you just ARE. You just exist.

I have found several valuable techniques over the years to help me slow down. They are: meditation, yoga, and "farting around." (Two of these are well-documented, respected traditions found in the moth-eaten texts of Eastern literature. The third comes from Ed's Encyclopedia of Living Well.)

The mind is the closest thing there is to a perpetual-motion machine. It never stops working unless a conscious effort is made to stop it. The practice of meditation is a conscious effort to stop it, at least to some degree. It can be looked at as a form of self-hypnosis that slows the mind down to a manageable speed so that we can be aware of what is passing through it. Instead of entertaining the many unconnected thoughts that pass through your mind, focus on one thing to the exclusion of everything else. It takes practice, but the benefit is increased clarity. Here is a specific exercise: Dim the lights. Sit cross-legged on a pillow or in a comfortable chair and begin to focus on your breath. The breath is always a good object of concentration because it is steady and reliable. Take a deep breath and slowly count to five. Hold it one moment longer, then exhale to a count of five. Hold it a moment longer, then inhale for a count of five, and so on. Try it for five minutes a day and notice how relaxed you feel at the end of a week.

This breathing meditation is one of the basic practices of yoga. Yoga is a methodology for expanding the mind and the body through breathing and stretching. As we age, our bodies lose the flexibility we need for optimal functioning. Many people like myself first approach yoga because of an injury that won't heal or some soreness that won't go away. For me it was the aches and pains from playing handball. The surprise bonus, however, is the overall calming and healing effect it has on the body as a whole. It slows us down and allows us to focus on our state of mind, right here and right now. One cannot perform the various stretching poses of yoga without constantly checking on the messages coming from the body. In this way, yoga is an excellent way to develop a relationship with one's gut. It helps answer Leslie Charles' questions: "What am I thinking? How am I feeling right now?"

What I have referred to as "farting around" can have the same result. What I mean by this is spending time with no apparent purpose, just being and observing. Most of our time is so filled with purposeful activities that we can only let ourselves fart around on vacation. And even then we keep ourselves surprisingly scheduled: sky diving at noon, snorkeling at two, buying souvenirs for the family, showering, dressing for dinner by six.

The flip side of this frantic scheduling is just to slow down. At work, do one project at a time. Consider getting in early to get a jump on the day. When you get home at the end of the day, don't rush to turn on the TV and do five things at once. Instead, slowly hang up your coat, turn on some music, pour yourself a glass of wine and go through the mail. When going on vacation, don't give your cell phone number to your supervisor. Instead, tell him you'll check in once a day. Be conscious of putting distance between work and play. On weekends, allot time for both leisure and work, and perhaps cut down on the amount of work you take home with you.

I know an awful lot of people who can't stand it if they're not occupied all the time. They can't relax unless they have something to do. In fact, *not doing* makes them anxious: "If I'm not keeping myself occupied, I'm wasting time." This compulsively busy behavior, this fast-paced mentality, are unfortunate symptoms of our time. A businessman can travel to Europe, a continent away, in only a few hours, and he will have his laptop turned on the entire time getting his accounts in order. By contrast, early in the twentieth century, the same man would have had to take a steamship and be en route for a week. He would have had time to stare out at the ocean and reflect. In our world, we seem to have lost that option. Time is now in such short supply that it appears to be a cardinal sin if we don't use every single moment for some specific purpose. Well, I am now certifying "farting around" as a specific purpose.

6. Wake Up to Your Own Awareness

Maintaining a gentle but vigilant awareness of the body's messages is a prescription for mental and physical well-being. You can walk down the street and easily spot people who are simply lost in space and not aware of themselves or what is going on in their surroundings. They're just like the nearsighted cartoon character Mr. Magoo, whose bumbling efforts to negotiate his way through a world he couldn't see always made me laugh. My view is that this Magoo-like quality of not being aware is a choice, not an accident. In dealing with the ups and downs of life, people make a variety of choices about how to cope. One is simply to keep blinders on and ignore whatever is unpleasant. By pretending that something they don't like just isn't there, they avoid having to deal with it and its consequences. Unfortunately, ignoring reality never makes it go away. It just comes around the other way and hits you in the back of your head. You must make the effort to reclaim your attention if you want to be able to tune in to your deepest intuitive urges.

Let's see how aware you are. Think about whichever room you visited last. It may be the bathroom or the living room or the garage. Without going back into it and looking, make a list of every item in the room. How many things are you able to recall? Can you re-create the experience of walking into the room? What were you feeling and thinking at the time? Can you remember, or were you sleepwalking?

In our culture, one of the most common ways of *not* being aware of reality is to ignore the messages sent by the gut. Yet if they are ignored for too long, a condition of imbalance will occur between mind and body resulting in the body going out of whack. I believe that many adverse health conditions are the result of having ignored messages from our bodies that an imbalance was taking place. It is a common belief, supported indirectly by the findings of health organizations and doctors, that stress leads to depression and disease. Extreme stress means the body is sending up a red flag that it's time for you to pay attention. If ignored, the body will eventually send you a bill saying "Payable immediately." The body's messages will not go away just because we speed up our activities and ignore these messages. They will go underground for a while, perhaps, when the body is treated by medication. But then they will resurface in some other way. The choice to be aware is a healthy one, better than multiple vitamins or a two-week stay at a health spa.

7. Talking to Yourself

In a sense, there is a kind of schizophrenic crack in human beings. There are two minds within each of us: the rational mind that speaks the language of the brain and the emotional mind that speaks the language of the body. The advantage of this duality is that it allows for conscious communication between the two parts of ourselves. I am recommending that we foster this communication between the "me" that thinks and the "me" that feels. In other words, *talk to yourself*. Create a dialogue so that you will have reliable access to the information your body is so uniquely qualified to provide.

The operative question to ask yourself is "What am I feeling?" Simple question. By answering it honestly, you enable the rational mind to achieve alignment with the emotional. Without constant practice, however, getting in touch with the emotional mind is difficult. After a person has been cut off from her emotions for a long time (since childhood, for instance), she may be terrified to find out what her real feelings are like. If she has been enclosed in the contained, innocuous realm of the intellect, she may find real emotions to be overwhelming. Many of the feelings may be distressful and even bitter and afflictive, but this is nothing compared to the hell of being emotionally dead. It was Oscar Wilde who said that the human heart was built to be broken; it just wasn't built to be closed.

Another exercise I learned in acting class can be instructive. One of the most popular exercises in method acting is using "emotional memory." The actor has to produce a specific emotional reaction for a scene, and to do so he must relive a meaningful moment from his life. I once played a scene that required me to project the emotion of sorrow. To accomplish that, I attempted to re-create for myself the physical context of a sad experience in my own life. I relived a visit I had made as a teenager to my grandfather when he was in a mental hospital, re-creating all the physical sensations of it: the hollow sound of my feet as I walked down the hospital corridor, the institutional yellow of the wall tiles, the stale smell of urine from the stairwells, the feel of my grandfather's frail body as I leaned over to kiss him. The combination of all these recalled smells, sights, and sounds brought on real tears.

If you are thinking about an upcoming event and having trouble figuring out how you truly feel about it, try re-creating the physical sensations of that kind of event in the past. For instance, perhaps you are about to begin interviewing for a new job. Relive the experience of going on job interviews in the past. You walked into a room and met a new person. What did it feel like to shake his hand and say hello? Were you confident? Was it a firm handshake? What did the new surroundings smell like? How comfortable was the chair? As you bring these memories to light, keep in mind these questions: "How am I feeling remembering these things? Do I feel optimistic or troubled? How is my body feeling about being in a new situation where I'm being tested?" You may sense anxiety, hopefulness, and excitement. This technique can help you sort out the jumble of emotions that attends facing a new experience.

8. Learning to Understand the Message of Dreams

Intuition is fortunate to have a sidekick: dreams. Dreams are the body's ultimate creative product. They offer a glimpse into your unconscious mind and a barometer of your emotions. If we can pay attention to the story in a dream, it will give us important clues about our life, about who we are, and about the hidden views we have with respect to our world.

My friend Carl was facing a major decision. He could either keep his business as it was or he could expand it and take on more hours, responsibility, and risk for himself. His wife, brother, and sister were all urging him to do the latter. One night he had a dream. He was driving a car across a bridge over a river. His brother was in the front passenger seat. Suddenly Carl lost control of the car, and it crashed through the side railing and over the bridge into the rushing waters below. The car began to fill with water and sink. Instead of saving himself, Carl tried to save his brother by pushing him through an open window. The harder he pushed, though, the more his brother pushed back, trapping Carl in the sinking automobile. He could feel the dark waters surrounding him, pulling him down, down, down. Then he woke up.

The dream provided my friend with some crystalline observations about himself. First, he realized that he had devoted his entire life to taking care of the people in his family, often ignoring his own needs in the process. His father had died when Carl was a teenage boy, and as the eldest he had looked after his younger siblings. He had become an adult before he ever had time to grow up. Second, in his adult life, the demands of his business had taken a heavy toll on him.

The dream showed Carl that he was "drowning" in work. It revealed his desire to finally take care of himself by breaking free from overbearing responsibilities. There was no missing the message that he had to cut down on the anxiety and stress in his life or he would be engulfed by it. The dream also brought to light the nature of his relationship with his brother and the other people in his life. He had thought they were in his corner, but in reality they were always using him for their own purposes, pulling him into a sinking vehicle instead of letting him float to the surface. Ultimately Carl got a divorce, sold his business, and distanced himself from his demanding family. Today he is a happy man, and he credits that one dream for waking him up to the reality of his emotional state.

Why are dreams able to furnish us with information that is not available via the conscious mind? In truth, we do not know for sure where dreams come from. Freud said they were dispatches from the unconscious mind, which contains repressed information. Another famous dream theorist was Carl Jung, who believed that dreams represent "archetypal" images—those expressing innate or universal ideas in the psyche—which are derived from the "collective unconscious" of the human race. What we do know for sure is that dreams use an associative language of images conveying information that exists in the form of nonlogical impulses and emotions that cannot be expressed in the verbal language of the conscious mind.

Whatever dreams are and wherever they come from, the only thing that matters is the significance our own dreams hold for us. I believe they translate the innate intelligence of the body—which is a deeper form of information than that which resides in the conscious mind—into a story whose message the conscious mind can unravel. It so happens that the format or language of dreams is metaphor. For instance, the dream metaphor in Carl's dream was "drowning in work." Metaphors are attempts by the body to present an image that says, "Listen up. Pay attention to what's really happening." They are here to guide us to overcome the obstacles to our personal happiness, and lead us to successful lives. Jeremy Taylor in his book, *Where People Fly and Water Runs Uphill*, writes: "All dreams come in the service of health and wholeness, always in the context of moving you further along in your growth and development."

We dream several times every night, but many people report that they cannot remember any of them. Here is an exercise to help you remember yours. Place a pencil and paper next to your bed. As you are falling off to sleep, tell yourself that you will remember your dreams that night. As soon as you first awaken, whether it is in the morning or in the middle of the night, write down whatever details you can recall from that night's dreams. If your notations seem crazy, chaotic, and undecipherable, remember that the dream's message comes in the language of metaphors. When interpreting a dream metaphor, pay attention to the very first thing that comes to mind; it is an associative process, not a linear one. You can also try discussing a dream with your spouse or a close friend. Sometimes another person listening to you talk about it can reveal the dream's secrets. Ask the other person to finish this sentence: "If this were my dream, I think it would mean . . ." That will encourage them to help you without projecting their own subjective interpretation onto you.

9. Taking on a Partner

"Examination of the world without is never as personally painful as examination of the world within," writes Scott Peck, "and it is certainly because of the pain involved in a life of genuine self-examination that the majority steer away from it."

Yet sometimes life itself drags people kicking and screaming into self-examination. I hit bottom when I transitioned out of show business. I had pinned so many hopes of happiness and success on my show business career that when I began to be disillusioned by it, this proved to be a low point of my existence. However, this also provided the impetus for me to look within myself for answers as I had never done before. When I found that I could not take on all my issues alone, a caring friend found me a psychotherapist. Prior to this, I used to think that therapists were for crazy people. My stubbornness was overcome by my need to cope with the terrible pain I was in. What I ended up receiving was, fortunately, more than I had signed on for. I discovered the tools that allowed me to follow my intuition, which in turn led me to be successful according to my wildest dreams.

My inner search was a subtle and difficult process, and I could not have done it alone. We all need help to become self-actualized. As I will discuss in Chapter Eight, we need many forms of support, including people who can help us through the rough spots and validate our value and uniqueness. One kind of support is affection-based: one good friend, a caring relative, or indeed anyone to provide unconditional love (including a trusted dog). Psychotherapy, however, provides a unique kind of support because it comes from someone who is trained in the ways of the psyche and whose only job is to be on your side and assist you in your journey of understanding. I have used psychotherapy to strengthen my inner life the same way I use handball and yoga to strengthen my body, the dentist to keep my teeth healthy, and the accountant to keep my finances in order. It is simply a tool for a healthier, more functional life. I probably could have done without it, but why would I want to have made the transition harder on myself? "It is possible to build a house without a hammer and nails," Scott Peck says in *The Road Less Traveled.* "Similarly, it is possible to achieve personal growth without employing psychotherapy, but often the task is unnecessarily tedious, lengthy and difficult. It generally makes sense to utilize available tools as a shortcut." If you are interested in energizing and nourishing your inner life, you too may want to consider teaming up with a professional who can help you in your search to find yourself. Believe me, when you're trying to communicate with and translate the messages of your own gut, it's nice to have help.

While you are deciding whether or not to go into therapy, here is an exercise you can do by yourself. Go into a quiet room or a place where you feel at ease (for me it's the beach). Pose this question to yourself: "What if my doctor told me I had only six months to live, how would I spend the time I had left?" Try not to censor yourself. What is the first thing that comes into your mind? Would you continue your life as it is, or would you make certain changes now that time was suddenly precious? Without editing or judging the answers, write down whatever comes to mind. It is amazing how that six-month deadline can put your life in a different perspective. If you realize, as I did, that there are definite changes you would want to make, then consider all the possibilities. Let your imagination run free. Again, do not abridge or amend your answers according to what all your conditioning says you "should" do with your time. Don't try to be logical. Just be honest with yourself. It's your life—and it's the only one you've got. As the saying goes, this is not a trial run. You deserve to be in charge and conduct it any way you want.

DARING TO BE YOU ▼

It would be very difficult for me to be Japanese. Although I like and admire the Japanese people, there is one aspect of their culture that would be an insurmountable stumbling block for me. It is reflected in the saying: "The nail that sticks up gets hammered down." Japanese society is based on all the little nails being willing to stay the same size and not stand out or slant in different directions. Even in their looks, people are encouraged to conform. For instance, while 90 percent of the people have straight black hair, the other 10 percent have curly brown hair. But to avoid being singled out in the school system, girls with curly brown hair will dye and straighten it so they can look like everyone else. While it cannot be denied that the Japanese people and their traditions have achieved much, I wonder what price the individual pays for submitting to such uniformity.

Despite the American myth about ours being the culture of the rugged individualist, in many ways we are not that different from the Japanese. As I discuss further in Chapter Nine, I see a lot of sheep out there. It just seems easier to do what we're told, to do what is safe, secure, right, proper, constructive, proven, and known. We are a society of organizations, and organizations tend to hammer down the individual like the proverbial nail that sticks up.

If, however, you want to follow your bliss, you can do it only through the course of your own individuality. You have to think for yourself and risk the unknown by following your gut feelings. As Scott Peck says, "It is only when one has taken the leap into the unknown of total selfhood, psychological independence and unique individuality that one is free to proceed along still higher paths of spiritual growth."

It cannot be denied that Americans have achieved a great deal of success by being team players. It is a strength we cannot afford to let slip away. Humans are, after all, pack animals, a gregarious species that plays on the group's strengths. I am in no way suggesting that we abandon team membership in favor of isolation and aloneness. What I am saying is that the distinction every person must make is, in the end, to choose his own values instead of having them thrust upon him. To be a success on your own terms, you must find the courage to honor your own principles and your own uniqueness. Your beacon in this effort is intuition. All you need is the courage to use it.

Part Two

ABUSED

Chapter 6

ABUSE WILL NOT MAKE YOU SUCCESSFUL

People put you down enough, you start to believe it.

JULIA ROBERTS IN THE FILM
PRETTY WOMAN

When the actor Donald Sutherland was about to enter high school, his father passed on to him a rather dubious piece of advice: "Keep your mouth shut, and no one will know how stupid you are." I saw Sutherland sadly recount this little episode on a television talk show and thought it was a perfect example of the abuse we endure in our growing years that is camouflaged as "just kidding," "helpful advice," "necessary punishment," "discipline for your own good," and "lessons for survival." Regardless of how the mistreatment, whether physical or verbal, is represented, it does not go unnoticed by the child's psyche. These things hurt, and they have a lasting effect on our identity. As adults we carry the burden of our damaged identity throughout every stage of life. This kind of upbringing saddles us with a little demon in the back of our head that reminds us, "It doesn't matter what you do, you're still a stupid little kid. No matter how you try, you can't escape it. You can fool other people, but I know you're a fraud and you'll never be a real success."

Some readers may take umbrage at my using a strong word like *abuse* to describe the general treatment that so many children receive. First, let me start by recording how Webster's *New World Dictionary* defines it. As a noun: "mistreatment; injury; a bad, unjust, or corrupt custom or practice." As a verb: "to hurt by treating badly; misuse."

We all *know* what the word means, but that doesn't mean we recognize it when we see it. Sometimes we just think of poor treatment as a necessary part of life, as "the way things are." Abuse is so prevalent that it becomes invisible, and often, unfortunately, acceptable. We live in a world in which abusive thinking and behavior are not only tolerated, but regarded as normal. It is so built into our lives, we simply endure it from the time we're born till the time we die without putting up much of a fight.

Many readers will find it especially difficult using the words *abuse* and *my parents* in the same sentence. Even people who can be quite critical of their parents tend to defend their body of work as a whole, usually contending that "they did the best they could." If we stood back and looked at the effect of their behavior on our well-being in a cold light and we told the truth, we would probably feel as if we were betraying them. The child in us is deeply loyal to our parents. Consequently, most people will put up all sorts of excuses to defend the treatment they received. "Yeah, Dad was kind of tough. But those beatings made me a stronger person." "Mom couldn't help yelling all the time. She was under a lot of pressure." "They had four other kids. There was no time to pay attention to me. I did have to take care of myself most of the time, and I couldn't go to them with my problems, but I did okay."

I am not saying that there weren't extenuating circumstances, and that parents all over the world don't have a great number of difficulties to contend with when raising their children. Nor am I saying that many parents aren't doing the very best they can, given the way they were raised and the limitation of their resources. However, that should not keep you from acknowledging the impact on you of being yelled at, belittled, bullied, humiliated, hit, berated, neglected—or subjected to any other acts of mistreatment. This chapter is not about blame. It is about acknowledging the truth and moving on from there. When you were growing up, you were entirely dependent on the good will of the "giants" around you. Sometimes those adults were cruel, hostile, neglectful, crass, and unsympathetic. They did not always serve your needs, and that has had a significant effect on your development.

Parents of the twentieth century did not invent abuse. It has been handed down as a human legacy. If you look at child-rearing practices throughout history, you see that children have been mistreated for thousands of years. Yes, we have survived and even thrived as a species, but at what price do we carry on? History is crowded with the inhumanity of war, slavery, crime, and intolerance. Sometimes a culture even applauds cruelty and condones it as part of the social order. If you have grown up with the usual level of abuse, it will be difficult to acknowledge how much you have accepted it on a daily basis, just because this is how it has always been.

THE BATTLEGROUND OF EVERYDAY LIFE ▼

The following is an example of what Susan, a sales representative for a furniture company, has to suffer through in the course of her day. After the shrill of the alarm jolts her out of sleep, she fixes breakfast for her husband, Bob, who is also cranky from lack of sleep. Susan accidentally drops the pitcher of orange juice, which shatters, and its contents spill out on the kitchen floor. "You are a piece of work," Bob observes sarcastically. "They must love you at the office."

As she moves to the front of the line to buy a subway token, she fumbles in her purse for the correct change. Those behind her immediately begin to grumble, and within seconds one calls out, "Lady, get your act together. We have a train to catch," making her feel that sixteen strangers see her as a klutz. Susan finds a window seat and ten minutes later out of half-closed eyes she glimpses a billboard of a supermodel with a doll-sized waistline sipping a diet drink. An unwanted memory of her aerobics teacher telling her to work on her "cottage cheese thighs" slips into her mind. She looks down at her body and cringes slightly at how far she is from perfect.

At the office, before she even reaches her desk, her boss waylays her, and in front of her peers reminds her that she has failed to meet her quota for the third month in a row and that he is beginning to question his judgment in hiring her. As she stows her purse in the bottom drawer of her desk, her cheeks are burning at the loss of face she has just suffered. "We're not running a rest home here," he says as a parting blow, and she tries to calculate how hard it will be to win back respect at the company after this dressing down. With her confidence at an all-time low, she spends the morning making sales calls to customers who fail to respond to her pitch. She cannot sell her product because she is in no shape to sell herself.

Finally—lunch. She goes out with the girls and, remembering the towering picture of the supermodel on the billboard, orders only a green salad. Everyone else orders a full-course meal, so when it is time to pay, Susan asks the waitress for a separate check. "I'm sorry," the waitress replies, "we don't do separate checks." "I'm out of cash," Susan lies, not wanting to reveal her lack of finances to the others who will surely think less of her for it. "I need to use my credit card. Can't you make an exception?" At this point, the conversation has caught the attention of those at the table who are uncomfortable with her making a public fuss. The waitress snaps, "Sorry, it's the restaurant's policy." Just as Susan opens her mouth to answer, one of her friends cuts her off. "Don't pay any attention to her. She just likes to give people a hard time." Susan feels like a five-year-old.

It is now only one o'clock, and Susan's ego has been assaulted at every turn. She has been made to feel inadequate about her work standards, her body, her functioning capacities, and her attitude. Each of these incidents, in and of itself, may appear innocuous, but try stacking a hundred of them a day and you have a campaign of destruction of a person's self-esteem. We are supposed to be autonomous and strong and somehow raise ourselves from the ditch of degradation, buck ourselves up, and carry on. We are supposed to defend ourselves from the constant harassments of daily life and insensitive, impatient people. We are supposed to be driven toward success no matter how inadequate we are made to feel personally. And all the while we cannot even see the barrage of assaults we have to withstand every single day, nor do we have compassion for our own pain.

WHERE IT ALL STARTS ▼

Children are ideal objects for abuse. They are in no position to prevent it and they seem to survive in spite of it. In her book *Banished Knowledge*, Alice Miller describes it: "This great adaptability of the newborn infant to our cruel world, this toughness has since time immemorial misled people to believe that one can inflict anything on a child with impunity: completely neglect him, hold lighted cigarettes against his skin, shake him, throw him against the wall, yell at him." Yes, we survive, but we carry the injuries inside us until we finally manage to purge ourselves.

Some children are exposed to physical abuse, which, at least now, is condemned by society and illegal. They are beaten and tortured and left without food or warmth. The more prevalent kind of injury, however, is emotional. Essentially, whenever a parent refuses to assist a child in meeting his or her needs, emotional abuse has occurred. In his book *Healing the Shame that Binds You*, John Bradshaw lists some of the ways in which children are mistreated emotionally:

- **Being shamed.** Bradshaw defines "toxic shame" as becoming endowed "with a sense of worthlessness . . . the all-pervasive sense that I am flawed and defective as a human being." No matter what you do, you're not good enough. The wound that Donald Sutherland must have sustained fed the feeling that he had nothing to contribute because he *was* nothing.
- **Being abandoned.** Children are abandoned in far more subtle ways than being physically left behind. Some parents are so taken up with themselves that they practice wholesale neglect of their children's developmental needs. The child isn't nurtured, accepted, praised, or

even taught how to function and survive. "To be abandoned by someone who is physically present is much more crazymaking" than to be physically abandoned by a mother or father walking out the door never to return.

- **Being prevented from experiencing a healthy range of emotions such as jealousy, rage, sexuality, and defiance.** When a child expresses a feeling that touches off an unacceptable trigger effect in a parent, the parent will try to silence his or her own reactions by silencing the child.
- **Being prevented from developing healthy psychological boundaries.** When a parent is using her child to act out her own dreams, she does not allow the child to separate in a healthy way. This is one subtle form of abuse that often goes unrecognized because to all the world it appears as if she is giving her child nothing but support and encouragement. But the question is: *What* is she supporting? His own individuality or her agenda? The child becomes nothing but an extension of her, living *her* life instead of his own. Whatever success he achieves in life, it will never feel real because it is not sourced from within himself.

THE SPIRAL OF ABUSE ▼

How does all this mistreatment prohibit success? Chapter One describes the obstacles that make it difficult for the average person to get her real needs met and achieve the kind of success that carries personal meaning. Overcoming those obstacles requires inner strength, healthy self-esteem, and an affectionate attitude toward oneself. If we are trying to make it in an abuse-based environment, all these qualities are precluded. We are focused on filling in holes of deficiency instead of building mountains of achievement. We cannot center on the positives and how to build on them because our attention has been commandeered by the negatives and how to overcome them. To find real success, you must—quite simply—feel good about yourself.

That's fairly difficult to do if you have been conditioned to think of yourself as flawed and defective. You really have nothing to work with.

Whatever self-concept you harbor on the inside, it will manifest itself in the outside world. If you view yourself as defective (whether you've recognized it or not), you will expend a tremendous amount of energy suffering the slings and arrows of your inner critic, and then overcompensate for your lack of self-worth. No matter what you appear to accomplish, you will never experience success in a positive way because you're just trying to make up for your perceived defects. The fact is that no amount of accomplishment will equalize a negative self-concept. You may find yourself the CEO of a Fortune 500 company, but if you have not healed the wounds that bind you, then you will secretly regard yourself as a failure. Of the many ways in which we pay a price for having been emotionally abused, none is more subtle and insidious than the way we are prevented from being the kind of success we would like to be, and then from owning it when it does come.

This is what the negative spiral in which most people are caught looks like: First, you have already been conditioned to perceive yourself as flawed. Think of a plot of land where the water table was poisoned for years by a steel mill. No matter where one travels on that land, the water tastes slightly bitter. Everywhere you go, everything you do, you have a vague feeling that nothing is quite good enough. Of course, your perception is in no way objective. It is all filtered through this fundamental sense of deficiency. You may score ninety-five on a math test, but you will focus on the five percent of answers you got wrong. A small voice will say, "What's wrong with me? How could I have missed those?" Perhaps you were second best in your class. You will tend to lose sight of all those students you soared ahead of and myopically concentrate on the one person who did better than you. People operating from this dark hole will always find an excuse to beat themselves up. They'll go out on a first date, and if they're silent for a few moments, a voice will rush in and say, "God I'm boring. Don't I know how to talk?" At the slightest bump, they jump to a negative conclusion.

Second, you feel ashamed of the flaw. The human psyche cannot tolerate feeling flawed. A person needs to feel acceptable and sufficient for who she is. If she doesn't, what comes up automatically is shame. It cannot be otherwise. The thought is, "I crash-burned on that interview. It's all my fault. I have nothing to show for myself. I'd like to crawl into a hole and disappear." More than anything else, one who feels shamed does not want her real self to be seen. She cannot afford to be genuine because her real "defective" self will be exposed. To cover up the flaw, she might try to be as perfect as possible in ways she can control. She is not only trying to fool other people in her drive for perfection, she is trying to fool herself. "If only I can make it through life without screwing up, then perhaps I can relax about myself." At least her mistakes won't stand out as testimony to her basic worthlessness. With some people this leads to grandiose behavior. Because they feel so lacking on the inside, they must project a superhero on the outside, someone who can leap tall buildings with a single bound, and certainly someone who never makes a mistake. They cannot afford to acknowledge being wrong because that would be allowing a crack to appear in the egg. One crack and it's all over. With people like this, grandiosity is just the twin brother of outright deficiency.

Third, shame propels you to have a hostile relationship with yourself. You cannot help attacking this person who is in such poor shape, who ought to be doing so much better. How can you possibly leave yourself alone? You have to improve this defective product. Who will ever love her?

Fourth, by treating yourself as your own worst enemy, you cannot possibly look out for your best interests. That stands to reason. You cannot plan for or achieve real success. That is not to say that people who hate themselves don't go out and make a lot of money. They do—they just lack all capacity to enjoy it. When people cannot enjoy being themselves, it is fundamentally impossible for them to enjoy their wealth. They possess all the external manifestations of success, but they live in a private hell where they feel inadequate and wanting at every turn.

The problem with a spiral is that it endlessly winds back on itself. It is a self-perpetuating system. The person spends his life spinning round and round on a merry-go-round he cannot get off. Once he is conditioned to perceive himself as flawed, it is inevitable that he will become an adversary to himself. Picture having your worst enemy locked in your head, the person in your life who likes you the least. Is this enemy going to behave in a caring way toward you, worry about filling your needs, comfort you when you hurt, tout your accomplishments, attain the goals of your heart and soul? No! And if you have a moment of forgetfulness, the demon in your head will remind you of your worthlessness. As summed up by Julia Roberts' character in *Pretty Woman*, "People put you down enough, you start to believe it." The demon that lives inside you is merely the internalized collective voice of all those who have disparaged your worth as a human being.

If you're having trouble visualizing just how powerful this demon really is, try taking a major risk in your life and it will appear in all its glory. Just in case you have no major risks on the horizon, do this exercise: Imagine you are about to make a life-changing decision. In other words, the stakes have to be high. Then stand back and notice the flood of thoughts that come rushing in. "You can't do this because . . ." "You shouldn't do this because . . ." "If you go ahead and foolishly do this . . ." Write down the thoughts in exactly the words they appear. Just let them pour out without censoring them. Now put your notes away. Wait a day or so without thinking about it. Then take out the notes and read what your internal dialogue looks like in black and white. I can guarantee you that the level of shrillness of the threat of doom will be in direct proportion to the level of risk you are proposing to take. The bigger the decision, the higher the decibel. This goes a long way in explaining why people have so much trouble overcoming their own resistance toward making major changes in their lives.

ABUSE-BASED THINKING ▼

What is our primary way of communicating with each other? Talking. The way we communicate with ourselves, though, is through thoughts. We have an ongoing inner dialogue traversing our brain every waking moment. It's a little like having a talk radio show on and not knowing where the off-switch is. Now think about listening to an obnoxious talk radio host who hates *you personally* and cannot help broadcasting his opinions over the air. Think of the barrage to your psyche. "Can't you do anything right? If they were handing out cash for brain size, you wouldn't make enough for a cup of coffee. When are you gonna wise up? My dog could live your life better than you do. Why aren't you making as much money as Jack and Jill? If you had invested in valley real estate in the sixties, look at how rich you'd be right now." The voice points out not only all the mistakes you have made but also the mistake that you ARE.

Now ask yourself this: Would you really let anybody else talk to you like that? Would you just stand there and take it? Picture this honestly. Wouldn't you turn around and walk away? As strange as it may seem, we rarely let anyone treat us as badly as we treat ourselves.

This steady diatribe is what Dr. Robert Luthardt refers to as *abuse-based thinking*. It is characterized by a sharp, critical tone that one directs at oneself, by a generally pessimistic attitude toward one's capacities and outlook for the future, and by a universally adversarial relationship with oneself, and consequently with the world. If your relationship with yourself is hostile, it cuts you off from yourself, interrupting the natural flow of information from the body to the mind.

Let's examine some of the ways in which abuse-based thinking manifests itself in our lives.

First, there is the understandable expectation that the world will be a hostile place. We don't expect abundance so pleasures don't come easily, if they come at all. Life is generally viewed as a battleground in which "I have to fight for what's mine because no one will give an inch." This accounts for all the colorful metaphors in the business world such as "Nuke the competition!" When I finally worked up the courage to quit my corporate job in favor of an acting career, the members of my family were downright appalled: "You can't make a living doing that!" And what else could I have expected from them? They had been disappointed by the universe at every juncture. What would cause them to believe it would treat me any better? The world is perceived by many people as a jungle, a place where you had better not get too comfortable while eating because someone will come up from behind and eat you. Arthur Miller, in *Death of a Salesman*, describes this mentality when Willy Loman is advised by his brother, "Never fight fair with a stranger . . . you'll never get out of the jungle that way." When the world is your enemy, defeat and disappointment are always at your heels.

Second, abuse-based thinking manifests as a congenitally pessimistic attitude in which the glass is never seen as half full, but always as half empty. A Hindu teacher once said that people are born crying, they live complaining, and they die disappointed. "And get used to it, folks, because that's life." A great-aunt of mine was the perfect example of this attitude. She was born with the proverbial onion under her nose. Even as a small child I could spot her as someone to avoid if I didn't want my mood soured. She cast off such a negative aura that she was unpleasant to be around. Whenever there was an opportunity to project how things could go wrong, she was a champ. Not surprisingly, for her they usually did.

Third, abuse-based thinking manifests as inner complaining. People just have no idea how harmful inner complaining is to quality of life. The reason it is so harmful is that it represents a rejection of your life as it is right now. Don't kid yourself: NOW is all there is. The past is a memory in your head and the future hasn't occurred yet. There is *only* this moment. Are you going to keep saying no to it? If you believe you don't complain very much, pay attention to the steady stream of thoughts in your head and notice how many contain a note of complaint. How many suggest that things just aren't quite right and that somehow they should be better? *"It's too cold. Oh . . . now it's too hot. Jerry still hasn't called; I hate to be kept waiting. My boss's feedback on that report this morning was less than glowing; I think I deserve better. I'm having a bad hair day. This dress doesn't fit. The steak is overcooked."* Does it ever stop? How many times in a day do we really allow ourselves to sink into the moment and say, "I accept this just as it is." Yet think of how much better life would be if we weren't busy rejecting practically every single increment of our experience.

For most people, inner complaining is all but invisible. Even more fundamental than a thought process, it is a state of mind in which reality is experienced as "not enough, not enough, not enough." This state is like a black hole that can never be filled no matter how much is shoveled in.

Fourth, abuse-based thinking manifests as a knee-jerk tendency to find fault with the world, blindly, and usually without reason. While inner complaining is a way of experiencing reality, finding fault is an attitude, a critical approach to the world at large. Quite simply, there is an orientation toward first *not liking*. Before you even realize the words are out of your mouth, you have just criticized someone or something. It is, in fact, internal complaining turned outward. Here is a joke that illustrates the point. A young man takes his mother to a restaurant. "I'm getting married," he says happily. "To whom," his mother asks. "Well, do you see that table over there, the one with six women? She's sitting right there. Can you guess which one it is?" Without skipping a beat, his mother says, "Is it the redhead?" The son is shocked. "How did you know?" His mother answers, "She's the one I don't like."

The joke is funny because the mother is being her usual self in that she is unabashedly hard to please whatever the situation. It doesn't matter which woman the son had chosen, his mother wouldn't have liked her because for one reason or another she doesn't like any of them. What is also telling about this joke is that it is a mother relating to her son. The pattern within family systems is that the tendency to criticize goes unchecked. People don't feel the same need to protect the feelings of family members, or even to observe some common courtesies, as they would for outsiders, probably because they feel their brother, sister, mother, father, son, or daughter is not going anywhere. Bound for life, as they say. Your sister will always be your sister.

Fifth, abuse-based thinking manifests as a pattern in which the behavior leads to more of the same. Whatever is fed into you, and is processed by you, ends up coming out of you in pretty much the same form. People who have to live on a steady diet of mistreatment believe it is normal to mistreat other people. There is almost no awareness that it could be otherwise. Shortly before my grandfather died, he fell and nearly broke his leg. Naturally, he was old and frightened. The doctor poked around and examined him, and then said, "You know what they do with horses, don't you?" This was an unmistakable allusion to the fact that when a horse breaks a leg, they shoot it. My grandfather, who was one of the bravest men I've ever known, was destroyed by this thoughtless comment. I don't even think the doctor who made it was trying to be cruel. He just never stopped to sensitize himself to the condition and frame of mind of his patient. He was either too busy or too callous. Like many physicians, he had gone through a miserable internship during which he was overworked and humiliated. Trained to be insensitive to his own emotional needs, he became insensitive to those of his patients. Such cold, uncaring treatment toward those at their most vulnerable happens far more often than it should in our healthcare system.

Each of the above five manifestations is the predictable outcome from people whose thoughts are intrinsically hostile. I learned firsthand from my own family the sorrows that are heaped onto a person who looks at life through a dim, gray lens. A kind of bleak picture inevitably forms. For my family, the world was a hostile place; it was implied in every exchange that nothing would ever work out well, that everything was slightly rotten. Even when conditions did improve, it was never good enough. The world turns out to be what we perceive it to be, nothing more and nothing less.

"Abuse-based thinking is artificial to the human condition," says Dr. Robert Luthardt, who originated the terms *abuse-based thinking* and *affection-based thinking*. "We have to be taught to be abusive, and it must be constantly reinforced."

Once we have expended so much energy initiating and reinforcing a negative approach to living, we are almost forced to believe it is the natural way of things. We have an investment in it being "the right way." The payoff, then, is a jaded form of comfort and a fortification that our whole lives haven't been a lie. "The misery I know is better than the misery I don't know." Abuse-based thinking shelters us from a fear of the unknown. However bad things are, it seems to be a human idiosyncrasy that we find it easier *not* to change them. And so we have good reason not to even acknowledge how bad things are because to do so would be to force one's hand. "If I really admitted how desperately unhappy I am living here, I would have to look for a new place. I couldn't kid myself about it anymore." In the prison film *The Shankshaw Redemption*, James Whitmore portrays an old convict who has been in jail most of his life. The paradox is that as harsh as it is, prison has become comfortable for him because it's the only life he knows. He goes into his parole hearings afraid to be released. When he finally is, the changes freedom brings are so intense that he commits suicide rather than begin a new life.

As an abuse-based thinker, your main problem is that you lose whether you succeed or fail. Many people who are "successful" have simply created a cozy little niche in hell. It's still a cave in the pit of the earth, but they've put a throw rug on the floor and reupholstered the furniture. They're so proud of their little spot. They don't really enjoy their life, but they won't give themselves permission to change it. There is the technically proficient surgeon who secretly detests being around hospitals and sick people, the partner in the investment banking firm who really wants to be a violinist, the guy flipping burgers who wants to run his own bookstore, the housewife and mother who really wants to be a real estate mogul. All of these people might be highly functional in what they are doing now. It just doesn't bring them the satisfaction they crave on a deeper level. When the unspoken payoff is "It's easier to stay where I am and be miserable," life is never going to live up to its potential.

As I discuss all the sources of abuse-based thinking, you may be wondering, "Am I surrounded by these people myself?" The answer is probably yes and no. The issue is not whether people are sometimes negative, it is whether they can be characterized as primarily negative, hostile, and pessimistic. I was in New York on a business trip a few years ago and made the mistake of calling my eighty-five-year-old aunt to say hello. "Where are you staying?" she asked. "At the Westbury," I replied, naming one of the loveliest hotels in the city. "Oh," she said, "the Westbury is a beautiful hotel." There was a pause, and in the back of my mind I knew she was launching the missile. "Of course, it's not as nice as the Carlyle." Pow, right in the kisser! If I had been staying at the

Carlyle, it wouldn't have been as nice as the Plaza, and so on. I knew from long experience that this woman could not let anyone be happy with what they had; she had to let the air out of their balloon. After I hung up, I realized that every conversation I had ever had with her had been characterized by the same "not good enough" mentality, and that it would never be any different.

My aunt is a clear-cut case of an abuse-based thinker. However, not everyone is as dyed-in-the-wool as she is. Some people have undesirable tendencies, but they're not hopeless cases. It is feasible to actively influence the behavior of most family members and friends and improve on the relationships you have with them. Even in the midst of a single conversation, you can literally change its course simply by modeling the type of behavior you prefer. I had a close friend who was in the habit of beginning every conversation with a "funny" insult. It was his way of saying hello. One day I came right out and told him that I was genuinely hurt by his sarcasm and would be grateful if we could be more affectionate to each other. At first he was shocked, but then I watched the awareness sweep across his face as he actually "got" my point. That one comment caused a metamorphosis in our relationship, and he has never insulted me since that constructive confrontation.

It is well worth evaluating which people in your life are predominantly steeped in abuse and beyond help. The following is a ten-question test. Score each person for how consistently every question applies. Rate each question on a scale of one to five—one meaning "not at all" and five meaning "all the time."

1. Do they make small remarks that undermine my confidence?
2. Do they stonewall me whenever I bring up a problem and want to work it out?
3. Do their first remarks about people and ideas tend to be critical?
4. Do they seek out opportunities to complain?
5. Do I feel diminished in their presence?
6. When I express my dreams and aspirations, do they discourage me from acting on them?

7. Do they pay inordinate attention to their own needs and ignore mine?
8. Are they pessimistic about life and how things will turn out?
9. When there is some dispute, do they always make me the wrong party?
10. When I attempt to be open and sincere, do they slap me down with sarcasm?

Even if the person scores a four or five on some of the questions, remember that we are all occasionally guilty of human frailty. What you are looking for is not haphazard imperfections, but a consistent pattern showing that the person is stuck in a cynical, pessimistic, and morose attitude, has no desire to change, and seems to want everyone to be just like him. If someone has an overall score of 35 to 50, he is probably an abuse-based thinker.

WHY WE BLINDLY ACCEPT ABUSE ▼

To me, the fascinating thing about abuse is not merely its prevalence in our culture, but the fact that the majority of adults continue to tolerate it whether they have to or not. The key word in the above heading is *blindly*. When I say we are blind, what I mean is that our self-esteem is assaulted by abuse on a daily basis, and often this process goes largely unnoticed by the conscious mind. Some readers may be thinking, "Well, what's the problem then? If my conscious mind doesn't know it's happening, I have nothing to be concerned about." That is not precisely true. It takes energy to activate a defense system, and that energy has to come from somewhere. When abuse is being dealt with, whether we are consciously aware of it or not, vital energy is being leached away from the entire body. A person who is defending against abuse has almost no energy left over to enjoy her life, to engage in healthy goals, and to pursue her bliss.

For those of you who are making your way through a minefield of very real offenses and staving off harmful behavior, it is worth examining why you waste your energy defending yourself when sometimes you could just move on. Why do you blindly accept abuse?

REASON NUMBER ONE: *You're not aware that you are being attacked.*

In the classic Bela Lugosi movie version of *Dracula*, one of the actors says, "The principal strength of the vampire is that people refuse to believe in him." The principal strength of abuse-based thinking is that we refuse to acknowledge it is there. It is so deeply imbedded in how we were raised that it has become an integral part of the dynamics of our mind. In other words, we are so used to the sinister whispers we hear inside our head, and the subliminal urgings are so much a part of us, that we don't recognize them as anything that needs to be purged. There is an old saying, "The devil is right behind you." The devil is that little voice in the back of your head that throws you into constant self-doubt. It is not the devil, however, who is speaking. It is you speaking to yourself, you doubting yourself, you poisoning the content of your mind, and you selling yourself short.

Once in a while someone else points out your self-destructive patterns, telling you that you're being hard on yourself or causing yourself needless suffering. How often do you shrug it off? "I'm okay. It's no big deal. It doesn't affect me. I don't pay any attention to it." We don't take our own suffering seriously, and because of that we perpetuate it. In turn, we are insensitive to others because we don't take their suffering seriously either. I constantly overhear people trading subtle insults, especially husbands and wives. This is a conversation I witnessed the other day: Wife: "Your taste is all in your mouth. You wouldn't know a good suit if you saw it." Husband: "The only thing you've ever been any good at is shopping. They should hand out degrees for using the credit card."

This tendency to diminish begins, of course, with parenting. The parenting rules that have been passed down from generation to generation tend to make children feel unworthy. These rules lead children to believe that their needs are demands, their desire for value is conceit, their activity to get attention is "showing off," their healthy expression of will is "destructive willfulness," their youthful spontaneity is wildness, and their desire to have fun in life is frivolous. In short, the child is taught to be *against* himself because he is so unacceptable for what he is—even though he cannot, of course, be anything else. This forms the core of shame. In *For Your Own Good*, Alice Miller refers to these parenting rules as the "poisonous pedagogy." Some of its tenets are:

- Children are the property of parents, who determine what is right and what is wrong.
- If the parent is angry, it's the child's fault.
- The child's life-affirming feelings are threatening.
- The child's will must be "broken" at a very early age so he won't realize how badly he is being treated, and so he won't be able to hold the parents responsible for their cruelty.

The last point is particularly important because it illustrates the original point of this section: The truly insidious aspect of abusive parenting is that we don't recognize that it has occurred, and we are unlikely to acknowledge it fully as adults because of our deep sense of loyalty. Says Miller, "This early conditioning makes it virtually impossible for the child to discover what is actually happening to him." It all happens preverbally, before we have any mental ability to formulate an opinion about it. Children can only take their parents' word about what type of treatment they are entitled to. Their faith in their mother and father is so overwhelming that they believe them above their own experience. It is easy to see, then, how dependent children are on parenting for their sense of worth. If Dad says Joey is a good-for-nothing little boy, and Joey would like to believe otherwise, Joey is going to lose. If Joey feels he is good with his hands, but his father says he's incompetent, Joey will distrust his own experience of competence and trust his father's assessment instead. Parents who teach children to doubt their own experience make it particularly difficult for them to be in alignment with reality, because after all, experience is the only thing one has to learn from, the only real foundation from which to deduce the truth.

Miller also comments on why adults cannot look back on their childhoods with objectivity. "The child's dependence on his or her parents' love also makes it impossible in later years to recognize [what has occurred], which often remains hidden behind the early idealization of the parents for the rest of the child's life." This means that as adults, we are inclined to keep justifying our parents' hurtful behavior out of the stubborn belief that they "did it for our own good."

In the popular HBO television series *The Sopranos*, Tony Soprano, who is the head of the New Jersey mob, is a classic example of the kind of person Alice Miller described. He is from a traditional Italian family where the mother, no matter what her character, is cast somewhere between a saint and an angel. Because Tony is subject to unexplained panic attacks, he is forced to see a psychiatrist so that he can be medicated for his condition. This is not the kind of man for whom revealing vulnerable and personal secrets about his childhood is comfortable, but he has to do it because it is part of the therapeutic process. In session after session, the psychiatrist listens to Tony complain about his destructive, toxic, overbearing mother and suggests, rather gently, that perhaps she has been a negative influence in his life. "Your mother," she says, "is clearly someone who has great difficulty in maintaining a relationship with anyone." Despite his anger, Tony evenhandedly defends the woman who raised him. "But she's my mother," he says. "You're supposed to take care of your mother. She's a little old lady . . . she's an old sweetie pie." For those who follow the series, this line makes them gag; she is an ogre. But Tony is incapable of admitting that his mother is both loveless and joyless, that she cannot tolerate joy in anyone else, and that she never gave him or his siblings an ounce of love. After Tony sulks for a while, the shrink inquires, "What were some of the loving, warm experiences you remember as a child?" Tony thinks for a few minutes, and then he can remember only one. "One time my father tripped and fell down the stairs . . . and my mother laughed."

While I think it's safe to say that Tony Soprano's mother represents a worst-case scenario, I can certainly see similar patterns in my own life, and I suspect that many readers will be able to do the same. I was always able to acknowledge my anger at my father, who had abandoned me at an early age, but not at my mother. I regarded her as someone who had my best interests at heart. One day in therapy, my psychotherapist suggested that my mother was, perhaps, an abusive woman. I reacted the same way Tony Soprano did. I leaped in to defend her: "My mother loves me and she's always sacrificed her own needs to take care of me. It wasn't easy for her to raise a son on her own. It would be ungrateful for me to label her as abusive just because of some of the things she's said over the years. That's just the way she talks. She doesn't mean anything by it."

Even as I was saying all this, I knew on a deep level that my therapist had a point. I just wasn't ready to bring the realization into the light of day. Understanding this, my therapist suggested putting his theory to a test. He asked me to record my next telephone conversation with my mother so that he and I could analyze it together. I did as he asked, and after we listened to the recorded exchange, I was staggered. My therapist, who had no investment in being right or wrong, demonstrated for me how virtually every word out of my dear old mother's mouth was disdainful, derisive, and undermining.

Hearing the implied attack in nearly everything she said through the objective ear of my therapist constituted one of the defining moments in my life. It brought so many things I had been confused about into complete clarity. I could see why my defenses were so often on the alert when I spoke with people: I expected to be under attack even on the most trifling subjects. When I asked my mother how she was feeling, her response was, "What do you care?" Analysis: She took a genuinely caring question and turned it back on me as an insinuation that I was actually an uncaring person asking an insincere question. When I attempted to share with her how successful my business had become, she said, "Well, I suppose you know what you're doing." The tone was unmistakably sarcastic, and it threw a monkey wrench into my machinery, causing me to question my own decision-making process even though it was producing sterling results. Suddenly I had the feeling that tomorrow, my business strategy might not work at all. At one point, feeling thoroughly despondent, I tried to defend myself by showing her that I did know what I was doing. Her response? "You never did listen to what anyone told you." Now I was not only ungrateful and incompetent, but narrow-minded as well. And on and on. I could not win. Obviously, this is a conversation that had been repeated in one form or another for years—all my life, in fact—but I was unable to accept how toxic the dynamic between us was, and therefore to do anything about it, until my therapist pried my eyes open.

How do you effectively defend yourself with someone like this? If you are a victim, you sit there feebly through the conversation making halfhearted attempts to regain some of your self-esteem. After you hang up, you fix yourself a double martini to numb the pain, pig out on chocolate cake because you're desperate for something sweet, or try to have sex to bring a little affection into your experience. You do whatever you can to make yourself feel better. I don't recommend any of these. A better approach is to face the beast. Try to recognize that the reason you're feeling lower than a piece of gum stuck to the bottom of somebody's shoe is that your self-esteem has been under attack. If you walk away from a person and you are unclear about whether you were attacked or not, a good indicator is whether, in the course of the conversation, you felt yourself growing smaller and smaller. Whenever you experience yourself being diminished, that is the red flag.

Once you learn how to recognize an attack, how do you put up a powerful defense, one that places you on sound footing? There are effective ways to disarm people and regain control of the conversation. For example, when my mother asked, "What do you care?" I might have reacted in several ways. First, I could have thrown the question back on her by confronting her comment directly. "I do care how you feel, and I would appreciate an answer." Second, I could have confronted her on the hostility of the question. "I asked you a perfectly sincere question and, instead of answering me, you attacked me. Was that your intention?" If she replies no (very few people will admit to attacking you), my reply could have been, "Then in the future, would you please refrain from making sarcastic statements when I ask an open and honest question." The simple truth is often the best defense.

As I suggested after the above questionnaire, if you find that a person is completely unresponsive to your needs and is utterly unamenable to dropping his hostility, it may be necessary to exclude him from your life. This is an extreme step, but I will venture to say that it is worth considering in some circumstances. Finding genuine success in life sometimes means discerning when to rid yourself of people who don't want you to be happy and have been actively discouraging your happiness for years. It is not surprising that millions of people wake up when they are middle-aged, wonder why they don't feel successful in the least, but don't do anything about it. Often it boils down to the fact that they don't want to make the necessary changes. Some readers will feel threatened at the thought of aggravating the people around them. If those people are being abusive now, when you are behaving within the norm, how will they act if your behavior changes radically? Then those friends and family members will really be threatened. Nothing, in fact, threatens people more than when one of their "own" attempts to break away and actually become healthy. You may find that you justify not making the changes necessary to create a genuinely successful life for yourself because you're simply afraid of bringing on additional criticism and reproach.

REASON NUMBER TWO: *As a child, you were educated in an environment where punishment was completely acceptable, and you are conditioned to accept it.*

While it is true that adults need to set boundaries and establish consequences with their children, punishment is of a different order altogether. It is demeaning, shaming, and hostile, and it is designed to make the child feel as if there is something wrong with him. Punishment is, by nature and by definition, punitive; it is designed to make the receiver suffer, not teach him right from wrong.

The educational system is based upon the liberal use of punishment. Although corporal punishment has been discouraged in recent years, shame, ridicule, derision, humiliation, bullying, and criticism are still used freely. The very pedantic attitude of teachers—that they have the answers and that students are merely empty receptacles—shows a lack of respect for children as thinking beings. This attitude is designed to discourage any challenge to the teacher's authority. If I had not seen it before, this became most obvious to me in law school where it was a time-honored tradition for professors to ridicule and threaten students. Since our entire future rested on the grades they gave us, there was no fighting back. One of my professors had a habit of singling out one student per day for individual hazing, which was unbearably humiliating for the recipient. Even in acting classes ridicule was a popular tool. In one instance, when I finally spoke out against an acting teacher for his egregious cruelty, the other students could not bear the threat to authority and came to his defense. "He's doing us a favor," they assured me. "That's how tough it is in the real world so we may as well get used to it now." If the teacher had begun beating students with a club, I half expected the students to say, "Well, that's reality. Get used to it." It was troubling to see that the way they framed this treatment in their minds was that it was something they had not only to accept, but to be grateful for.

The tone set by parents and teachers is picked up on by children, who act it out with each other. Just watch the pecking order on the playground and you will find it unmistakable. *Lord of the Flies* is a frightening novel by William Golding that describes how well children learn to pass on cruelty as if it were part of the natural order. The book describes a group of English schoolboys who are marooned on a deserted island and left to themselves to survive. Eventually, even the least aggressive of them reverts to savage behavior just to be part of the group and avoid being picked on himself.

As you grow up, you find that the whole wide world mimics the behavior of parents in that mistakes, failure, and nonconformity are met with a hostile and, in a way, demeaning response. In a perfect world where people are free to be their best, most decent selves, there would be kindness and neutrality as a response to mistakes. There would be an overall appreciation for the fact that mistakes will be made. A healthy response is to correct the mistake without insulting or assaulting the offender. Sometimes behavior must be censored and decisions must be criticized, but these responses can be delivered in an objective, affirming, and kind way. This makes the person want to do better, not feel shame about the past.

A few progressive schools—The Dalton School (New York), Advantage Schools (Boston), and the Waldorf Schools—have begun to teach their students a "kinder and gentler" way of interrelating and resolving conflict. These children learn to respect and listen to each other. If, however, that healthy behavior is not being mirrored in the home, there is little that teachers can do. They can have some positive effect, but parents are a far stronger influence.

Those people who were not treated fairly in the home or in school will not expect to be treated fairly as adults. They will put up with the same treatment from bosses, spouses, and everyone around them. In turn, they will dish out the same. Abuse begets abuse.

REASON NUMBER THREE: *Mistreatment of human beings is an institution, and therefore it seems impossible to escape it.*

Because it has been handed down by tradition throughout history, the practice of abuse has been institutionalized and labeled with the safe and comforting phrase, "That's just the way it is."

Years ago, Shirley Jackson wrote a short story for the *New Yorker* that became famous. It was entitled "The Lottery." In the story, the residents of a small town in a peaceful area of the country hold a lottery every year. The conditions of the lottery are not described at first, nor is it told what "the winner" actually wins. But not far into the narrative there is a sense of foreboding that this is not any ordinary lottery. In the end, the reader finds that all the villagers draw lots and the winner is stoned to death. No one can remember when the tradition began, nor do they know why it is kept up. There is some unrest about it, especially as the time of the actual stoning draws closer. It is clear that nobody actually wants to play the game and that everyone feels intrinsically that it is wrong. Yet they all participate freely. When someone does speak out to question the practice, the voices of the crowd converge to silence him. The tradition is too firmly rooted, and it is actually more threatening to them to stop it than it is to stone a human being to death. It is not that the perpetrators are not rattled by what they are about to do, but they move inexorably toward the gruesome end because the status quo must be protected at all costs, even at the expense of the poor individual whose turn it is to die.

When the story was published, the *New Yorker* received a glut of letters from disturbed readers. They were angry. What could this story possibly be suggesting? Even you are probably thinking, "I would never participate in anything like that!" You can hold that position only because the barbarism of your own society is so invisible to you. War, poverty, and injustice—in spite of the fact that each bestows unspeakable suffering on the recipients—do not create any particular level of outrage in the average person.

One way, perhaps, that we can see the lesson of this story illustrated in life is to take a short look back in our own history books. In the pre–Civil War United States, shiploads of human beings were brought across the Atlantic Ocean in worse conditions than livestock were transported. They were chained, beaten, bought and sold, and forced to work without pay. Today it sounds contemptible, but at the time, even decent people who didn't quite approve of slavery nevertheless thought of it as a necessary part of the economic system of the South. How could a moral populace have tolerated treating human beings like property? After all, this was not the Roman Empire where human life was cheap and even meaningless. This was a democratic nineteenth-century America; slavery was diametrically opposed to the democratic ideal.

Just like in "The Lottery," no one could remember exactly when the system of slavery started or even why it started. But once the tradition had taken a firm hold, it took a war to uproot it. The reason slavery could be so easily accepted was that it was an institution, just like central government, organized religion, and a market economy.

For a rare few, the injustice of such an "institution" just becomes too much for their conscience to bear, and they must strike out against it. It isn't enough to engage in polite murmurings of dissent. They must do battle and put themselves at risk to dislodge the system. It takes a cataclysm to overturn an institution, and the American cataclysm of the nineteenth century was the Civil War. When history looks back on our own time, what traditions will they find abominable?

Most abuse does not take place on the scale of slavery. It occurs in subtle ways in everyday interactions. I grew up on the East Coast where many people seem to thrive on mutual debasement. They even express affection by beating each other up, figuratively speaking: "Hey, asshole. How ya doin'?" It is so commonplace for people to insult and ridicule each other that I did not become aware of it until I moved to the West Coast, where I found people to be more affectionate and "laid back." (The one exception is Hollywood, which is East Coast in spirit and where competitive backbiting is the norm.) Now, when I visit New York, I am sometimes appalled at the unbridled disdain and cynicism. A cynic is a person who sucks the life out of life. Often it is done through humor, but even when it's funny, it has the same effect. The price we pay for cynicism is a loss of joy and contentment and a lessening of the ability to simply appreciate the small pleasures of life. The one capacity cynics cannot allow themselves is appreciation, and they cannot stand it in those around them.

There are many more institutions than we would like to acknowledge that support the notion that abuse is normal. Besides the public school system, there are, among others, the military, the legal system, the corporate world, the media, and sports. Wherever we find our niche, it seems, we just learn to survive. One of the reasons I survived at Marine Corps boot camp, where recruits are worked over royally by drill instructors, was that I was so used to being mistreated in my childhood that a little bit more didn't seem to make any difference.

As anyone who has been there will attest, abuse-based thinking abounds in corporate America, which functions on what I call "management by intimidation." No matter what your job, the sword is always dangling over your head: "Produce or (gulp) we'll fire you!" Last year, my friend Hal took a job with a six-figure starting salary.

He was the number two executive in a new ad agency, which he soon found was a pressure cooker. If he made it home by ten at night, he considered himself lucky. His boss, the president, was the mistress of abuse. She criticized him without offering constructive advice. She ridiculed him at meetings. "Why don't you understand this point about market shares? Joe understands it." She pointed the spotlight on his every gesture. "You're shaking your head. I want input, not head shaking!" She took him to task for the slightest oversight. "Why didn't you send that client a Christmas card? Do you realize how big his account is with us?" She would even call him at home on weekends just to yell. It took a year of bullying for Hal to acknowledge that he was being bullied. He had been in the corporate atmosphere long enough to accept that bullying was just part of the way business was conducted, so his boss had to step far over the line before he was willing to walk away. By the time he resigned, he was a wreck.

This man's story, and the fact that he accepted such outrageous behavior for so long, illustrates how acceptable inhumane treatment has become in the corporate world. It is no wonder that road rage, domestic violence, alcoholism, drug abuse, and depression are so common. The stress of the work world is overwhelming. It has to leak out somewhere, and miserable people will either explode or self-medicate.

Even if one is not working in an environment where abuse is common, one is exposed to it in the media. This demonstrates our infatuation with ill treatment. Famous people are routinely savaged by journalists, guests are interrogated and browbeaten by hosts, and common courtesy appears to be a thing of the past. The prevalence of violence in movies and television is renowned. An extreme example today is professional wrestling, which is becoming increasingly popular. It takes Three Stooges slapstick to a frightening new level of savagery and mayhem. Wrestlers relish verbally beating each other up and then breaking chairs over their opponent's head. Small children in the audience sit on their father's shoulders and cheer them on. Then they go home and practice choke holds on their little sisters.

REASON NUMBER FOUR: *The person accepts abuse because he has no choice.*

Reason Number Four is short because, unfortunately, there is not much that can be said. There are segments of the population who can do nothing about their predicament. Life is hell, and that's all there is to it. Small children who are neglected and/or abused are doomed to endure it. Inmates in prison have no place to escape to. And those in extreme poverty often have few choices. All that these people can do is minimize their losses and get out when they can.

REASON NUMBER FIVE: *The person is too afraid to either fight or leave.*

Many people who are on the receiving end of mistreatment prefer not to rock the boat out of fear that things will just get worse. The classic example is the wife who, in spite of repeated physical abuse by her husband, refuses to leave him. "Where would I go? What would I do?" Some people are naturally passive and are not temperamentally suited to standing up for themselves. It takes a special act of nerve for them to show any sort of aggressive behavior. I have seen from my negotiation seminars that most people do not relish the thought of confrontation of any sort. If they can avoid a fight or an argument, they will.

REASON NUMBER SIX: *Because of low self-esteem, the person doesn't feel she deserves to be treated better.*

Abusive treatment creates low self-esteem, and in turn the abuse-based thinking that follows maintains this diminished sense of self-worth. Deep down, people with this mentality believe they are simply getting what they deserve, that they are actually being treated fairly because someone as worthless as they are can't expect much. Naturally, their lives are abysmal failures because their life manifests straight out of their philosophy: "I'm no damn good. I deserve to be a failure." They have a chronically negative self-image, and the continual lack of success they meet with reinforces what they already feel is true. Receiving few riches, material or otherwise, matches their internal picture of themselves as poverty-stricken individuals. They are nothing, so they should receive nothing. Even within their own minds they don't disparage being treated poorly. "I am flawed, so I'm in no position to complain." This attitude will be discussed further in Chapter Nine on the subject of victim mentality.

▼   There may be others, but these are the most common reasons for accepting abuse. The entire social system can be so toxic that we mistreat ourselves and we mistreat others without ever taking note of how much suffering is being caused needlessly. We can no longer perceive the level of suffering that is taking place because we are inured to it. "Not to take one's own suffering seriously, to make light of it or even to laugh at it," observes Alice Miller in *Banished Knowledge*, "is considered good manners in our culture. This attitude is even called a virtue, and many people are proud of their lack of sensitivity toward their own fate." In the next chapter, we will visit an insensitive, abusive concept that can get in the way of our success.

Chapter 7

A NEW PERSPECTIVE ON FAILURE

Success and failure are both difficult to endure. Along with success come drugs, divorce, fornication, bullying, travel, meditation, medication, depression, neurosis and suicide. With failure comes failure.

JOSEPH HELLER

One of the most abusive concepts human beings live with is called "failure." According to *Webster's Dictionary*, to fail is "to be lacking or insufficient; fall short." "To be unsuccessful in obtaining a desired end." A failure is "a person who does not succeed." We are all aware of the conventional associations with the word *failure*. Here I would like to debunk five different myths about this awesome and often fearsome concept.

MYTH NUMBER ONE: *Failure is the opposite of success.*

As we revere success, so do we abhor failure. In Western culture, failure is regarded as the direct opposite of success. In truth, it is an integral part of success because it contributes to the learning process. You cannot improve your knowledge, refine your expertise, bolster your competence, or perfect your technique without failing and learning from the experience.

Life can be looked at as a series of small and large failures punctuated by success. If life required you to wait till you were perfect before you were entitled to act, you would never get out of bed: "I'm still waiting. I surely don't want to make any mistakes. I don't dare get up yet." Life is, in fact, a process of learning *through* our mistakes, not in spite of them. It is a dynamic process in which you cannot get it right until you get it wrong first. So in spite of its usual negative connotation, failure is actually the catalyst for success. Look at any inventor, any pioneer, and you will see that they tried and failed and tried and failed until they finally figured out what they were doing. A classic example is the famous inventor Thomas A. Edison. Edison tried over a thousand materials until he found the one that would make a filament for his light bulb that would not fizzle and burn in seconds. We do not remember Edison as a failure for the 999 substances that were a miss. We remember him for the one that was a hit. Another example is Richard Nixon. After losing the 1960 presidential election to John Kennedy, he was written off completely by many pundits. He did disappear from the national scene for a while, but never lost his famous ambition. Years later he re-emerged and won the presidency twice. To paraphrase a line from the movie *Gigi*: Sometimes instead of succeeding at first, we succeed at last.

MYTH NUMBER TWO: *If you fail at something, the only appropriate response you can have is shame.*

If we look at failure as a means of learning, we can respond to it in a constructive way and still feel intact after it. Unfortunately, since shame is usually inextricably linked to failure, it means that if a person feels she has failed in some way, she will be moved to avoid or deny it. People will do anything to avoid feeling shame. It is the one emotional state most people cannot seem to tolerate. A person might outright hide from it. She may go in the opposite direction and overcompensate by becoming supremely competent in other ways. She might exhibit

hostility or anger toward anyone who dares point out the so-called failure. The one thing she won't do is face the failure because the feelings
that come up will be too painful.

Sometimes a single failure dogs a person's heels for life. When my
father was only twenty-one, his mother, who was a savvy businessperson herself, set him up in his own jewelry business in midtown Manhattan. Unfortunately, he was not ready for the responsibility, and
because of his youth and inexperience the business went bankrupt
within six months. He was devastated to such a degree that he was
never able to pick himself up and try again. He worked on and off as a
jewelry salesman, but he never bounced back from this "personal failure." He could not see it as merely a learning experience and move on.
For the remainder of his life, most of his money and energy were
sucked into compulsive gambling. He managed to get by thanks to his
army pension, and by sponging off his three sisters, but the shame of
failure crippled him until he died.

The way to deal with this kind of shame is to heap kindness upon
it. If you had a three-year-old who was ashamed of something, how
would you treat her? Wouldn't you be kind, affectionate, nurturing, and
supportive? Why do less for yourself? You can treat yourself with affection by reminding yourself that it is okay to fail, that failure is a catalyst
for success.

MYTH NUMBER THREE: *Success can only lead to more
success, failure to more failure.*

Not necessarily. Sometimes success leads to stagnation because it creates the comfortable illusion that you don't have to change. There are
legendary stories of individuals and companies that pursue the same
strategy endlessly into the future and miss the fact that it's time to
change. A dramatic example of this is IBM. In the sixties and seven-
ties, it was impossible to find a more successful corporation. It seemed
that it couldn't miss. Its aggressive marketing mowed down everything
in its path. By the mid-sixties, computers were even being referred to as
"IBM machines." It was such a behemoth that the government stepped

in to prevent a monopoly. But success bred slothfulness. From its original motto, "Think," they sank to "Don't rock the boat." Management thought the company owned the market. What they failed to realize was that if they were not going to be a crucible for new ideas, they could not stay on top. They were so enamored with their prize product, the mainframe computer, that they did not foresee the emerging dominance of personal computers, leaving the field open for the "little guys": Apple, Microsoft, Sun Microsystems, Oracle, Dell, and Compaq. Today, IBM is fighting to catch up.

While success can lead to stagnation, failure can lead to success. Failure makes you hungry, watchful, and alert. It keeps you on your toes and forces you to keep moving because you can't afford to sink. It points you in the right direction by declaring, "That way was wrong. Try again."

MYTH NUMBER FOUR: *If you're genuinely good at something, you can't fail.*

If you build a better mousetrap, Emerson said, people will beat a path to your door. Not true! Some people are terrific mousetrap builders, yet they never achieve fame or fortune. Their failure to rise to the top was just the way the dice rolled.

There is no better place to look than the world of acting to see that talent doesn't necessarily lead to success. In the Screen Actors Guild, many members are brilliant at their craft, yet more than 85 percent are out of work at any given time. An actor named Bill O'Brien is a prime example. Not only has he done extraordinary work onstage in New York's Off-Off-Broadway theater, but he is a talented screenwriter as well. With all of his ability, he has never been able to attract the kind of attention that puts the star machine into action, and so he supports himself by driving a cab. He lives in a small walk-up apartment on New York's West Side.

On his own terms, Bill is living the life he wants, but in the eyes of some he is a failure. To cope with this perception, he has had to adopt a healthy perspective on his lifestyle. It is essential that the talented

O'Briens of this world not allow others to define for them the meaning of success. They must focus on the satisfaction they derive from the fact that they do the work they love. For Bill, hell would be living in an expensive loft in SoHo for which he would have to work at an office job. In his life, success lies in the fact that he doesn't have to contend with climbing to the top of corporate America, which would send him to a mental institution. He does, however, live in New York—a city where people are highly influenced by image and power. He has to keep healthy emotional boundaries and stay grounded in his own values. If he were to let himself be overly influenced by the culture around him, his self-worth would be damaged.

How many people who are dissatisfied with their position in the world would feel differently about their status were it not for external influences? Ask yourself this question: "If I were the only one evaluating how I live, if I had no exposure whatsoever to the criticism of others, would I be satisfied?" The answer might surprise you.

One other aspect of Bill's life that contributes to his overall feeling of success is that he has a creative outlet, even though the job that brings in the paycheck is noncreative. The majority of his time is spent acting, writing, and sculpting, all of which provide nourishment for his soul. Acting is so satisfying that he takes pleasure in the process whether he receives recognition for it or not. In the film *From Here to Eternity*, Montgomery Clift's character wants to stay in the army in spite of the brutal treatment he receives there. When asked why, his response is, "A man loves a thing, it doesn't have to love him back." If you love what you're doing, failure ceases to be an issue. The word loses its power entirely.

The opposite story to Bill's is that of Henry Parkhurst, who is an excellent sales manager and makes more money than he can spend. He is so talented he could sell a cowboy the horse he's riding. But he drinks too many dry martinis at lunch and I've never seen him relax. Success has undermined his willingness to take new risks and prevented him from giving up the "success" he knows to pursue the success he doesn't. Henry's real love is roses. He has over 150 different varieties in his backyard, and all he really wants to do is cultivate new ones. If he pursued this path, it would make a far greater contribution to his life than what he's doing now. People who are really good at something and reap tremendous rewards for it are not necessarily doing what makes them happy. They're just doing it because they're good at it. And the better they get, the more investment they make, the harder it is to give it up and pursue the unknown or the untried.

MYTH NUMBER FIVE: *Failure is never acceptable.*

It is actually important to fail at things that are worth failing at. They are intrinsically useless to you, and in pursuing them, you are throwing your time away.

In the working world, nothing carries the stigma of failure more heavily than getting fired. My own unique take on this subject is that getting fired from a job is often the best thing that can happen to a person. It is the universe's way of telling him that it's time to move on. When most people find a new job, it turns out to be a better fit, their talents are more appreciated, and frequently it even pays better.

And let's face it, there are some jobs it is a pleasure to be fired from, particularly the ones that require you to turn your back on yourself. Never be ashamed of being fired from a job that made you go against your own values. During one bleak period in my acting career, I took a job at night selling water purification systems. It turned out to be a scam. People were baited into attending a seminar by the promise of a free trip to either Hawaii or Las Vegas. (Naturally, it always turned out to be a bus trip to Las Vegas.) After the audience was subjected to a "fire and brimstone" lecture that exaggerated the dangers of tap water, each buyer was assigned a salesperson who ran a chemical analysis of his or her tap water. Not surprisingly, the sample was always declared to be as polluted as if it came from a stream running through Chernobyl. At that point, we zeroed in with a $5,000 water purification device that would "save their lives." On my first evening at the job, my "prospect" was an eighty-year-old woman attending with her retarded forty-year-old son. If I had been willing to knock over this unfortunate pair I would have made a handsome sales commission, but my conscience wasn't willing to pay the price. This was not a company where I wanted to be successful. I didn't even wait to be fired. My first night was my last.

Sometimes we need to fail. Our conscious mind might not know it, so the unconscious will have to step in and engineer failure for our own good. When I left law school, it wasn't entirely voluntary. I was carrying on at an adequate level until I met my nemesis—a course called "Family Law." Part of it focused on Catholic canon law and was taught by a priest. No matter how hard I tried to conform, something in me rebelled at sitting through the sheer irrelevance of listening to a priest pontificate on an esoteric branch of legal theory I would never use. I tried to stick it out, but you can only force yourself to stomach so much. When it came time to take the final exam, my intellect basically said, "I am not going to pass this test." My intellect was entirely capable of grasping the information, it just didn't want to succeed at something that was so nongermane to real life. Not only did I flunk it once, but I suffered through the class a second time, only to flunk again. I was somewhat puzzled at the time because I had excelled in classes that were far more difficult. I am now certain that my unconscious forced me out of law school for my own good. Since I wouldn't listen to my intuition in any other way, this was its attempt to go behind my back and assert itself. It worked. I was invited to leave law school.

To borrow from Dickens, it was the best of times and it was the worst of times. Getting kicked out of law school was a devastating blow to my ego at that time. I was relieved on some level, but the stigma attached to failure dogged me just as it had my father. Years later, it occasionally still bothered me that I hadn't succeeded in earning a law degree, even though it would have trapped me in a profession for which I felt no joy. However, this "failure" actually marked the beginning of my authentic life. Everything I had attempted until that point was based on my conditioning. After that, my mind and my life were open to the field of infinite possibilities. In short, it was the best thing that had ever happened to me.

HANDBALL AND
THE EVILS OF COMPETITION ▼

The opening scene of the movie *Patton* is famous. A medal-festooned General George S. Patton, standing as if a two-by-four were thrust up his spinal column, addresses his audience. "The reason America will never lose a war is because Americans will never tolerate a loser." The audience does not seem to question his pronouncement, and is, in fact, proud of it. Our national spirit is very competitive and this, when channeled in a positive direction, has yielded remarkable results. Indeed, the impact of American ingenuity and creativity on the world front is probably unprecedented in all of history. Virtually every invention that made the twentieth century what it was—the telephone, electrical appliances, the automobile, the airplane, radio and television—was born here. The dark side of competitiveness, however, is an abusive, dog-eat-dog, cutthroat mentality that says, "I win and everybody else loses." It is clearly destructive for the "losers," who have failed to win; and in the end it can be self-defeating for the winner—who is often trapped in the compulsiveness of his achievement.

The American belief that there can be only one winner is easily seen at the Olympics. The buzz ahead of time is always, "Who will take home the gold?" The American press is virtually suggesting that the other medals are booby prizes. If it is clear that an American cannot possibly aim higher than a silver or bronze, that event garners less interest. Silver and bronze medalists, then, are the people who are "sort of winning," but they aren't really winning. The glory of gold is even illustrated visually at the moment of acceptance when the gold medalist is seen standing on the highest platform with his head raised. The other two winners are on appropriately lower platforms, and sometimes their heads are actually turned down in defeat. Any silver- or bronze-winning athlete who was myopically focused on the top honor cannot appreciate what he has accomplished instead. This attitude is also infused into the language of TV sportscasters: "Joe worked so hard to win this event, but he'll *only* be taking home the silver." The silver medalist, of course, has pulled off an amazing athletic feat beyond the scope of mere mortals; he is the second best in the world at his event, but this fact doesn't seem to impress anyone. He is considered a failure.

In American athletics, which represents the essence of competition, winning *must* create losers. This is one other unfortunate effect of abuse-based thinking in our society. One person wins, but 700 losers lie in his wake, often disappointed and unrewarded. In each Olympic category, an advertising dollar amount can actually be placed on the winner, depending on whether she wins the gold or the "other medals."

Many sports enthusiasts are not professional, but harbor the same destructive attitudes as the pros. For almost thirty years I have played a fiercely competitive game known as four-wall handball. The rules are the same as in racquetball, but there are two major differences. In handball, you use your hands instead of a racquet, and the ball is smaller and harder. It takes endurance to play, and skill to win. Handball is to racquetball what chess is to checkers—more difficult and challenging. So much so, in fact, that it is a dying game. Few young people want to attempt it, which is a pity because there are few games that provide such a high level of physical conditioning.

Because it is such an inherently difficult sport, it attracts certain kinds of players, who tend to fall into two categories: those who play to fit in a good workout and have fun, and those who have a compulsive need to win at all costs. Unfortunately, the very nature of the game seems to attract the latter in hordes. Compulsive players gauge their success by how well they do *against* their opponents, not by how well, objectively, they play. "Losing is not an option," as the saying goes. If (gasp!) they do lose a game, they take it as a personal affront, and they pout, yell, and ridicule themselves. During one game, my opponent was so angry after losing a single point that he banged his head into a wall half a dozen times until his forehead bled. "You moron," he screamed at himself, "why didn't you make that shot?" Those who were watching were stupefied to see a grown man act like an angry child. He took competition from the sports realm into the hell realm. Fun and good sportsmanship were transformed into a destructive force. People like this are not just trying to win, they are trying to destroy their opponents; and when they don't, they take the hostility out on themselves. Those on the court that day watched this man verbally abuse himself as though the person speaking the words were not the player himself but a separate person, an angry parent berating his child for putting on a less than perfect performance.

This competitor's need to win can only be described as compulsive, a trait that is a distinct sign of abuse-based thinking. According to the dictionary, compulsive behavior is marked by "an irresistible impulse to perform some irrational act." The irrationality of the player described above is found not in wanting to win, but in *basing his entire sense of self-esteem on winning.* Why else would his reactions to a simple mistake in the game be so violent? To enter the true spirit of a match, the self-esteem of the players must rest on a healthy relationship with themselves, not with the outcome of the game. Affection-based handball players compete against themselves and take their misses in stride. They want to win, but in the end it's only a game. If they lose, yet feel they played well, they will walk away exhilarated because they gauge their success by how well they lived up to their own potential.

A newspaper story published several years ago sums up the compulsive nature of competition very well. Its objective was to determine how much money a person needs to consider himself "rich." The first person interviewed earned $100,000 a year. "Are you rich?" the reporter asked. "No way. I can't even afford to buy a house in my own neighborhood. If I made two hundred and fifty thousand a year, then I would be rich." The reporter sought out a person who made $250,000 a year. "Are you rich?" he inquired. "Are you kidding? I can't afford to buy a yacht. If I made a million a year, then I would be rich." Finally, the reporter found a man who earned a million dollars a year. He was in his early thirties and had founded a prosperous, high-tech company. "Are you rich?" the reporter asked a third time. "Hell no," was the answer. "I can't afford a private jet."

These people were too preoccupied with comparing themselves to others to enjoy their wealth. The compulsive nature of the achievement robs it of all joy. Compulsive people don't keep going because they really need to get somewhere; they keep going because they cannot stop. They can't afford to because the guy next door isn't stopping. They never feel like a success, no matter what they do, because, in the words of Joseph Campbell as retold in *The Hero's Journey*, they "have climbed to the top of the ladder and found it's against the wrong wall."

The evils of competition can be seen everywhere. What we observe in athletes on the field is mirrored by the population in general. There is a dichotomy between the enlightened minority who play the game of life to enjoy the experience, and those who fight and scratch their way to the top of the heap, standing on the bodies of everyone they passed. Earlier in the chapter, I suggested that readers ask themselves how they would feel about their lives if they were the only ones evaluating them. The predators of the world would not know how to compute that question. They have no inner yardstick for measuring success; they can only judge how they're doing by comparing themselves to the guy next to them.

For an example of the need to win gone awry, look no further than the bizarre story of Tonya Harding in the 1994 Winter Olympics. Tonya was an extremely competitive skater from a poor family who perceived herself as a kid from the wrong side of the tracks who was pitted against society's darlings. Her teammates were girls who knew how to look the part, and that is essential in ice skating because female skaters are expected to possess all the physical ability of other athletes, but come across as princesses in pink tights. Tonya was probably the only girl on her team who regularly fixed her own truck. She developed a complex about her image, convincing herself that she couldn't win against her arch rival Nancy Kerrigan because Nancy was picture perfect and the judges loved her. To even the odds, Tonya allegedly plotted with her husband to incapacitate her rival by having her kneecaps broken by a hired thug. The fact that the plan was even hatched, let alone carried out, shocked the world. This was taking competition too far by anyone's standards. One element that contributes to how far a person will go to win is how high the stakes are. For women's ice skating singles, the stakes are very high indeed. In endorsements and future engagements, a gold medal is worth millions. Sometimes a silver medal is worth a tenth of that.

Personally, I was as appalled as others were at the viciousness of the plot, but not particularly surprised. Given the high stakes and the destructive atmosphere of competitiveness, something like this was bound to occur sooner or later. What will be difficult for readers to do is acknowledge that there may be parallels in their own lives. Have you ever sabotaged someone else at work to get ahead? Have you recklessly jockeyed for position on the freeway? Have you pushed somebody else out of the way to win yourself a seat on the subway? These are all versions of "getting what's mine," of "winning at any cost." Tonya's story is only an exaggerated example of how our values have become so distorted that pushing others around to take care of ourselves is considered acceptable. It is an extreme example of negative competition theory taken to its logical end.

Everyday examples abound, and they are far more subtle. What we see an athlete doing on the field, and a businessperson doing in the marketplace, we can also see, in another form, a couch potato doing. Picture a man sitting on his patio in the middle of his garden sipping a cold lemonade. The sun is shining, the birds are chirping, the geraniums are in purple bloom. For a minute, all is bliss. Suddenly a discordant sound rips through the peaceful setting: the four whirlpools, each on its own separate setting, start up in the neighbor's hot tub. At that moment, the ugly little snake of envy rears its head and the man's contentment is shattered. He doesn't have a hot tub, let alone one with four settings. He couldn't afford one after putting in the patio.

Thanks to that harmless sound, the man goes from total relaxation into an involuntary muscle spasm. And on his day off too! Envy is an insidious form of competition gone bad. It arises only because the person has compared himself against someone else and found himself wanting. It makes him disparage what he has and wish for what someone else has. And often, he *only* wants it because the other person has it. The desire has very little to do with the object and very much to do with "winning out" over the competitor, which in this case is the man's neighbor. The rampant envy of people in our culture accounts for an untold amount of stress, which contributes to our high rates of mental and physical disease. In the next chapter, we will discuss the smart way to deal with these abusive practices.

Chapter 8

THE AFFECTION-BASED SUPPORT SYSTEM

Love is all you need.

THE BEATLES

ffection-based thinking is the opposite of what has been described in the last two chapters. It is characterized by positivity, optimism, and a loving relationship with oneself and the world. One perceives the glass to be half full. One feels a natural warmth and tenderness for all of life. An affection-based thinker gets the most out of life because he can both win *and* lose, yet still retain his equanimity. He doesn't have to stack trophies on his mantel to feel good about himself for he knows his value from the inside. While he still must suffer the pain of life, going through its ups and downs like everyone else, his general state of mind is stable and centered, peaceful and blissful. Since he does not have to expend all his vital energy propping up a sagging sense of self-worth, his energy is freed to create happiness for himself and others. Uninhibited access to one's vital energy is what lets a person feel fully alive and present.

Affection-based thinking also promotes a healthier relationship with the body. A person who is not at war with herself can stop and quietly listen to the messages from her body. When abuse-based thinkers stop to listen, all they hear is harassment and belittling. It is little wonder that they run themselves into the ground rushing from one accomplishment to the other. Just being with themselves in a quiet way is neither relaxing nor friendly. In fact, just being with themselves with no distractions is often a downright painful experience. But in failing to listen to their own bodies, abuse-based thinkers keep themselves from attending to their own needs. In contrast, affection-based thinkers are able, by listening to their bodies, to attend to their needs and thus create a far healthier lifestyle.

Affection-based thinking is both the sign of, and a contributor to, a strong ego structure and a solid sense of self. It feeds the psyche the right kind of food to be healthy and self-sustaining. It is no different than feeding the body every day from the major food groups or taking multivitamins. To build and sustain a healthy system, you must nourish it.

There are three major challenges that life throws our way—*rejection*, *change*, and *abuse*—and affection-based people are far better prepared to deal with all three than those afflicted with abuse-based thinking.

Rejection is a fact of life. No one goes through life without it. As one small organism in a big, big world, you are more or less likely, depending upon your circumstances, to get both your basic and your more complex needs met. No matter how well you are set up in life, every day will be full of unmet needs of one kind or another. You are subject to rejection whenever there is something you want and somehow aren't going to get—a new car but you didn't get the raise you were expecting, a compliment but one was not forthcoming, a chocolate soufflé with raspberries but you're on the plains of Nairobi, a buyer for your Girl Scout cookies but everyone's on a diet, a quiet afternoon but your neighbor is running his leaf blower, the correct time but your Rolex is on the blink. Either *you* can be rejected or *your demands* can be rejected. Either way, it creates suffering. What you must focus on is not whether you will have suffering in your life—you will—but how you will face it. If you can reach a state of mind where you can maintain a certain level of serenity and equilibrium whether you get what you want or not, overall your life will be immeasurably better than if all your happiness depends on getting what you want when you want it and as often as you want it.

One other way that an affection-based thinker deals with rejection is that she doesn't take it personally. This makes her life easier. Most people don't take the time to observe the fact that rejection is rarely genuinely personal. Most of the time, it's just the way it is: What you want and what you can actually have just aren't coming together simultaneously. Not taking rejection personally releases you from the stress of feeling that you, as an individual, have been singled out for denial. It takes the sting out of rejection, so that while you may still not be getting what you want, at least it doesn't have to offend you.

Another fact of life is change. How one deals with it is largely a matter of perception. You can perceive it as an opportunity either for gain or for loss. An abuse-based person is afraid of change. His well-being is held together by keeping every comfortable little piece of his current life in place. In fact, the conditions of his life have been assembled for just that purpose. If a piece is moved around or goes missing, his inner peace is shattered. No wonder he experiences enormous stress at even the thought of change. No wonder that, for him, change equals loss. An affection-based person, on the other hand, is not depending on external conditions for her peace of mind. It is internally controlled and is based on her relationship with herself. When circumstances change, she makes her adjustments and then looks for the opportunity for new gains and new knowledge from the experience. No wonder that, for her, change equals opportunity. When I quit my corporate job to become an actor, my abuse-based friends thought it was a disastrous decision. My affection-based friends were excited for me. One said, "Ed, if anyone can pull this off, you can." He knew that change didn't scare me and that whatever adversity I faced, I would use it to my advantage.

Abuse, which has been discussed extensively in the previous chapters, can come in a number of different forms; some are subtle while others are glaringly obvious—criticism, sarcasm, yelling, intimidation, bullying, reproach, scorn, reminders of past mistakes, statements that trigger self-doubt, and more. Because life is full of these, a person has to learn to withstand them and yet still emerge in one piece. An affectionate frame of mind helps the person weather the storms of abuse. The inherent sense of value and worthiness he possesses enables him to retain a high opinion of himself even though it is not being mirrored by those around him. Some criticism, of course, is justified. An affection-based thinker can review feedback from others objectively and decide when it is helpful and when it is merely belittling. He can assess when a comment "belongs" to him and when it belongs to the person who made it.

The ability to hold up to the "slings and arrows" of life with our self-esteem intact is called resilience. The reason those arrows hurt so much is that they strike a chord within us. For a critical remark to injure us, it must match something we have already been saying to ourselves. In other words, it reactivates a wound that already exists. If there is no wound, the criticism ricochets off of us and shoots back to the person who made it because it clearly doesn't belong to us.

CREATING AN AFFECTION-BASED SUPPORT SYSTEM ▼

As I said before, abuse-based thinking is a habit. You have probably been doing it for most of your life. Even small habits are hard to destroy, as anyone who has tried will attest. Ingrained habits of thinking are far more difficult to break, and to do it you must consciously decide to change your life in favor of finding support for your new, affectionate way of relating to yourself. If you don't make a deliberate point of changing, nothing will change. Habits are self-perpetuating and will continue on as they are unless you intentionally try to derail them. It takes focus and a contribution of time, effort, and attention. If front-loading your time and energy seems like too much trouble, bear in mind the pay-off: As a result of what you ante up now, you will be able to coast along for the rest of your life with more peace of mind and a greater sense of well-being. The process of creating support is two-pronged. It is both internal and external.

The internal effort consists of two stages. First, we have to recognize the negative thought patterns for what they are. Since we are so used to them, this may not be easy at first. It involves training our attention *on* the mind itself and witnessing our own thought processes without interfering. Just observe your mind as if it were on a glass slab under a microscope. What do you actually see going on? It is important to observe what is there without criticizing or trying to change it. First, criticizing it won't do any good; and second, it interferes with the observation process.

Once you have learned to see the destructive voice coming from the back of your psyche for what it really is, you can replace it with an affectionate, loving voice. "An abuse-based system resists change," says Dr. Robert Luthardt. "Fighting won't do any good. You have to replace it." The mind, like everything else, abhors a vacuum, so you don't exactly evict destructive thoughts, you simply replace them with new tenants.

Do not expect overnight change. Do not expect to accept the affectionate thoughts immediately. The process is gradual. The demonic voice that issues the destructive thoughts was planted over a period of years, and they happened to be the most impressionable years of your life. The process of doing a make-over is step by step. An abuse-based thought will, at first, be replaced by one that is less malicious. Then by one that is more neutral. Then by one that is slightly favorable. Then by one that is affectionate. Eventually, only an affectionate voice remains. For example, suppose that you have just begun a new job and the first thought that enters your head is "I'm not good enough to take this on. I'll never make it." The simple act of seeing and acknowledging the thought is the first step to the cure. Next, whenever it crops up, replace it with one that affirms your self-worth. "There is a reason why they hired me. This job and my talent are a good match." After a while, begin saying "I know I'm going to be a success at this place." Over a period of time, when this technique gradually erodes the demonic voice, you will begin to experience affection-based thoughts automatically.

Of course, your demonic voice won't give up without a fight. It will focus on the difficulties and convince you that they're overwhelming. It will tell you you're not up to the task and try to make you feel defeated so you'll give up. Remember, this part of you doesn't want to change. The obstacle to changing is the fact that a habit of mind represents the status quo, and the very nature of a status quo is to stay the same. To overcome that obstacle, you must focus on the positives and wrench your attention from the negatives. This helps you motivate yourself to keep up the effort, and it puts you in a favorable frame of mind to continue. Don't focus on how much work you still have to do on yourself. Focus on how far you've come, the improvements you've already made, and how much stronger you already feel.

There is a more proactive method of banishing abusive thought patterns. You can use affirmations whenever you have a free moment. A particularly productive time for affirmations is the transitional period—the semi-awake state as you are going to sleep and as you are waking up—when your unconscious mind is most open to suggestion. It is a time when an affirmative thought is most likely to take hold.

You can find models for affirmations, but it is best to design your own so they are a fit adversary to combat your own unique destructive thoughts. No two people have the same devil in their head. Here are a few examples to give you an idea:

"I am a worthwhile person who deserves to be loved. I am lovable."
"I am a capable, intelligent person."
"I can do anything I put my mind to."
"The universe is on my side and supports my endeavors."

The second stage of your internal effort is to examine your goals. As was stated in the first chapter, so far in life your goals have probably not been of your own making. All facets of your life—work, hobbies, relationships, diet, workout habits, and so on—were built on society's model of success. Now it is time to create goals in those same areas that support your own reinvented model of success. This is difficult because you've been brainwashed to adopt all the socially approved patterns of living and to create your goals accordingly. The conditioning can be reversed by making a commitment to reach a set of personal goals that are in alignment with who you really are.

Creating an external support system is just as important for your personal growth as creating your internal system. Externally, affectionate support comes primarily from the people in your life. If you surround yourself with angry, negative, sarcastic people, you are merely supporting your abuse-based condition, and whatever work you try to do internally will be sabotaged. Exposure to such people is equivalent to breathing polluted air. They create a toxic environment that is unhealthy for a living being.

It may feel threatening to evaluate the people around you because you won't want to acknowledge how abusive some of them can be, especially if you have a close relationship with them. But thinking about people and rating them will help you when you have to defend yourself against subtle forms of attack by them, and it will inform you when it's time to modify their behavior with a gentle reminder that you would like to be treated better.

Most people you know will probably rate somewhat midrange on the toxic/healthy scale. Some people, however, are so incorrigible in their negativity that you have no choice but to banish them from your life, and this is a tough moment to face. To muster the strength, you will have to remind yourself that you are making a significant step in the direction of your emotional well-being. I had such a friend once. For years I knew that he had a Jekyll/Hyde personality. Depending on his mood, he could be either very supportive or very hostile. The fact that he was sympathetic and reassuring once in a while is what kept him my friend for as long as it did. But I always vacillated about how much he actually contributed to my life. The straw that broke the camel's back occurred during the opening night performance of an Off-Broadway play in which I had a starring role. My friend sat in the front row of the audience and kept speaking to me when I was onstage, breaking my concentration. His obstructionist behavior helped me to realize, once and for all, that he was not really my friend. It was clear that he was actually lobbying for me to fail. In the words of John Barrymore, I needed to "close the iron door" on him. My life has been richer without him, and since then I have learned that we all have more choice than we let ourselves admit about the kind of people we allow into our lives.

To get an idea of which people in your life really are affection-based thinkers, you can conduct an inventory. Here is a ten-question test for evaluating whether the people with whom you live and come into contact are affection-based. Score every person for how consistently each question applies. Rate each question on a scale of one to five, one for "not at all" and five for "all the time."

1. Are they nurturing?
2. Are they open to discussing problems and working them out?
3. Are they tolerant of other people, ideas, and me?
4. Do they provide constructive, friendly criticism?
5. Do I feel encouraged in their presence?
6. Do they support my plans and goals?
7. Do they listen to me when I speak, and really hear me?
8. Are they optimistic about how life will turn out?
9. Do they look at the positive side of a situation?
10. Are they able to laugh at themselves?

If someone scores in the middle range (twenty to thirty-five), don't give up hope. Remember, it is in their own best interest to become more affection-based, and you can influence their behavior in that direction. The more you change, the more you will lead others by example. The miracle is that once you begin treating yourself better, it provokes improved behavior in others. As you become healthier yourself, you will also find that the people who surround you will either conform to your new paradigm or they will drop out of your life. The key to working out your differences, of course, is to do it in a constructive way.

The following are some of the categories of people who will form your support system.

Family

The family system—a group of genetically related members—is still the foundation of every culture on earth. Humans have evolved in family systems, and no matter how much we may kick and scream about individual family members who drive us crazy, it is still the best way we know to bring little humans into the world and let them grow into adulthood. At its best, a family is made up of team players, all of whom contribute to and support the system.

In healthy families, there is a kind of basic trust that can be found nowhere else, a respect for individual talents, a balance of dependence and autonomy, and a fabric of intimacy. Our family is the basis for our identity, good or bad. When it is functional and serving its true purpose, it provides us with a solid platform for the initiative and the industry it takes to create the life we truly want for ourselves.

Friends

"You can't choose your relatives, but you can choose your friends." An old saying that still holds true. Real friends are those people who care enough about you to be there when you need them, in spite of the fact that they're not obligated. Unlike family members, friends choose each other consciously because they see something they value. This means that your friends accept you and like you for who you really are; otherwise they wouldn't have chosen you. In some ways, no one knows you better than, say, the brother or sister you grew up with. But in a different way, a friend may see you with more objectivity just because he *didn't* grow up in the same family system. The members of one's immediate family often have identities that are so merged, they have trouble viewing each other as unique individuals. If this is true in your case, they will certainly have trouble letting you change because it means you will break out of your traditional family role. With longtime friends you grew up with, you can be seen as an individual and yet still retain the unique bond of all those shared experiences and rites of passage you went through together. These people know you intimately, but they can allow you to grow and change. In fact, the support of close friends, both old and new, is necessary if you are to be infused with the inner strength you need to make significant changes in your life and to seek out meaningful personal success.

Psychotherapist

Even the best of friends may not be equipped to listen dispassionately and wisely to your problems, or to be perceptive about your issues. A caring therapist is. The value of spilling your guts out to an objective, educated listener has been proven over and over. For one thing, you are more likely to tell the truth to someone with whom you don't have a relationship outside the office. For another, therapists are trained to understand how the mind works so they will be cognizant of your behavior and the motivation behind it in a way that others won't. Family and friends may have an axe to grind or a hidden agenda when advising you; a good therapist does not. This is especially helpful for someone trying to create an affection-based lifestyle because a therapist can be an important sounding board, helping the person identify what is healthy and what is unhealthy in her life.

Numerous influences prevent people from facing their deeper personal issues. Because therapy consists of a series of one-hour sessions, it forces people to use that time to focus on what is important without any distractions. It's their dime, and they aren't there for any other purpose than to work on themselves. This makes it very hard to run away from themselves. Finally, a good therapist embodies the concept of affection-based thinking and can help clients to cultivate the same habit. His or her influence should be completely supportive, constructive, and productive.

Professional Advisers (Accountants, Attorneys, Physicians, Architects, etc.)

The people you hire to look after your finances, legal affairs, health, and so on, can make a significant difference in how well prepared you are to tackle the search for success. They should not be merely competent, but sensitive to your needs as well. Whatever the specific reason they are being hired, remember that their ultimate purpose is to contribute to your overall sense of well-being. It is worth your time to interview such people until you find the ones who can best provide the kind of resources that will enhance your lifestyle. When I was looking for an accountant, I didn't want just a good number cruncher. I interviewed several people until I found one who genuinely cared about who I was as a person. In the course of our relationship, he has become very supportive of my work and my lifestyle choices. I actually look forward to meetings with him. That, in fact, is the litmus test. When you have arranged for a meeting with the person, do you look forward to it?

Keep in mind that when you hire a professional, you are giving her power over a certain area of your life, one where you have a real and distinct need that you are asking her to fulfill with her expertise. You have an emotional investment in your relationship with her because when you offer to pay for her advice you are, in effect, saying, "Tell me how to run my life." Something is at stake in her answer, and how she treats you will influence how you feel about yourself. Because so much weight is placed on what she tells you, it is important for your well-being that she does not convey some subtle message of abuse in her communication. You are more vulnerable than you realize, so take the time to choose people who take an interest in you as an individual and genuinely care about your welfare.

Teachers

Growing up, you lacked the ability to choose your teachers. Your parents chose your school. Your school chose which classroom you had to appear in. Now that you are an adult, this has all changed. People who want to continue growing find themselves taking adult courses to increase their scope and knowledge. The choices are endless: computer programming, Spanish, kickboxing, investing, gardening, cooking, and on and on. The subject matter, however, is not the only choice you should be making. In also choosing a teacher, you should be choosing a person with the right attributes because what she says can have a huge influence on how you feel about yourself. When the actor John Hurt was in school, he had to pay a visit to the headmaster and tell him what he wanted to be when he graduated. Hurt mustered all his courage and sputtered, "I want to be an actor." The headmaster laughed and said, "That's all very well to do in school, but you'll never make it out there." Hurt, now a middle-aged man and a very successful actor, acknowledges, "That is a terrible thing to say to a boy." This one comment has haunted him throughout his entire career, right up to the present.

While we are less impressionable as adults, it is still important to choose affection-based teachers, ones who support the learning process, respect our intelligence, create a friendly atmosphere, understand that every student is at a different level of expertise, and are attuned to each student's unique passion. But when you come across a teacher who reminds you of the abuse-based teachers you often had to put up with in grade school, drop out. One of my hobbies is yoga. In one class, I had a teacher who stood over me like a drill instructor, and when I performed a certain yoga posture incorrectly she said, "Ed, what are we going to do with you!" It was a clear tip-off that she did not respect her students as equals. I went on to find one who was able to give me constructive criticism in a way that made me feel good about myself. When I say constructive criticism, I mean comments that make you want to improve yourself, not comments that are designed to show you how to fix what's wrong with you.

People at Work

Part of the message of this book is that you have a choice about where you work and with whom you work. If you work in a corporate environment, you are likely to spot certain abusive tendencies, and you will want to re-evaluate from time to time whether you are in the right place. Take a look at your bosses and co-workers and the general system under which you work. Use the test on page 138 to appraise whether these people form a real affection-based support system. If they fail the test, you have an obligation to your emotional and physical health to seek a paycheck someplace else, where the price isn't so high to you personally.

In many surveys, employees report that the most consistent source of stress on the job is their boss. Your boss affects your life both on the job and off because very few people leave stress behind at the office. An abusive boss is still in your head on the weekend when you're at the lake with a fishing pole in one hand and a beer in the other. The kind of boss you need is someone who appreciates your worth to the company and who can focus on your strengths instead of your weaknesses. Look for someone who wants to mentor you and who can inspire you to do your best. The same rule applies to co-workers. Are you surrounded by people who think affectionately and offer constructive feedback? Are they upbeat or do they spend most of their time back-biting and complaining?

Hobby Co-enthusiasts

The people who share the time you devote to hobbies have an important role to play in your support system. After all, these are the pastimes you love. You have chosen them because they contribute something important to your life. This is when you let your hair down and have fun, so the people you hang out with should not be sucking the joy out of your pleasure time. Don't throw these precious hours away by spending them with someone who is sour, angry, or resentful, someone who is a poor sport or who has a negative agenda that has nothing to do with the pure enjoyment of the activity. One of the saddest things that can happen is that a person who loves doing something finds that the joy of it is being sapped out by an abusive person. You owe it to yourself to preserve and even fight for the activities that you love.

Support Groups

We are fortunate to live in a time when we have support groups—collections of two or more people who share a common concern and meet regularly for the purpose of giving comfort, inspiring and embracing each other, consoling and nourishing each other. The group can be for personal or career growth, or for mutual support in times of crisis. These groups probably arose in modern times to fill the vacuum that was left when close-knit communities and families began to disintegrate. Nowadays, it is all too easy to become isolated in our struggles and our suffering. Belonging to a support group provides the much needed sense of community and fellowship that is lacking in so many lives. It also provides an opportunity to hear regular feedback on how well you are dealing with life's ever-changing problems, goals, and commitments.

The advantage of joining one of these groups is that the people are all there for the same reason, so you can count on the fact that when you go to a meeting, you will all be working on the issues you genuinely care about. The purpose—to promote each other's goals, offer useful advice, listen, and sometimes suffer through the same losses—is clear.

▼   Here is a recap of the techniques that will help you change from abuse-based to affection-based thinking:

- Discontinue the practice of accepting abuse from other people.
- Learn to recognize your negative thought patterns, replacing them with positive ones.
- Invigorate your self-esteem by creating your own positive affirmations.
- Redesign your personal goals so they are in alignment with your real needs, instead of paying homage to the values you were brainwashed to accept.
- Don't take rejection personally.
- Convince yourself that change is healthy.
- Fill your life with affection-based people.

After everything I've said in Part Two, the choice is yours. You can ignore every word. You can fall headlong into the rest of your life following your old patterns and making yourself miserable. You can keep pursuing some vision of success using compulsive, adversarial behavior to achieve it. You are free to say, "What's the point in putting all this effort into changing the way I think? It'll never work, and even if it did, I don't deserve a better life." You are free to put this book down and go watch a bloody bout of pro wrestling. But I hope you won't. As an affection-based person, I don't want to be on an island of happiness; I want to see everyone be happy. Affection-based people are not selfish about finding bliss. Because they feel expansive and open, they tend to want everyone to have a good life and find the success they deserve.

Part Three

VICTIMIZED

Chapter 9

THE VICTIM MENTALITY

*Though they may outwardly appear to be adults, even suc-
cessful adults, perhaps the majority of "grown-ups" remain
until their death psychological children who have never
truly separated themselves from their parents and the
power that their parents have over them.*

M .   S C O T T   P E C K

In this society, you must achieve some level of status, wealth, or
power because they are the only standards of success that are
genuinely recognized. If you fail to meet these criteria you will
suffer for it. You will feel insufficient in some indefinable way, as
if you're not quite good enough and it shows.

The question is: Why? How is it possible that not achieving *someone else's* goals, reaching a generic idea of success, can make *us* feel miserable? Because we have allowed ourselves to be defined by the culture's
values while we dismiss our own. After a lifetime of this, we don't even
perceive what our own values are anymore. They remain invisible and
inaccessible to us because we are so caught up in the rat race that we
don't have time to look inward and see who we are as individuals. It is
as if we lose our own fingerprints.

On a very deep level, however, people become aware that something vital is seeping out of them. That vital something is *us*, who we truly are, our unique and idiosyncratic identity, untouched by cultural influences. If we want to escape this fate, we have the uneasy task of acknowledging to ourselves how much we have surrendered to the collective.

A person who is internally validated makes his key life decisions based upon a value system he has worked out for himself. More than we like to admit, most of us have been dependent upon external validation of our self-worth rather than being the autonomous, self-validated people we would like to think we are. There is a reason for this, of course. We are social beings, and we see ourselves in the context of the whole. Consequently we tend to see ourselves through the eyes of others, to be externally validated by using others as a mirror rather than being internally validated. That is to say, we take more cues about how to live from what we see around us than from an internal yardstick. Much of our interior world—our values, our identity, our consciousness in general—is tied to the culture in which we live.

What this all boils down to is that we abdicate our right to judge whether we are successful in life, and instead we adopt the standards and values of others. Trying to attain a sense of worth by meeting other people's standards is, in my view, an inherently false way to live, and it leads to a basic dissatisfaction. The reason is this: The definition of a satisfied person is one who has gotten her needs met. If the criteria you use for making your decisions are based on another's values of good/bad, right/wrong, the result of the decision cannot possibly address your own needs.

A DAY IN THE LIFE ▼

What happens to our quality of life when we gear all our time and effort toward goals that have no personal meaning, and when we lose ourselves in trivial details? To find out, we can look at a typical "day in the life."

We stagger out of bed at seven in the morning after being shaken from sleep by a rude-sounding alarm clock. On the financial page we find out that our stocks have dropped yet again this week, putting to rest any idea of pursuing a membership in that new and exclusive exercise club. We eat a rushed breakfast of sugar-glazed doughnuts and slide into the front seat of our car. As we approach the entrance to the freeway, we hold our breath and hope for the best. But no! Traffic is backed up all the way to the bridge. We sit there stewing, tapping the steering wheel impatiently while we listen to the traffic update on the car radio.

When we get to work we are pleasantly surprised that at least someone made the coffee already. We pour the first of a dozen cups for the day and sit down at our desk waiting for the first rush of caffeine. Without that, we'll never rouse ourselves into action. As we look down to face the pile of paperwork, there is a moment of silent resignation. This is a job in which we always seem to be in the middle of something, never at the beginning when the task seems fresh or at the end when there is a sense of satisfaction. We don't know where the project goes once it leaves our desk, or even whether we did a good job. At the end of the day, as we stop at the water cooler and listen to the usual snippets of complaints, we realize once again that our job offers no sense of completion, no inkling that we've made a contribution that means anything to anybody.

As a reward for getting through another day, we stop at Macy's on the way home to buy that new DVD player we've been thinking about all day. Even on sale, it's more than we can afford, but what the hell? You've gotta find a little enjoyment in life . . . somewhere.

This is a snapshot from a day in the lives of too many people. They do all this just to pay for a packaged life and to project the right image. But this is a store-bought life, and a profound feeling of diminishment accompanies it.

It isn't that society actually wants people to be unhappy. It's that society can't afford to have you pay attention to the unhappiness you experience while working to achieve the American Dream. If you did, you might bail out. That's why Madison Avenue NEVER shows a guy in a new Lexus looking depressed. He has to radiate the happiness you're supposed to feel if you work your butt off so you can afford a Lexus. Every message we receive from the mass culture advertises the packaged life as the quick route to happiness. A market economy is based on as many people as possible buying into it, keeping the money circulating for goods and services. It is based on a kind of compulsiveness that keeps us so busy, so tied up, that we can't focus on our true state of mind. We work compulsively and we spend money compulsively, all to fill up the emptiness of an unrealized and unempowered existence.

Society, then, holds itself together through a mutually supported idea that it is actually better to look good than to feel good. Such an idea can only support image-based values. But what happens to a human being who lives out of an image? He stays on the surface of himself. He may sense that something is missing, but he doesn't know what it is. And it seems vaguely threatening to even try and find out. It's so easy to avoid the trouble of looking into the void and discovering what's really wrong. After all, one is offered so many tempting ways to deflect one's attention from this depressing emptiness: TV sitcoms, video games, the play-offs for the World Series, the rise and fall of the stock market, end-of-the-month White Sales, nude pictures on the Internet.

Nothing really works, of course. The person cannot be truly happy because he is removed from the depth of himself, from his authentic core. He has his STUFF, but he doesn't have his SELF. Every day, his actions express a set of values that do not come from his core, but from the world around him. He is playacting, being a puppet. Somewhere inside himself he knows this and it haunts him. But he spends so much time frenetically doing more, getting more, achieving more, looking like more, that he can't quiet down long enough to understand what is happening to him. When his own real needs cry out to be heard, he dismisses them because they don't fit into his lifestyle. In so doing, he is dismissing and abandoning himself.

By buying into and living according to society's values, he is giving the world his power. He can't break away because he is dependent on (a) the judgment of the world to determine whether his life is acceptable; (b) society to create the standards he will live up to; and (c) those around him to tell him whether he is a worthwhile person deserving of respect. Although he may even appear to be successful, his body eventually will let him know that he is not centered in himself. This communication usually manifests itself in the form of what we loosely refer to as depression. Depression is described as a feeling of emptiness, a lack of energy, an absence of caring. It is a signal from your body that it is time to wake up and make changes.

So the first thing this person, who is just waking up to his condition, must do to heal the pain and deal with the emptiness is to reclaim his power. He must give himself the authority to decide whether he is worthy of respect and admiration, and then make his decisions accordingly—decisions about work, money, and life. In many cases, this means an entire change in lifestyle because so much of the previous life was based on an idea of success promulgated by society.

As long as a person gives that authority away, she is making herself into a victim and rendering herself helpless. But if she can retain that authority, she becomes the director of her own movie, so to speak. She charts her own course toward success.

MASTER OF YOUR OWN FATE ▼

Unfortunately, many people do render themselves helpless. There are a number of reasons for this, but at the root of them all is the fear of not fitting in to the system. It's safer to be a cog in the machine than to be at the controls. This fear ties directly into the survival instinct. The assumption is that only by being part of the machine can one survive. "After all," we think in the recesses of our mind, "what happens to a part in the engine of my car if it doesn't work? I throw it out. If I'm not working as a functioning part of the machine, fitting in just right, I'll be thrown out." The first machine we were a cog in was the family machine. We were completely dependent on it, and we carry that feeling of dependence into adulthood. But as adults we are part of an even larger system, the society machine. We are certain we can't survive without it. In some ways, this is true. We are all interdependent on each other. What I am saying is that such a reliance should be a healthy one and not detract from our individuality. Human society is not a termite mound. We're too complex to be interchangeable the way termites are. The message I want to send is that you can be successful on your own terms and still be part of a greater whole.

Nazi concentration camps are the closest human counterpart I can think of to a termite mound. People were treated like slaves, worth nothing as individuals except for the labor they could provide. And yet even in these extreme circumstances, one can preserve one's identity. In Viktor Frankl's book *Man's Search for Meaning*, he describes his experiences in a camp. He survived unthinkable brutality, yet came away believing that it was the person himself who ultimately determined whether or not he would be stripped of all individuality. The Nazis couldn't possess the prisoner's inner core without the man or woman's acquiescence. "Even though conditions such as lack of sleep, insufficient food and various mental stresses may suggest that the inmates were bound to react in certain ways, in the final analysis it becomes clear that the sort of person the prisoner became was the result of an inner decision, and not the result of camp influences alone." He concluded that "everything can be taken from a man but one thing: the last of the human freedoms—to choose one's attitude in any given set of circumstances, to choose one's own way."

As much as we fear that asserting our individuality will threaten our survival, the fact is that a person actually stands a better chance of survival in this world by acting like a human being than by acting like a termite. Individuality is nature's way of giving us the incentive to look out for ourselves. It is our internal mechanism for actively seeking to satisfy our needs. Whatever culture you live in, that societal system has its own survival requisites, and they might clash with yours. There are times when it is noble to sacrifice your needs for the greater good, to give in to society's demands at your own expense. If you want to make a conscious decision in certain circumstances to do that, it is not a bad thing. But don't make it a lifetime practice to ignore your own needs so that others may thrive.

In Aztec society, it was common practice to haul people up a set of stone stairs to an altar, upon which they were tied down and had their beating hearts ripped out. The belief was that this was necessary to appease the gods. These were amazingly thirsty gods; they needed twenty vats of blood a week. Hundreds of thousands of citizens were sacrificed to satisfy their lust. Would I have willingly let myself be sacrificed for the blood lust of the high priests? After all, they said it was for the good of the whole. I'd like to think I would have talked my way out of it and gone on permanent vacation in Mazatlán.

On the other hand, during World War II when there was a risk of the world being taken over by Nazi Germany, American soldiers really were fighting for the future freedom of their families. Many of them lost their lives for the good of their country.

It is worth looking at a third scenario—Vietnam. Here the boundaries are not so clear. The American government was telling people they were fighting for their country, just as in the Second World War. If you were a termite, you packed up your gear without thinking and headed for the jungle. As a twenty-one-year-old Marine lieutenant, I was one of those who decided that was the correct decision. But for a person with "full inner liberty," as Frankl puts it, it was necessary to think long and hard about whether he was being told the truth. In this circumstance, many chose not to become what they considered to be sacrificial lambs. They asserted themselves and refused to go. Upon looking back, although their choice was not my choice, I can respect their position.

WHO'S GOT YOUR POWER? ▼

By not exercising their individuality and taking care of their own needs, people participate in what I call a victim mentality; that is to say, they unwittingly allow themselves to be used, hoodwinked, and exploited by others. This may seem to fly in the face of the survival instinct, yet many people lead their entire lives this way. There are several influences that sway people to act counter to their own best interest.

Family Background

To fit into the family, many children learn to mute the expression of their own needs. They are discouraged from being assertive and encouraged to "go along with the program." As explained in Chapter Six, authors Alice Miller (*For Your Own Good*) and John Bradshaw (*Healing the Shame that Binds You*) show how the parenting rules we have all inherited from posterity contribute to the victim mentality. Children are thought of as possessions, chattel; they belong to their parents. In other words, they are objects without rights. Their wishes are belittled as childish and unreasonable. This is abusive. It is not that a child's every wish must be granted, but it should be acknowledged. The message a child receives when her wishes are invalidated is that she has no right to her needs, and this is a form of abuse.

Personal Temperament

Temperament is a person's pattern of characteristic behavior that reflects his or her natural disposition. It affects how we think, feel, and act in the world. Temperament may be somewhat affected by our outer environment, but primarily it is not something that is acquired but inborn. Some people are, by temperament, more passive than others. This means that they are automatically less likely to invite confrontation or stand up for their rights than is someone with more aggressive tendencies. If you are one of these people, it is important to recognize it and know that there will be times when you will have to overcompensate for your own inborn disposition. You will have to initiate assertive behavior, even though it does not come naturally to you, or you will find yourself preyed upon and upstaged whenever your interests are at stake.

Low Self-Esteem

People with low self-esteem are particularly susceptible to exploitation because they secretly believe they deserve the short end of the stick. If you hold yourself in low regard, it is easy to accept being treated badly. The poor treatment you are receiving is in accordance with your own self-image, so the alarm doesn't go off in your head that something is wrong: "I'm a worthless person, so the behavior I am receiving matches who I am." An analogy for self-esteem is the immune system, which is there to protect you from harm. A strong immune system will fight off infection; a weak one will be overwhelmed by opportunistic diseases. A person with no confidence in himself as a human being will be overwhelmed by people who are out to take advantage of him. Such a person will be easily intimidated from standing up for his rights.

Sociological Influences

We live in a culture that often rewards a victim mentality. If you can make a case that you are not responsible for yourself or your actions, you may be entitled to the privilege of being taken care of. Many able-bodied people on welfare are deemed "unemployable." The proof, of course, is that they have never been employed, and so they are supported by the government. Some minorities are deemed incapable of being competitive, and so they have to be protected by affirmative action. When I worked for IBM, an African-American colleague articulated his sense of outrage that he couldn't compete without being given a leg up. He was offered a promotion for a very desirable job, yet he was conflicted about accepting it. "Ed," I remember him saying, "I know they're only giving me this promotion because I'm black and they have a quota to fill. I don't feel right about it. I want to be promoted because of my qualifications, not because of my skin color." While affirmative action may be a well-intentioned attempt to deal with legitimate issues of discrimination and poverty, often it merely reinforces the degrading idea that minorities aren't powerful or smart or competent enough to make it on their own. The message that was sent to my IBM colleague was, "See yourself as a victim and we'll give you the chance to move ahead."

Current Cultural Notions

Many contemporary schools of thought thrive on the concept of victimhood. In fact, selling people on the idea that they are victims is a cottage industry. The legal profession couldn't do without it. One perfect example of the trend of abdicating personal responsibility and placing the blame elsewhere is the case of Dan White. In the 1970s he gained notoriety for killing the mayor of San Francisco, George Mosconi. His defense was that his blood sugar was unnaturally high from eating a Hostess Twinkie only hours before the murder. It became famous as "the Twinkie defense." When he got off with a very light sentence, that sent a message to the community at large about how the culture views personal responsibility. That, and many legal rulings since, are a clear indication that the trend in America is away from individual answerability in favor of "It's not my fault. The devil made me do it."

MAGICAL THINKING ▼

A clever way to avoid the effort, challenge, and upheaval of taking responsibility for oneself is magical thinking. The person has an unrealistic expectation that life is going to deliver him from his discontent without his having to lift a finger. He sets a goal before him, and instead of creating a plan to attain the goal, he visits a psychic and gets a reading: "What do you see in my future? Will I be a success?" Or he has his astrological chart read: "Are my stars lucky this month?" Or he asks "yes" people to give him an answer, knowing full well that they always tell him what he wants to hear. What he doesn't do is attend to business. He thinks the universe has magical powers and it secretly wants him to attain his heart's desire without him having to work for it. This is akin to a child thinking he'll get a cherry-red bike with a racing stripe for Christmas because Santa Claus will leave it under the tree. Or another child believing the Easter Bunny will put a chocolate egg in her basket and when she wakes up Sunday morning, there it will be. There are adults out there who have brought in "acceptable" substitutes for Santa Claus and the Easter Bunny. They always seem to believe that somehow their dreams will come true if they just wish hard enough.

Magical thinking is appropriate for children. Their brains have not developed sufficiently for conceptual thinking. When they see a magician pull a goose egg from behind their ear, they believe it really happened. An adult is supposed to know that it's a trick. When an adult starts to believe the egg really was behind his ear, he is in trouble. And that is an apt metaphor for people who think success will occur on its own.

The most perfect example of magical thinking today is the idea of winning the lottery. A woman in Boston recently won $172 million. Does this ever happen? Yes. Does it happen to you and me? No. A famous newspaper columnist once quipped, "You have the same chance of winning the lottery if you *don't* buy a ticket as if you *do* buy a ticket." In other words, forget about it. Millions of people waste valuable time and money that they could be investing in themselves by buying lottery tickets. In a July 1999 study sponsored by the Consumer Federation of America and Primerica Corporation, it was found that more than one out of four Americans actually count on winning the lottery as the main component of their retirement plan. For people with annual incomes of under $35,000, that number jumps to a staggering 40 percent. Since the probability of actually winning the big jackpot is about twenty million to one, how can their stubborn belief in winning not be magical thinking? Of all those surveyed, less than half believed that saving and investing was the most reliable route to wealth. What this means is that most people are passing their days hoping for life to turn out as they want it to and squandering the resources they could be using to actually make it happen.

When life is difficult, magical thinking can be used as a coping mechanism. Growing up in a depressing Brooklyn neighborhood, I used to fantasize that my bedroom was Tahiti. My imagination had been ignited by a TV program about a man who sailed a schooner around the South Seas. I allowed myself to believe I was in Brooklyn when I was outside my room, but once inside, it was Tahiti. Outside Brooklyn, inside Tahiti. Get it? I actually made this work in my mind. I visualized the warm, sandy beaches, the palm trees swaying in the breeze, the silky tex-ture of water in the lagoon, the topless Polynesian maidens. For a short time, this fantasy let me forget the three armed thugs who had just chased me down the block. As a coping mechanism it worked for a time, but if I had remained stuck in the fantasy it would have arrested my development. At some point, you have to face life—warts and all.

I wish I had a magical answer to this problem. If trust in the magi-cal powers of the universe is a firm part of your belief system, and you don't want to give it up, your only solution is to go one step further. You have to include yourself in the equation, seeing yourself and your natural capacities as part of the magic. This one little alteration will change you from a passive bystander—a victim—to an active agent. There is magic, but it takes your own magic to make it happen. And when you are proac-tive, you will find yourself interacting with the world like an adult, not a child. You will inspire a different kind of confidence in those around you, in people who can help you attain your goals. The world of adults tends to trust in and reward people who think and act like responsible adults.

THE ARGUMENT FOR VICTIMHOOD ▼

What price do you pay for acting like a victim? You place unnec-essary limitations on yourself, not venturing to go where you can in life, to change what you can change, to measure up to your full potential. It's like suiting yourself up in a straightjacket. You are stuck. You have a limited range of movement to solve problems and create success. Whatever kind of success would really mean something to you will remain perpetually out of reach. When a person feels helpless to attain her goals, she will not even bother to try. She will just keep taking Prozac to dull the pain of an unrealized life.

What do we really need in order to feel that we have made a success of ourselves? First and foremost, we have to meet our own needs. Without that, we are simply living in a state of constant dissatisfaction. I don't care how much money you have, if you are fundamentally dissatisfied, you are a failure at living. To just feel passably all right is akin to waking up in the morning in a ditch you have to dig yourself out of. That's not living; it's getting by.

You cannot meet your needs, however, if you have not claimed your own power to marshal your resources and act in your own best interest. If you have not recognized your right to exercise a reasonable amount of control over your life, you are going to go without quite a few valuable things.

The question that needs to be answered is: Why would anyone choose to give up his or her power? Why do people make decisions that render them helpless? The first thing to understand is that the vast majority of people who are doing it don't know they are doing it. They take the wind out of their own sails by the way they talk to themselves, by the habitual utterances that issue from their unconscious minds. There are certain kinds of comments we have been making to ourselves for years that we are not particularly aware of. They are more like whispers in the back of our minds that we cannot exactly make out, although they influence us enormously. Often they are shrouded assumptions, arguments, or justifications that we hide behind so we don't have to meet life head on. We use these subliminal messages from the unconscious to avoid confronting reality.

The only way to release ourselves from their power is to bring them out into the open and examine them in the light of day. They work primarily because they are never challenged.

Argument Number One

"I don't dare appear different or I'll be ostracized by the community."

There is an old Sufi story about a village whose well becomes inexplicably poisoned. Ingesting the poison affects the mind and causes the person to go insane. One by one, as the villagers draw water from the well in the town square, they go mad. This occurs over a period of days. The last people to draw from the well observe what is going on around them in confusion. Why is everybody acting like this? Once they have drunk the water, however, their neighbors' behavior seems perfectly normal. After a while, people continue on with village life in a state of collective madness without anyone objecting. Then one day, a traveler passes through. His perfectly sane behavior strikes the villagers as very odd, alarming even. Soon they arrest him as a troublemaker. The traveler quickly assesses that the source of the population's madness is the poisoned well and refuses to touch the water. Days pass. He grows increasingly lonely, and tired of sitting in a cell by himself. Finally, he makes the choice to sacrifice his sanity by drinking the water so he can escape his isolation and become a part of the community.

This story illustrates the strength of the collective to influence the individual to give his mind away so that he will fit in.

Argument Number Two

"There's no point in being assertive because no one will listen anyway."

My masseuse, Melissa, finally realized she needed to join the age of credit and get herself a credit card. Naturally, she applied to her own bank where she had been doing business for years. They turned her down with a form letter. She called her bank manager who responded with, "Sorry, you don't have any credit history. You've never borrowed money." "But," Melissa protested, "I have two thousand dollars in my account." He apologized again and said he could not give her one. For six months, Melissa accepted the bank's decision, and then decided to apply again. She got the same reply. Six months later, she tried again with the same negative result. Each time she accepted their reply as gospel, she gave her power away. She permitted them to keep her at the receiving end of their unfair business practices and yet allowed them to keep her money on deposit.

Why did Melissa give up her power? She made several incorrect decisions. First, as one customer of many, she assumed she had little leverage to influence this behemoth of a corporation, that her mere two thousand dollars didn't mean much. She didn't use her leverage because she didn't realize she had any. Second, she assumed that the person she was dealing with at the bank had the last word on the subject. Consequently, she did not challenge his authority by asking to see someone else who might be persuaded. Third, she assumed she had no place else to go. If this bank turned her down, so would others.

Eventually Melissa got tired of being turned down and answered the bank manager's rejection with, "Fine, don't give me a credit card. I'll take my money, which now amounts to six thousand dollars, and go somewhere else." The manager put her on hold. He returned several minutes later and told her she had been approved. She had not resorted to calling out the National Guard or writing her congressman. In the end, she simply used what collateral she had, and it worked.

Argument Number Three

"I have to behave properly or it will destroy my image of myself as a good person."

Fred and Marie went to the Toyota dealer to buy a new car. Having heard that salesmen respect male customers more than they do females, they decided to let Fred do the talking. As the contract was being drawn up, Marie noticed that her husband was giving in on every point, and the tally was adding up. They were paying a lot more for the car than they needed to. She quietly began to intercede and go over each point again, this time negotiating for better terms. Whenever she saw that the salesman was trying to pull the wool over her eyes, she held her ground and insisted on a lower price for that option. Fred grew embarrassed. He thought his wife appeared obnoxious and pushy, not the image he wanted to project of them as a couple. He thought of himself as a well-mannered person and didn't want that picture tarnished. Even though he would have saved thousands of dollars, he was afraid of asserting himself and appearing brassy. What he really needed was to go home with a good deal, but he could not get that need met because he was so concerned with appearances. The trouble with Fred was that he was not in present-time reality. He was stuck back in childhood when his mother used to say, "Freddy, don't make a scene." Marie was in present time. She was forty-two years old and buying a car, not a little girl being polite in front of company. She did not stand on ceremony.

Argument Number Four

"I'm not supposed to challenge authority."

A famous psychology experiment was conducted back in the early 1960s by Stanley Milgram at Yale University. Male students were recruited on campus to participate in a study. The stated purpose was to test the effect of pain on a person's ability to learn. A subject was seated in a room with electrodes attached to him. If his response to a question was wrong, the volunteer sitting in a booth was to administer a small shock. The volunteer had access to controls that allowed him to raise the volume of shock as required.

In fact, the "subject" was not another volunteer at all, but one of the researchers, and the electrodes were not hooked up to an energy source. The real purpose of the study was to see if the volunteers could be persuaded to perpetrate real harm onto a human being they did not even know just because they were told to do it. The volunteers were given instructions through a speaker in their booth by a deep, authoritarian male voice. The voice purposely never yelled or threatened. It just insisted in a steady, dictatorial way that the volunteer administer increasingly severe doses of electric shock to the "subject." The researchers were amazed to see how far the volunteers could be persuaded to go in turning up the dial on their instrument pad, clearly against their will. One man, who had turned the dial up to nine and watched the "subject" spasm under the electric shock until his body went still, was actually weeping and begging the man behind the voice not to make him go any further.

This revealing study illustrated just how powerful the influence of authority can be, even if there is no significant punishment for disobedience. The only thing that hung over the volunteers for not complying with the authoritarian commands was that they would not get their measly pay for participating in the study.

In my career, I have been surprised to see how many strong and seemingly self-reliant people will walk away from a conflict with an authority figure rather than stick up for their own interests. What they don't realize is that by walking away, they have just participated in their own victimization.

Argument Number Five

"I must have done something to deserve this abuse, so I have no basis to defend myself."

Peter was speaking in a therapy group about something very personal. At one point, a fellow member, Suzanne, interrupted with an erudite and opinionated analysis of what his problem was. Her remarks *were* ill-advised and somewhat insensitive, yet it was clear that she meant well. Peter paused a moment and then erupted. "Just shut up! You're a fool, you know that? What you said was so stupid I can't even comment." Suzanne went red in the face and did not say another word for the rest of the meeting. Days later she recounted to me a casual conversation she'd had on the phone with Peter that day. I was surprised that all had been forgotten so easily. "I think I would still be upset with him," I said. "Upset about what?" Suzanne asked innocently. I pointed out to her that Peter had lashed out at her and insulted her in front of the whole group. It was evident at the time that she had felt humiliated. "Well," Suzanne admitted, "I did feel awful when he called me a fool, but he had good cause for his attack. After all, I did interrupt him." "But Suzanne," I replied, "just because you did something inappropriate doesn't mean his response can be brutal. He could have just told you in a neutral way not to talk to him then."

Within seconds, tears were pouring down her cheeks. She admitted that when she was a child, her father could punish her as severely as he wanted and she was always told that her behavior justified his cruelty. She went through life believing that if she made a mistake, people were allowed to react abusively toward her and she was not supposed to defend herself.

People like Suzanne were never given the right to be treated with respect; only the other person, her father for instance, was accorded that right. To carry this mentality as an adult is a recipe for failure. Suzanne does not understand that she has rights, even if she is not perfect. Everyone makes mistakes. If she thinks this condemns her to a life of maltreatment, she will always be beaten down. How can she ever get ahead and be a success if she allows herself to be treated this way?

Argument Number Six

"If the other person flinches when I make a request, it means I'd better back down."

Josephine went into her boss's office first thing Monday morning to ask for a raise they both knew was long overdue. After a few minutes of small talk, she got straight to the point. Her pay had remained the same for years, even though her duties had increased and she had several subordinates working for her now. She should have gotten not one, but two salary increases by this time. She told her boss that, as she estimated it, her annual salary should now go up to $60,000 a year, a jump of 18 percent. Her boss reacted as if he had just sat on a tack. "Sixty thousand dollars!" he gulped, jumping from his seat. Josephine immediately receded into the back of her chair. *My request was entirely too high*, she thought instantly. *That's obvious from how shocked he is. I must have miscalculated.* Before the man behind the desk said another word, she began to backpedal. "Well . . . maybe I misspoke . . . that number is a little high." And down the negotiations went from there. Josephine had four thousand dollars lobbed off her asking price before she had even made a case for herself.

In negotiation parlance, her boss's technique is called "the flinch." It is effective because it contains a hidden message. He nonverbally communicated to Josephine that she had done something outrageous and that her request was so ridiculous it didn't bear discussing. The only logical retort was to dismiss it summarily. And because the message was covert and nonverbal, she could not easily respond overtly and verbally. The manipulative part of the act is to cause the other person to back up immediately in their negotiations or risk looking like a fool. Unfortunately, it worked because Josephine reacted too quickly, not giving herself a chance to assess what her boss was doing. He laid a trap and she fell for it.

Argument Number Seven

"They're more important and they know more than I do, so I'd better not argue."

As a child, I was taught that doctors were all-knowing, god-like figures, and it was an affront for mere mortals to disagree with them. In Norman Cousins' book, *Anatomy of an Illness*, he describes the doom-and-gloom diagnosis he received from his doctors. Clearly he was expected to accept their proclamation that he had a terminal illness, give up all hope, and put his affairs in order in time for his funeral. At that time, in the 1960s, it was considered highly out of line to do anything but follow a doctor's advice obediently. But Cousins decided to claim his power and take responsibility for his own fate. He took the unorthodox approach of using humor to heal himself. Ultimately he proved his doctors wrong and went right on living.

It cannot have been easy for him to chart such an independent course. What he understood was that his doctors might have known a great deal more than he did technically, but they didn't know everything, and they could be wrong about him. He did empower these professionals to help him through his crisis. That did not mean, however, that he abdicated the right or responsibility to think for himself. On some level, people *want* to give their power away in a situation like this so they don't have to take responsibility. Taking responsibility often makes a person uncomfortable. Cousins gave his doctors only enough power to influence him, not enough to control him. He was always aware that on the doctor's side there was general knowledge and expertise, but on his side there was specific awareness of his own body, gut instinct, faith, and the right to investigate for himself and ask for a second opinion. Cousins was willing to challenge the popular wisdom that "the doctor is always right." He stood as an individual and succeeded in living against the odds.

Argument Number Eight

"If I insist on my rights, it will backfire and I'll end up worse off than I am now."

At one of my seminars, whose subject was the art of negotiation, I told people that they needed to challenge unacceptable behavior. Afterward a woman came up to me to ask a question. I could see right away that it was something that had been bothering her for some time. She worked in a bank. Several months earlier she had devised an idea for expediting the process of approving home loans and presented it to her boss. She told him about the plan while he was standing at her desk, and right in front of her co-workers he told her it was an idiotic idea. It was not the first time he had dismissed her with contempt in the office, robbing her of the respect of others. Yet she felt powerless to stop him. My obvious response was, "Why don't you tell him that if he doesn't treat you with respect, you'll quit and get another job." The woman said, "Oh, I couldn't do that. He might call my bluff and fire me. I don't want to put myself through a job search. And what would I do if I couldn't find one? I can't fall behind on my rent."

I responded by relating a similar story of my own. Years earlier when I worked for a computer company, I had finished a project improperly. My boss approached my desk and pointed out the mistakes, which he was right to do. But his tone of voice was derogatory, and after the pertinent comments he literally said, "You're bad, bad, bad." He returned to his office, while I sat there fuming. Several minutes later I marched into his office and said, "I quit. I'm not going to let anybody talk to me like that." I was not making a threat. I honestly felt that quitting was a response that had integrity. Suddenly, however, my boss had a change of heart. Overall he liked my work and didn't want to lose me. He called his boss in, and together they persuaded me to forget the incident and stay. My boss never used that tone of voice or language to me again.

When I finished my story, I told the woman that she might want to rethink her position that she had to stay and put up with the abuse. I pointed out the extremely low unemployment rate in the country at the time, and said that many employers were clamoring for new employees. "They probably need you a lot more than you need them," I said. The woman beamed and made up her mind on the spot to confront her boss. "I thought I was helpless," she said, "because I assumed I was easily replaceable."

Most companies are run on fear. They utilize the victim mentality of employees who assume they have no options or control. Historically this has been shown to be untrue. Many of the privileges we enjoy today—the forty-hour work week, paid vacations, child labor laws— are the result of employees who rose up amidst great opposition and decided they had a right to be treated better. They took power even when it looked as if there was none to be taken. The fact is that people always have more power than they realize. They don't know how much they have until they assert themselves.

Argument Number Nine

"If other people would only be nicer to me, then I could be happy."

I overheard a young woman in a movie theater say to her sister, "Mom is always criticizing me and making me unhappy."

The assumption she is making here is that other people have control over her emotions, and she has to accept whatever emotional state they leave her in. The truth is that no one can make you unhappy except yourself. A feeling is your emotional reaction to an outside occurrence based on your interpretation of it. The woman's interpretation of her mother's criticism was "I must be a bad person." After that thought, of course, she felt bad and then believed that her mother had caused the feeling. In reality, in order to feel bad, she had to collude with her mother's criticism. If she had separated from her mother emotionally in that moment, become autonomous, then she could have left the critical comments where they were—in her mother's mouth.

A Zen story illustrates this perfectly. Two monks who had taken the vow of chastity were walking down the road. They came to a small stream that was the result of a sudden rain and found a young woman standing there, unable to cross. One of the monks put down his load and carried her to the other side. The two men then continued their journey in silence. When they returned to the monastery, the other monk immediately went to their superior and reported that his fellow student had touched a woman. The offending monk appeared in the superior's office and said to his traveling companion, "I left the woman back at the stream. What about you?"

The helpful monk is telling his critical companion, "This criticism belongs to you, so you keep it." The young woman in the movie theater, on the other hand, accepted her mother's criticism as her own. While the helpful monk owned his power, the young woman did not own hers, and thus allowed her mother to control her.

We are the ones who carry the burden of other people's opinions around with us, not realizing how much they weigh, how much they take away our freedom, and the fact that they can be put down. If you let others control you through their judgments, you will have very little power of your own. The woman in the theater will never be a success in her own eyes if she continues as she is. She will only be able to do it on her mother's terms.

Argument Number Ten

"The world is a dangerous place, so I'd better keep my head down and not take any unnecessary chances."

Rick was a systems engineer at IBM. He developed the systems that I sold to the customer. One day a major airline company was having trouble with errors in their reservation system, and we sold them a solution. Instead of creating something innovative to meet the demands of the problem, Rick fell back on what was tried and true. To him, this was a way to ensure that he didn't get into trouble. If his mothball solution didn't work, he could simply say, "This is how we've always done it. It's not my fault if it didn't work this time." When I got to know Rick, I found that everything in his life exhibited this habit of clinging to safety and conformity—his clothes, his car, his hobbies, his wife. One day at lunch he said to me, "I like working for IBM. I enjoy having the corporate umbrella over my head." In all my years in the business, I had never heard anyone actually use that trite phrase "corporate umbrella" before. He was admitting in the most obvious way possible that he was the poster boy for playing it safe.

For all Rick's conviction that this was the best way to meet his needs, he was wrong. What he really needed was more money because his kids were ready to enter college. The job he had would never provide enough; he had to move up in the hierarchy. Because his performance was always so lackluster, though, he was never even considered for promotion. Rick did not give himself the option to go on to greater levels of achievement in his profession. He was forced to be satisfied with what he had. And in the end, things grew even worse for him than stagnation. When IBM did the unthinkable and downsized, he was let go. Other employees who had developed their skills at IBM went on to better jobs, but Rick had grown utterly dependent on the behemoth corporation. Being fired devastated him to the extent that it was difficult for him to pick himself up and find another job.

▼   These arguments for victimhood are compelling, but the next chapter will offer an equally compelling rebuttal.

Chapter 10

THE CONFIDENCE MYSTIQUE

Man is ultimately self-determining. Man does not simply exist but always decides what his existence will be, what he will become in the next moment.

VIKTOR E. FRANKL

In life, many forces are trying to exert an influence over you and take away your power to be an individual, your power to think for yourself. This makes you extremely susceptible to becoming a victim to any person or group that wants to exploit you. While it's easy to fall under the influence of others, it is worth the effort to resist.

There are a number of sources that disseminate information to the public: government, news organizations, corporations, unions, educational institutions, medical associations, religious groups. And whether you are aware of it or not, they are impacting how you view the world. Just because you can't put your finger on who it is that told you to think this or that, or when and how they told you, it doesn't mean they haven't exerted a great deal of influence over you. They've gotten into your brain and there they stay.

You may ask yourself what difference it makes if an outside source forms your worldview: "How does that affect my life? Why is it important for me to keep control over my own worldview?" One of the central ideas of this book is that success, power, and individuality are interconnected. If you do not have the freedom, or enough control over your life, to be in alignment with who you really are, you can never count yourself as a true success story no matter how much money you've made. Another way of saying this is that your life must have a component of truth or you are not truly living. People who are not in touch with their own truth are disconnected from their inner core, and they go through their day like zombies. We've all met zombies; they have the qualities of dullness and apathy. They are spiritless, passive, and colorless. If you could look inside their minds you would see that they are not in direct contact with their own experience. The life they are leading is nothing but an empty shell, and they seem incapable of making conscious decisions on their own behalf. Instead, they are told what toothpaste to buy, what team to root for, what status symbol to crave.

A good visual example of this kind of person comes from the 1930s Buck Rogers movie serial with Buster Crabbe. Whenever the bad guys captured someone, they didn't kill him because they wanted him to work as a prisoner in their labor camp and be a slave to their wishes. To achieve total submission, they put a "special" metal helmet on the prisoner's head. He would immediately change from kicking and screaming resistance to docile and subdued acquiescence. His eyes would go blank, and he would move about in a trance-like state. At that moment, he ceased being an individual and became a body that would do things on command. This is an exaggerated example of a person who is outer-directed and not in possession of his own uniqueness or truth. For all intents and purposes, he is dead. We can see, then, that to be truly alive is to experience truth.

Everything must be in alignment with its natural state (or with natural laws) or it becomes the walking dead. The natural state of a human being is to be as unique as his fingerprints, to be self-determining, and to pursue his own idea of happiness. If you allow the world to impose on you a point of view, whether it is about global concepts like international politics and religion, or about personal matters like lifestyle, it will throw you out of alignment with your own truth. Even though it is sometimes a formidable task to challenge the powers that be and set your own philosophical course through life, it is worth doing.

What about people who are not living their truth? They watch TV, mosey along from one year to the next, stay where they are because it's comfortable, get through life somehow. They don't give truth or individuality a second thought. They aren't aware of how their opinions and views are formed or of who formed them.

Some people would make the argument that ignorance is bliss. If the problem doesn't seem to bother them, why is it a problem? The problem is that what you don't know will circle around and hit you in the back of the head every time. Whatever issues we are avoiding catch up to us eventually. For instance, let's take Betty, a woman who was tied to a bad marriage for twenty-two years. Her husband made all the financial decisions, chose their friends, and even told her how to vote. Her family and friends, all of whom attended the same church, reinforced the belief that a good wife deferred to her husband. Betty harbored a secret desire to leave her domineering husband, but was afraid to confront her fear of being alone and the disappointment others would direct toward her. When she turned forty, though, the marriage left her. Her husband dropped out of their church and wandered off in search of a second adolescence. By that time, years of resentment had built up from which she now had to purge herself, and she had wasted her youth by not developing her own resources. Consequently, she wasn't equipped to compete in the job market, and her self-esteem was somewhere on the bottom of the swimming pool.

Twenty-two years of denial had left this woman unprepared to deal with real life. In addition, she was a stranger to herself. In all those years as a zombie, Betty had only been connected to the surface of herself, unaware of her true inner resources, like courage and creativity. Her fear-based personality had made her inflexible, unable to roll with those punches life sometimes delivers. She had stayed as a child, emotionally, and now that she was alone and in pain she lacked both the wisdom to guide herself through the catastrophe and the depth to weather it. All she had as company were fear and inadequacy. This scene is replayed thousands of times a year across America. The moral of the story is that it pays to wake up and be aware of the true conditions of your life. Walking around with blinders on only makes it easier to get run over by a bus.

Sometimes entire countries are swathed in denial and out of touch with reality. The former Soviet Union is an example of a state where for many years its citizens were fed a steady diet of lies. "Communism is working." "All the citizens are provided for." Everywhere people looked they were bombarded with this propaganda and denied the right to think for themselves. The result was depression, apathy, and alcoholism on an epidemic scale.

Each one of us is born with the gift of self-awareness, the ability to tap into our own personal truth. Regardless of the extent to which we choose to develop this gift, it is always present in us to some degree, keeping us honest. No matter how much a zombie tries to convince herself that she is a success, because her choices are not in alignment with who she really is, she feels, deep down, like a failure. It is our birthright as human beings to actualize our uniqueness and be fully self-aware, rather than to walk through our life in a trancelike state.

CONFIDENCE AND CHARISMA ▼

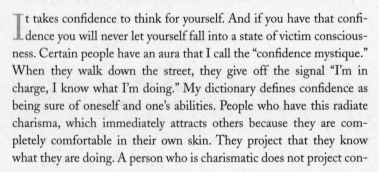

It takes confidence to think for yourself. And if you have that confidence you will never let yourself fall into a state of victim consciousness. Certain people have an aura that I call the "confidence mystique." When they walk down the street, they give off the signal "I'm in charge, I know what I'm doing." My dictionary defines confidence as being sure of oneself and one's abilities. People who have this radiate charisma, which immediately attracts others because they are completely comfortable in their own skin. They project that they know what they are doing. A person who is charismatic does not project conceit or arrogance, which has a defensive quality, but a relaxed self-assuredness.

Confidence is not a characteristic you're either born with or not. It is usually fostered by your parents in a loving environment, and it can wax or wane at various stages of your life. I grew up in a bad neighborhood where I used to get beaten up every other Tuesday. Unfortunately, my parents did not foster confidence in me. When I walked home from school, I was in a constant state of fear about which direction the first blow would come from. When I reached puberty, however, chemical changes took place that affected my mind and body. My physical stature grew and my attitude changed. I began to tell myself, "I'm through with playing victim." My inner sense that I had drawn a line on what kind of behavior I would accept, and the knowledge that I could take care of myself, had an impact on my physical bearing. Magically, from that time on I was never picked on again. I didn't have to have a big conspicuous fight so everyone could see my new strength. I simply radiated it. The neighborhood bullies no longer had my implicit permission to beat me up. I had traded my victim mentality for the confidence mystique. It was later refined in the Marine Corps by what is known as "command presence." This term refers to a way of carrying yourself that inspires confidence in others; it makes people want to follow you.

I never fully appreciated the power of the confidence mystique until I decided to trade in the pin-striped suit of a corporate executive for actor's jeans. What happened was nothing short of a revelation. I wanted to quit my job, but I needed severance pay to sustain me during my hungry days as a neophyte actor. It would be much better strategically if I were to get fired. With that in mind, I no longer cared what my superiors thought of me; I just wanted out.

I tried a myriad of ways to "persuade" them to fire me. I was outspoken and obnoxious, late for work, argumentative in meetings, and prone to long lunches from which I did not return. Unfortunately, my strategy backfired. My employers interpreted my brassy attitude as a superhuman level of confidence in myself which, by reason, must reflect superhuman capacity. "He's so sure of himself he must know what he's doing, and if he knows what he's doing, we want to keep him. He'll know how to meet any challenge."

Far from firing me, they bestowed two promotions on me, one right after another and each with an accompanying pay raise. Then something even more extraordinary happened. My division was sold to another company and 1,500 salespeople and managers were let go. Only six remained, and I was one of the notable six! That old phrase, "What does a guy have to do to get arrested around here?" kept popping into my mind. The irony of it all still makes me laugh.

It is clear that the result would have been entirely different had I not exhibited such a cavalier attitude, an attitude based solely upon my willingness to walk away. They sensed the confidence mystique and found it so irresistible they couldn't bring themselves to let me go.

People bow to confidence. What is behind the self-assuredness is secondary; what is important is the perception. In the movie *Patton*, an aide to the general says to him, "General, sometimes your officers don't know when you're acting and when you're not." Patton replies, "It isn't important for them to know. It's only important for me to know." I have often found that experts don't know half as much as they seem to know. They enjoy the prestige and the big paychecks because they make people believe they know more than they do.

ASSERTIVENESS 101 ▼

Confident people assert themselves in such a way that they are consistently able to meet their needs. Assertiveness, however, is different from aggressiveness. When being assertive, the central aim is power for your own good. When being aggressive, the central aim is power to control others. In both cases, some kind of challenge is involved, either of another person's decision or of his opinion. Intelligent opposition involves a confrontation for the right reason; you are searching for the truth or fighting for something that is rightfully yours. A challenge turns obnoxious when you are arguing just for the sake of being right, or trying to satisfy your desires whether you are entitled to them or not. You are thinking only about yourself and not considering the needs of those around you. Being assertive is a self-preservation tool; it is meant to help you meet your needs so you can have a better life. It is not meant to help you display a blatant disrespect for others.

Unfortunately, a large percentage of the people I come across are either unable or unwilling to be assertive. Many are afraid of disapproval, of not being thought of as Mr. Nice Guy, or of being the object of ridicule or anger. I believe this is because they have lost sight of certain basic principles of assertiveness that happen to be easy to apply. These simple ideas should have been taught in childhood, but all too often they weren't. These, then, are the eight fundamental assertiveness principles.

1. Know What You Want

You cannot succeed without knowing what constitutes success for you. This means delving beneath the surface and finding out what your *real* need is. It is surprising how often people fail to do this one simple thing. Here is an example. People often say they want to be in show business. When I left the corporate world for show business, I thought I had finally achieved true success. Yet eventually, even though I was working steadily as an actor, I found myself dissatisfied. Whenever I thought about quitting, however, I believed it would break my heart. What was it that I couldn't bear to part with—the glamour, the money, the beautiful people? Once I honestly analyzed what I was attracted to about show business, I realized it was the free time. Then I concluded that I didn't have to be an actor to procure that. I could look for better work options that provided the same major asset without the disadvantages of show business. The option I chose turned out to be professional speaking.

Whatever surface option seems to be the only choice for satisfying your needs, don't accept it without question. Look deeper. Find out what your true need is before you begin making decisions. Otherwise you will use your assertiveness in the wrong direction. Author Stephen Covey, in his book *Seven Habits of Highly Effective People*, understood this when he pointed out the importance of keeping the end in mind. You have to know exactly what the goal is or you will not take the correct steps to meet it. When I think about the railroad conductor mentioned in Chapter One, I can easily speculate as to which needs were satisfied by his particular job. He worked on his own with no one looking over his shoulder, he was around people all day, he was on his feet and not stuck behind a desk, and he was afforded the opportunity to travel. Some people would think they had to become a jet-setter like investor George Soros for their lifestyle to meet those criteria. But this man wisely picked a simpler lifestyle that gave him what he wanted without a lot of trappings he didn't want.

2. Ask for It

Observe how small children will continue to ask for what they want even when their parents have said no. Yes, they can be annoying, but there is a lesson to learn from them. They understand the value of persistence. Children are probably more in touch than adults are with the connection between needs and survival. As they are growing up the survival mechanism is very active, commanding them to find ways to meet their changing needs. It really is no different for adults, and yet many of us feel guilty about asking for something that will fill a need. The moment another person says no, many adults accept it and drop the subject. They give up too easily, and they need to recognize the value of persistence.

As a professional speaker, I spend half my life in hotels. I sometimes make a number of 800-calls from the phone in my room. I know these calls are free, but some hotels have a policy of charging seventy-five cents for them anyway. When I see that charge on my bill, I challenge it. Usually the clerk at the desk blandly answers, "I'm sorry sir. This is our policy." I ask to speak to the manager and explain my position. Most of the time the manager acquiesces in the face of my persistence. How many extras are you paying for because you don't challenge a policy? There are four conditions under which I believe it is usually worthwhile to take a stand:

- When the amount of money involved is more than you want to lose
- When the stakes are high; if it is a matter of life and death, don't let go
- When there is a higher principle involved
- When what you are asking for is simply fair and the other person's position is blatantly unfair.

3. Don't Undermine Yourself with Negative Self-Talk

Many of us don't need outside adversaries to sabotage our chances of success—we have ourselves for that. If we actually recorded the stream of self-criticism and abuse that goes on in our minds we would probably be shocked. It whittles away at our ability to be assertive, constantly telling us what we can't do, what we're not supposed to want. Unaware of how we make ourselves suffer, we put up with this negativity all day, every day.

Self-awareness is the key. To thwart these kinds of messages, we must first be aware of them. Simple awareness lessens the power of the message to chip away at our confidence. Every time you catch yourself in a negative thought, replace it with a positive one. If you hear your mind saying, "They'll never say yes," try substituting, "If I ask for what I want I have a good chance of getting it."

4. Practice Expressing Your Feelings

You cannot meet your needs if you don't express yourself, because needs and feelings are intermingled. If you keep quiet, you'll go hungry, figuratively speaking. Whenever you don't express feelings that are appropriate and honest, you are giving power to the other person in the sense that you are relinquishing your right to satisfaction. You are saying to him, "My needs are not as important as yours."

People have two main emotional obstacles to expressing their feelings openly and honestly: fear of an angry response and anxiety.

Many people are afraid that if they tell someone else of their displeasure, they will provoke an angry response. To rationalize their way out of the imagined confrontation, they say to themselves, "It won't do any good anyway. It will just make her defensive and she'll cut off all communication." If you are afraid to express a feeling because you think the other person will interpret it as an attack, try rephrasing it as an "I" statement. Instead of saying "You're wrong for doing that," substitute "I don't feel comfortable when you do that." This shows that you are not imposing a rule on the other person, but taking responsibility for yourself.

People experience anxiety about telling others what they feel because they don't want to reveal their vulnerability. Deep feelings show the core of who we are, and many of us are afraid that if that core were seen, it would not be found acceptable. We don't want to be rejected on such an intimate level. It does seem frightening at first to take such a risk, and certainly you want to pick the circumstances under which you choose to do it, but the more you get into the practice of expressing your real feelings the less frightening it is. The reason it is important to express them is so you don't stay hidden all your life, invisible to yourself and others.

5. Learn to Say No

To be an individual, you must establish clear boundaries of who you are: what you stand for, your preferences, your point of view. These distinguish you from everyone else on the planet. In other words, boundaries protect individuality.

Others step on your boundaries all the time. It can happen physically—someone pushes you in a crowded subway car—but most often it is psychological. People try to bully you into agreeing with them or giving them what they want. You are prone to accept it because you're used to it. When we are born, our boundaries are fairly transparent.

Babies don't know how to behave or function, and their parents have to step in constantly to function for them and tell them how to behave. When we grow up we do not need that level of intrusiveness, yet many of us continue to allow others to intrude with their opinions and their criticism even when it is completely inappropriate. The invasion of personal boundaries is suitable for a child whose mind is not fully formed. It is an acceptable intrusion because the parent is guiding the child. In other words, the crossing of boundaries is appropriate to the parent/child relationship. It is not appropriate, however, for adults to dictate values to other adults, or to tell them how to behave other than working out the necessary compromises of living together.

Quite simply, when someone is overstepping her boundaries and getting into your business, you must learn to say no. If you are the kind of person who typically says yes as a first response, you can compensate for that by giving yourself time before you respond. All you have to say is, "Let me get back to you on that." This provides you with a time-out zone for getting in touch with your feelings. "What do I really want here? Do I want to do this person a favor or do I want to turn her down?" Your immediate reaction of saying yes is just a habit. Becoming aware of your true feelings allows you to find out which choice is really right for you, and then to present an honest response.

If you see clearly that saying yes is not right for you and then you say yes anyway, you need to look at where you are placing yourself in the scheme of things. Are you really valuing yourself and your time? Or are you saying implicitly, "She's more important than I am. I should give her what she wants." If you do that, you are not respecting your own boundaries. Others can read this vulnerability in a person and some will take advantage of it. It is important for you to remember that if other people are taking advantage of you in this way, they can only be doing it with your collaboration. You must make a concerted effort to act in your own best interest and say no. If you cannot do it on your own, seek professional help.

Quite a few people believe that to convince another person to accept no for an answer, they have to deliver the message with belligerence. This is not true. The rule is simple: Be polite but firm. You do not need to be obnoxious to be taken seriously.

6. Open with an Extreme Position

Ask for more than you actually want. You can always settle for less later. This technique is common knowledge in business negotiations. For instance, when you are entering a salary negotiation with your employers, if you open with exactly the sum you are willing to accept, they are naturally going to offer you less, and things only go down from there. When you ask for more than you want, three things can happen. One, you might get as much as you asked for. Two, you make concessions but still settle for an amount above your goal. Three, you make concessions but end up settling for the goal you had your eye on in the first place. Asking for more gives you room to maneuver.

If asking for more makes you uncomfortable, it is worth examining your reasons. Don't you think you're worth it? If you think you aren't, you may want to consider how such a notion got into your head. Who told you that you aren't worth it? Or perhaps you are afraid of being perceived as unreasonable. Your asking amount will never be perceived as ridiculous or unreasonable if you can present some good reasons in support of your request. Remember, this is a kind of dance we sometimes have to do in order to meet our needs.

7. Approach the Problem from the Other Person's Perspective

On the face of it, this may not look like an assertiveness principle. What many people don't know is that it is easier to convince someone else to do what you want if the other person thinks she is doing it out of self-interest. By using language that shows her you understand the problem from her point of view, you can appeal to her self-interest. You show her what is in it for her if she agrees to comply with your request.

On the other hand, if the person with whom you are in conflict believes you are being negligent of her needs, she is more likely to hold out. In any conflict, two people's needs are butting heads. By approaching the problem from the other's point of view, you let her know she is being listened to. This eases her into a more cooperative frame of mind and encourages her to work *with* you on a solution.

8. Be a Good Listener

One of the biggest mistakes people make when they are attempting to win others over to their side is to *enter talking*. They go straight for the jugular, trying every line they rehearsed ahead of time to convince the other person they're right. Far from winning over their "adversary," they usually alienate the other person and put him on guard.

Instead, *enter listening*. As with the last point, this runs contrary to popular myth. The common belief is that talking is assertive and listening is passive. What many good negotiators know is that *the interviewer* has the power. The one who is asking the questions is the one in control.

People love to talk, and they are more likely to be open to what you want if you let them do the talking, especially about themselves. When people are listened to, they feel cared about. It is a natural thing. They tend to trust a person who appears to care about them. And once someone trusts you he is more amenable to engage in dialogue and to be cooperative. He becomes supportive of your needs because he feels you have been supportive of him.

▼ To be truly successful, we must retain our power. If we allow society to brainwash us into believing that all there is to success is fame and fortune, we abdicate our power. We become termites, zombies, willing victims of whomever seeks to control our minds. We distance ourselves from the kind of lifestyle we always hoped we'd have.

Did you begin life with a dream? Did reality then reach in and steal your dream from you? By the time we reach middle age, many of us have given up on the dreams we had in our youth. Unfortunately, those dreams represent all that was vital in our existence. Retain your power and you need never give up searching for what is truly important to you. You need never surrender your life.

Part Four

FREE AT LAST

Chapter 11

YOUR MONEY OR YOUR LIFESTYLE?

*The pursuit of the material has become our reason for liv-
ing, not enjoyment of living itself.*

MARLON BRANDO

I chiro Oshima, a twenty-four-year-old Tokyo advertising executive,
aspired to status, prestige, money, and power. Toward that end, he
worked six days a week until he was bone tired. He did this for a
year and a half at one of Japan's largest ad agencies. Whether it was
from self-inflicted stress or from the abuse of his bosses, we will never
know—for Oshima did not leave a note—but after falling into a deep
depression he hanged himself one night. This made him another statistic
of *karoshi*, a Japanese term meaning "death from overwork." The fact that
the syndrome is prevalent enough in Japan to have a name is a message in
itself. The sad truth is that between one and ten thousand deaths a year in
Japan are attributable to karoshi, not counting an additional thirty to fifty
thousand cases of stroke and other serious illnesses caused by overwork.

The fact that Japan has put a name to the problem does not mean
it is restricted to that country alone. Quite the contrary. In 2001, CNN
reported a study that found that 24 percent of American workers spend
more than fifty hours a week on the job; that almost the same amount

don't use their vacation time; and that 28 percent feel overwhelmed by their workload. It has been documented that the overworking of employees is the cause of serious mistakes in the workplace, higher costs in healthcare, and strain in family relationships. The term *overwork* should not just be taken to mean putting in long hours. The feeling of being overworked also occurs when the employee is pressured and pushed to produce, or when he feels that the work he does is not of any real value.

With our culture's overwhelming emphasis on making money, do not expect the workload needed to achieve that high income to go down any time soon. As a recent study (see Chapter One) demonstrates, young people today are just as eager to be rich and famous as their parents were. If this ravenous appetite for riches and recognition is any indication, karoshi and its look-alikes are going to be with us for a long time to come. People are seeking external and superficial goals that do not feed the deepest part of themselves. The irony is that this leaves them feeling impoverished when their goal all along was wealth.

The real cause of all this work-related stress is that we have forgotten why we work. In my opinion, there are only two valid reasons to work: first and foremost, to be able to create and maintain a desired lifestyle; and second, to do something that provides enjoyment or fulfillment. The money you make from working is significant only to the extent that it provides satisfaction and enhances your lifestyle. And that is what Part Four is about—lifestyle.

BAROMETER OF THE GOOD LIFE ▼

My friend's robust twenty-month-old son ran across the lawn. As he reached me, he was grinning from ear to tiny ear. "Ed!" he screamed with joy, recognizing me from the day before. Suddenly he tripped and fell. I expected him to cry, but instead he just lay there for a minute as though checking to see that all systems were "go." Then he struggled back to his feet and laughed. Like an adorable wind-up toy, he ran around in circles for pure joy as he laughed, and laughed, and laughed. All I could think was, "This is how we are meant to be. Life, essentially, is joyful, and we are meant to enjoy our lifestyle, whatever it may be."

Lifestyle refers to the totality of how you live your life. It includes work, leisure, friends and acquaintances, sexual preferences, location, dress, and food. In other words, the quality of your life is reflected by how you fill your days, from week to week, month to month. Our culture's obsession with working to make money has given birth to a narrow definition of success that excludes most of the elements of lifestyle other than work. By not paying due respect to the overall importance of the many different aspects of lifestyle, we deny ourselves the full satisfaction that is possible. When we label someone a success purely because of how much money he earns, we ignore the fact that he may be neglecting himself in many of the other areas, and therefore may not be a success at all. The real question is: What does a person do from the time he wakes up in the morning until he goes to bed at night? Are all aspects of his day a success or is he actually limiting himself? After all, Ebenezer Scrooge was considered an eminently successful man in his community, and yet he was abjectly miserable. If the satisfaction we derive from our lifestyle is the ultimate barometer of whether or not we have achieved the good life, Ebenezer was an out-and-out failure.

It should be clear by now that the message of this book is that each of us has the ability and the power to choose what his or her lifestyle will be. Not only do you have a choice, but, as Dr. Robert Luthardt says, "You are condemned to choose. You are either going to have the life you really want or you're going to have some other kind of existence." Unfortunately, "some other kind of existence" is what too many people limit themselves to. Because they remain brainwashed into accepting somebody else's idea of success, they do not deliberately choose a lifestyle that would really be fulfilling. And because they haven't seen the value of choosing it, they have not made the sacrifices necessary to create it. What do they do instead? They passively accept whatever flotsam and jetsam float their way, and suffer through the ensuing feelings of neglect and regret.

Yet there is certainly evidence that some people do take hold of the reins and change their lives. In my experience, it often happens after they have come face to face with the fact that they are not going to live forever—when they can no longer deny the fact that time is limited, which leads them to the inevitable conclusion that they had better make the most of it now. Robert Steinberg was a California physician who was diagnosed with incurable lymphoma. He was given, at most, ten years left to live. "It put me in touch with my own mortality," he said. After extensive self-examination, he realized that he no longer wanted to go on as he had been. "I made a global decision to do the things that I wanted to do." He walked away from his medical practice, went to Italy, and took lessons in Italian, piano, and drawing. "In some ways, there was an exalted quality to my life at that time. [The illness] raised my awareness and sensitivity to people and things around me. The understanding of a perspective of life and death allows a certain risk-taking and carefreeness. It became a kind of touchstone for me." Then Steinberg traveled through France, where he indulged a lifelong interest in cooking. He developed a fascination for chocolate, and upon returning to the United States he began producing his own gourmet chocolate with a high cocoa content. Today, more than ten years after his diagnosis, Steinberg runs a chocolate factory. He is absorbed in something he loves: making better chocolate, teaching others about it, and "expanding the chocolate universe." In Steinberg's case, the ten-year deadline of death by cancer catapulted him into a major change. The question is: Why wait for a death sentence? Why not do it now while you still have a long life ahead of you?

There is cause for hope that, in general, consciousness in this country is changing, that we are loosening our judgments about lifestyle. In the public forum, the whole concept of a different kind of success is continually being voiced, and if we are listening, some of it might get through to us.

In a recent interview, feminist Betty Friedan said:

There needs to be bolder thinking on how to measure the quality of life of men and women in the workforce. Currently, success is measured by material advancements. We need to readjust the definition of success to account for time outside of work and satisfaction of life, not just the dollars-and-cents bottom line.

Marlon Brando, the Godfather himself, says on page 456 of his autobiography *Brando*:

> We have an abundance of material things, but a successful society produces happy people, and I think we produce more miserable people than almost anyplace on earth. We have plenty, but we have nothing, and we always want more. In the pursuit of material success as our culture measures it, we have given up everything. We have lost the capacity to produce people who are joyful. The pursuit of the material has become our reason for living, not enjoyment of living itself.

It is far easier to find examples of people who have sought out this kind of individualized success in fiction than to find it in real life. Novelists seem to guess at the individual's need to self-actualize, and then they express it through their stories. Jim Harrison, in *The Man Who Gave Up His Name* (part of the *Legends of the Fall* trilogy), wrote about a prosperous, forty-something executive who is knee-deep in midlife crisis when he finally decides to examine his life for redeeming value. He comes up empty. After serious soul-searching, he gives up his job as vice president of an oil company to become a short-order cook in Florida. His new lifestyle, while it fails to fit any kind of image he ever had of success, is actually far more attuned to his real needs.

Today, in spite of the mad rush for the external trappings of success, more and more people wish they could emulate this kind of courage. Millions of middle-aged workers are discovering that their childhood goal of luxuriating in wealth doesn't meet with an acceptable payoff in their unsatisfying lifestyles. Many have reacted to the events of 9/11 by changing their lives. New Yorker Joe Gonzalez, like *The Man Who Gave Up His Name*, re-evaluated his career in publishing after holding down key editorial positions at *Vibe*, *Blaze*, and *Seventeen* magazines. He experienced the New York "celebrity circuit," appeared as a hip-hop expert on television, and wrote about famous people. After 9/11, at the age of twenty-nine, he realized that his heart lay elsewhere. He resigned his position as executive editor to do freelance work, travel, and write the novel he had started years before. Joe literally glows now that he's taken charge of his life instead of remaining trapped in the dubious glamour of Manhattan high life.

THE FIVE ELEMENTS ▼

The purpose of Part Four is to explore how to go about fashioning a lifestyle that is congruent with who you are, without having to wait for an external event such as a stress-related heart attack to act as a catalyst. One way to begin is to ask yourself, "What is the real meaning of my life? Deep down, what is really important to me?" This bigger philosophical question will lead you to one that is more practical: "What do I want a typical day in my life to look like?" Instead of focusing on false images and misplaced goals, place your attention directly on the five major elements that really do make up a successful lifestyle: work, location, leisure time, relationships, and health. If you carefully consider each of these in relation to an average day in your life, you can make them work for you. When your typical day actually fills your needs and mirrors your deepest intentions for a good life, you can truly call yourself a success.

You may wish to prioritize these elements according to their value to you personally. Some will rank higher than others, depending on who you are as an individual. For many people, family relationships carry more weight than work or leisure time. For some, location will take precedence. A famous example of two people who differed greatly are actresses Katherine Hepburn and Annette Funicello. The former revealed in a television interview that as a young woman she had made a conscious decision to forego family to pursue her career. The latter quit acting at the high point of her career (not an artistic high point perhaps, but a financial one) to marry and have children. Neither, in their later years, regretted their decisions.

1. WORK: A FOUR-LETTER WORD ▼

What is the real role of work? Principally, it finances our lifestyle and makes us responsible for our own upkeep. Both of these reasons center around money, but money is not the only consideration. What makes the problem of work so complex is that it takes time to make money, and it is the amount and quality of time that count. If this weren't true, it would barely matter what we did for a living. If we lived in a world where it took people five minutes a day to earn their daily bread, no one would care very much whether they picked up garbage or painted murals. We can tolerate doing anything for five minutes. But the fact is that most of us spend upward of eight hours a day (not including the commute) earning our living, and that is a significant chunk of life. It is, in fact, the largest chunk of awake time we spend at any single activity. Over a lifetime, that's a lot of time, and it had better count.

Contrary to popular belief concerning the hardships of life in the past, modern man spends more time working than his predecessors ever did. Before the Industrial Revolution, in rural societies, people put in fewer actual work hours in a year than we do now. And they probably couldn't even tell you exactly how many hours in a day they worked because nobody kept track. Work and down time were intricately connected. A person milked the cows at five in the morning, then chewed on a piece of grass thinking about what to plant next spring, then had a three-egg breakfast, then dug up a tree stump, then smoked a pipe, then ploughed the southwest corner of their land, then leaned on the fence with a neighbor talking about when the rains would start, then went fishing (which was either for fun or for dinner), then cleaned up and sat in front of the fire for a while. The farmer didn't wear a watch. Neither did the farmer's wife. Besides taking care of the children, she churned the butter, kept the vegetable garden, made the clothes, hauled the water, and tended household animals.

These activities weren't *work*, they were just *life*, and they were laden with meaning because they were directly connected with survival. No work: no eat. Work equals life. Today, because society and culture have become so specialized, we are ten steps removed from how our daily work actually results in food on the table. We know that we can pick up our paycheck, cash it, then go to the supermarket. But how does the food show up in cans and cellophane on the shelves, and how does the work we do have any kind of ripple effect on the farmer or rancher who produced it?

A person in a simple society may not have had much of a choice in what he did for a living. Women had children and did chores around the house—period. Men did whatever their fathers did or they joined the army or the clergy. But work still had meaning because, by the sweat of their brow, they met their own needs and fed their families. This kind of cause-and-effect relationship between labor and production makes inherent sense to most people, and provides them with much of the satisfaction they derive from daily activities. It is this very satisfaction that has been removed from so many of our lives because our jobs are so minutely specialized that they each form one tiny cog in a huge, chugging machine. We are locked into our little nooks of the machine and cannot see the whole, much less what we contribute to it. In the past, the cause-and-effect between work and survival gave work its meaning. Today, that has been stripped from us. So we have to find a way to put it back in.

We must, of course, make sure that our work is lucrative enough to ensure our survival. One who isn't surviving—in other words, who is out on the street begging for a sandwich—is not successful. But the work must also be enjoyable. Otherwise, there is no sense of fulfillment. You must be employed at a job where you feel you are making a difference, contributing value, achieving excellence, or in general adding to the lives of others as well as to your own. This brings the cause-and-effect back into our day.

Essentially, it is the cause-and-effect relationship that we are seeking to re-establish because that creates the conditions whereby people can feel enjoyment, satisfaction, and accomplishment. You hear this phrase all the time from satisfied people: "I have such a sense of accomplishment." What does this mean? It means, "I did it. I see what I did and how well I did it. And I see why it was useful."

In their book *Now, Discover Your Strengths*, authors Marcus Buckingham and Donald Clifton of the Gallup Organization concluded that most people do not enjoy their work very much at all. But they also found that people who are "both successful and fulfilled" are not merely skilled at what they do, but also enjoy using those skills again and again and "derive some intrinsic satisfaction from the activity." Somehow they have managed to reconnect the cause-and-effect relationship between their labor and the fruits of their labor.

What career path are you meant to be on? The challenge is to complete the circle by discovering something you are both skilled at and from which you derive satisfaction. In terms of discovering life's passion in work, most of us fall into three groups:

CAREER GROUP ONE: *"I knew what I wanted to do when I was in diapers."*

These are lucky people indeed. They did not have to twist and squirm through sessions with clueless career counselors in high school or wander aimlessly around after college wondering when, if ever, they will find out what they want to be when they grow up. It was in their blood when they were born, and they recognized it early. Their path was set. The biographies of many famous people tell this story. Mozart and Picasso, for instance, had identified their life's passions before the onset of puberty. This, however, is a rare thing. The majority of us stumble around looking for signs from the gods: "I love putting my make-up on in the morning. Does that mean I should be a cosmetician?" In the absence of clear signs, we fall into one career after another, only to find out it isn't *The One*. In this day and age, few people end up embracing the very first career they choose.

CAREER GROUP TWO: *"I had to flounder around for a while, but I finally found a career I enjoy."*

The path of another famous artist, Vincent Van Gogh, resembles that of the general population more than Picasso's does. Reading Irving Stone's marvelous biography, *Lust for Life*, one almost doesn't know whether to laugh or cry at Van Gogh's tortured search for his place in life. The poor man gave 100 percent of himself to every job he tried, but alas, he kept striking out. Only after he had exhausted all other possibilities—dabbling at being a teacher and a missionary, among other things, and looking like an utter failure—did he finally stumble upon painting. Then, although he couldn't sell any of his paintings, he knew he had arrived. He couldn't *not* paint. Many, many people today do not fall into the right career until they are in their forties or fifties. It takes a lot of living and a lot of mistakes to finally get it right. Although this may seem fruitless and even painful while we are still wandering in the desert feeling lost, it is actually a healthy process. Much of our pain is caused by society, which keeps pressuring its members to know what they want when they're still eighteen with pimples. An eighteen-year-old can barely parallel park yet. How is he supposed to know what his true calling is? The search for the right career, however long it is, should be considered an integral part of life.

CAREER GROUP THREE: *"I give up."*

There are different ways of giving up. You can find a job fresh out of college that is like slow death, yet stay with the company for twenty years until they downsize and kick you out. Then you finally are forced into searching for something different, but if you stayed where you were for that long, you probably won't welcome the opportunity to change; you will just go out and find another job like the one you lost. Then there are those who stick to a particular job for about two years before moving on. They seem to be getting somewhere as they play musical chairs, but ten years down the road they are as lost as ever. They are merely dabbling at different activities without the soul-searching that's required to know what they are really meant to do. These people are as dissatisfied as the previous group. They both run out of steam and grow old before their time. Instead of being pioneers and charting their own paths, they look through the want ads and find yet another job that serves the machine. Playwright Arthur Miller said, in response to a question about why his play *Death of a Salesman* had made such an impression on the public, "We are alone, valueless, without even the elements of a human person, when once we fail to fit the patterns of efficiency." Most pre-cut jobs do not respect the complex needs of a human being, and this makes it more and more difficult to connect to the jobs that are out there. "When you think about what people are actually undergoing in our civilization," said Joseph Campbell in *The Power of Myth*, "you realize it's a very grim thing to be a modern human being. The drudgery of the lives of most of the people who have to support families—well, it's a life-extinguishing affair."

▼ This is precisely why, for millions of people, work has become a four-letter word. You may not be lucky enough to fall into Career Group One, but whatever you do, don't fall into Group Three. What do I mean by this? Don't give up. Just because you didn't know that you wanted to be a writer when you were in preschool learning the alphabet does not mean that you won't find out when you're thirty-six. It's never too late. In our culture, the message is that if you don't make it by the time you're thirty-six, you're all washed up. But some people are slow starters. It's true that in certain professions, like being a pianist or a ballet dancer, one will not make it if she doesn't begin when she is young. But this is not true for most professions. Quite the contrary, in fact.

With many vocations, a person brings a lot more to the table once she has lived a little. As she grows older, she develops her instincts and her skills, which make her better at her job. All her prior experience, even if it was within a completely different area of expertise, makes a contribution to her new endeavor. In fact, there are things she can do at forty she couldn't possibly have done at twenty, like write a book that contains real wisdom. On a personal level also, finding and sticking with a particular career at age forty makes sense. The person has stuck her finger into a lot of pies. She knows what they taste like. Now, when she settles down, she has no regrets.

There are practical and legitimate reasons for not giving up on finding the right work for yourself. The important thing is to stay true to your values. If doing what you truly love places you lower on the totem pole financially, so be it. Fred Sloan, for instance, is an energetic forty-five-year-old man with a Santa Claus belly and the genial disposition to go with it. He has been teaching high school chemistry for seventeen years, even though he has a degree in pharmacy and has received many offers for jobs that would triple his paycheck. But he won't switch. Why? "I love to teach and I love the kids." Fred is as successful in his way as Mozart was in his.

Getting Your Money's Worth

One other important aspect of work is the money it earns you, and that means not just picking the right job, but making sure that the money you earn goes as far as it should. Even if you love what you do, you don't want to be forced to do it twelve hours a day to support unnecessary lifestyle choices when you would rather do it eight hours a day. By remembering my often repeated mantra—income is significant only to the extent that it supports your desired lifestyle—you will have no trouble keeping a steady focus on the right goal: quality of life. There are many categories of people who flush their money away on unnecessary luxuries. The following are four of the main follies that Americans waste their money on.

1. THE STATUS SEEKERS

I will go into the importance of living in the right location later in this chapter, but the point of this section is not precisely *where* you live, but whether you get your money's worth out of it.

Mr. X lives in Brentwood, an upscale community on the West Side of Los Angeles. He does live in an award-winning 2,500-square-foot house, but he paid $2 million for it and it sits on a tiny lot a block from a laundromat and a fast-food restaurant. He had to come up with $400,000 as a down payment, which cleaned out his savings, and now he is saddled with a monthly mortgage of $15,000. Yet what peace of mind has this Shangri-la brought him? The high crime rate in L.A. has forced him to install bars on his first-story windows to protect his family, and the poor air quality has racked up his children's medical bills because of the impact on their allergies.

Mr. Y, in contrast, lives in Eugene, Oregon. He paid $110,000 for his comfortable 1,800-square-foot house, which sits on a quarter-acre lot in a quiet, tree-lined, crime-free neighborhood. His down payment was an affordable $10,000 and his monthly mortgage is only $800. The air is fresh, and from his front window is a beautiful view of a park. With the money they save on the mortgage, Mr. Y and his wife were able to buy a cabin on a scenic lake, at which the entire family spends their weekends.

For some people there are compelling reasons to live in large, expensive industrial cities like Los Angeles, but for many residents, their reasons for living there are ill-considered. They could be making wiser choices.

2. THE OVERCOMMITTED

These are people whose accumulation of wealth has caused more problems than solutions. Their substantial income has placed them into such a high tax bracket that half their paychecks go straight to the government. They have purchased expensive adult toys for which they then have to pay upkeep, and which they have precious little time to enjoy. I was particularly struck by this one weekday when I was in Newport Beach, an extremely pricey community in Southern California. As I stood gazing at the harbor and the thousands of yachts and sailboats, I couldn't help noticing that, save one, they were all lashed to their moorings. Their owners were slaving away at work to pay for the docking fees and maintenance. I'm not one of those people who think toys are only for children. I believe in having fun until you draw your last breath. But it is important to weigh the cost of your playthings and to evaluate whether or not you couldn't find a way to squeeze the same amount of enjoyment out of something with a smaller price tag. So many of our expensive leisure-time distractions are more caught up in image than in a pursuit of that which genuinely interests us. Skiing, playing golf, and sailing, for example, all have a certain patina that broadcasts a person's membership in a tony social class. How many who engage in these activities would choose them without the high-class association?

3. THE ADDICTED

Certainly Americans have not cornered the market on addictions, but it seems that we are perennially vying for first place. In ever-increasing numbers we are being drawn into habit-forming patterns of behavior, and they are literally killing us. They are certainly draining our resources, both human and financial, as a nation. Besides their known dangers and drawbacks, addictions, at the worst, throw many people into debt, and at the least they gobble up extra money that could be spent more constructively. Gambling, illegal drugs, alcohol, compulsive shopping—and now, with the high price of cigarettes, even smoking—are the most common culprits. By the very nature of an addiction, it can never be satisfied, which means that we are basically working eight hours a day to throw money at a problem that will never be solved—at least not in this way. We all know that an addiction is never just what it appears to be on the surface; its presence always points to deeper, unre-solved issues. I've said it many times in this book, but it bears saying again: Your life will be more successful overall if you face your issues than if you compensate for them.

4. THE IMPULSIVE

Impulses can be very expensive, and months after that hasty moment of action, we find ourselves still paying for something we either don't want anymore or would have simply been better off avoiding. The most obvious category is impulsive spending. Stores are set up to prey on the weak, to seduce people into reaching for an item and paying for it before they have time to think about which closet they're going to shove it into when they get home. Credit card companies are equally culpable. They tempt consumers into overspending by making it feel painless at the moment of purchase, so that millions are pouring their hard-earned dollars into unnecessary bills and exorbitant interest charges. Another item that goes unnoticed in this category is "the need for speed." Many people with sporty high-powered cars cannot resist the temptation to let them do what they were built for. They endure the speeding tickets and the increased insurance bills to indulge their passion. It must be said, though, that few things provide less value for the money than a speeding ticket. Another area of impulsive spending that affects a certain segment of the population is getting married on impulse. Ex's can be expensive. One last category are people who make poor investments based on a tip from an "inside" source. They cannot resist the temptation to make quick, easy money without having to work for it, but usually they just end up spending the money they did work for to pay for the bad investment. Many who fall into this group are professional people who are fairly successful and are misguided into believing that their expertise in one area automatically carries over into another. An endodontist may know how to perform a root canal job, but that doesn't mean he understands the commodities market.

Retirement: Heaven or Hell?

People in certain government jobs or in the military have always had the option of accepting early retirement. Increasingly, others now have the same option because they work in industries where they can accrue considerable amounts of money while they're still in their thirties and forties, enough money to stop working at an early age if they want to. Consequently, the issue of early retirement now takes on greater significance than ever before. No longer is retirement reserved just for the aged. Everyone—from policemen to dot.com millionaires—is facing the decision. The big question, if the answer is yes, is "Now what?"

What I have found consistently is that the people who adapt the best to retirement are the ones who most treasured their leisure time when they did have jobs. Retirement offers them the golden opportunity they've been waiting for, the chance to finally do what they want all day. They can devote themselves to a beloved hobby. They can develop skills that have never been required for their job. Some people think of it as "time to travel." The kids are grown, the mortgage is paid off, and there is no reason to put a time limit on an adventure. As one woman who had raised five children said to me, "There is not a single living thing in my house that I now have to be responsible for. If my husband and I go to the Bahamas and we want to stay an extra week, we don't have to worry about the kids missing us or the dog going hungry or the plants needing to be watered. We can do what we want."

The people who retire successfully seem to be the ones who don't see it as a time to stop doing, but simply to start doing more of what they want. In other words, they are not inert. My uncle, who was an extremely busy man all his life running his pharmacy, did not grow less busy when he retired. He was just busy at different things. He played golf in the morning, took courses at the local university, mentored young people in the community, and traveled all over the world. In his eighties, he was busier than I was in my forties. His solution to the aimlessness that some people struggle with when they retire was to retain as much structure in his retired life as he had when he ran his pharmacy.

For many people, however, retirement is a curse no matter how they look at it. They have depended on the structure, meaning, sense of belonging, and feeling of making a contribution that their job has given them all their life. Their whole identity, in fact, has been based on their career. Once they give it up, what's left? They honestly don't know, and they're too depressed to find out. These are people who genuinely need to work. They cannot live without it—literally. The statistics on how many men, especially, die within a short time after they stop working is staggering. Said Paul Terhorst in *Cashing In on the American Dream*, "For years I watched partners from San Francisco's most elite firms put away their briefcases, get a new set of golf clubs, and move to Carmel. They were going to play eighteen holes with their wives in the morning and eighteen with the guys later on. They were going to relax and enjoy the money they had worked so hard to save. And some of them did—for six months or so. Then they had heart attacks and died."

Retirement is particularly hard on Type-A individuals who have been workaholics ever since they were young enough to be assigned a social security number. Asking people like this to *slow down* is one thing, but asking them to *shut down* is another. Many of them are highly successful at what they do because they've been living their work all their lives. Sumner Redstone, the feisty chairman and CEO of Viacom, said, "Retirement is not in my dictionary. What does it mean?" If you accept the culture's definition, it means he is supposed to stop using his mind productively and vegetate. Retirement, as we know it today, is an insult to the intelligence and capabilities of people who want to continue being productive members of society. Instead of mandatory retirement, what I propose is that we give people the option of continuing to engage in productive activities—in other words, choosing to go on working for as long as they are able.

Today we must adopt a new perspective on retirement because, for many of us, it will last a very long time. In the past, when life expectancy was about fifty, people retired to the cemetery. Now we have between twenty and forty years to fill up. The change I am suggesting can take place in two areas: in the kind of work you do and in the balance of work and leisure. First, when it's time to retire from the job you have always held, you could consider it the perfect opportunity to change careers. Use your pension or savings to coast on while you create a new line of work for yourself. Second, since you no longer need to work nine to five, Monday through Friday, why tie yourself to that schedule? Why not work two or three days a week and devote the balance of your time to leisure? In this way, you can acquire all the advantages of early retirement without giving up the benefits of work.

2. LOCATION, LOCATION, LOCATION ▼

Given the huge impact that location has on quality of life, it is surprising how little effort and consideration goes into the choice of the best possible place for us to set up housekeeping. The location of our home is not just a point on the map, it is the place we have chosen to plant roots and establish ourselves. This is where we should feel a sense of belonging and of community, or at least satisfaction when we walk out the front door in the morning. The litmus test for whether you have chosen wisely is this: When you return from a trip and set foot in your home territory, do you honestly feel that this is the best place on earth? Can you say, "There's no other place I'd rather be?" Unfortunately, many people cannot answer yes because where they live is the result of either a purely practical consideration or of plain apathy. As Paul Terhorst observes in *Cashing In on the American Dream*, "To my surprise, I found that most people had never thought about why they lived where they lived. After some stammering, they'd glare at me and say, 'We've lived here a long time.'"

Today, with all the possibilities available to us and with the flexibility of modern life, it makes no sense to abdicate the right to choose where we will live. At no time in human history have the possibilities for geographical mobility been as great as they are in post–World War II America. For most of history, people were chained to the land of their ancestors; if they did move out of pure necessity (usually to escape starvation or persecution), the first few generations in the new land suffered tremendous hardship. Just at the turn of the twentieth century, even moving to a different region within this country was as difficult as it was for Columbus to discover America. People had to reestablish whole new relationships in communities that were already formed and hard to break into, and just traveling to the new location was a saga. Thanks to the automobile and the airplane, as well as advances in communication, we now have the option of picking up and relocating to what we consider the most favorable part of the country without losing touch with family and friends.

And yet with this increased mobility, it is still important to reestablish roots and provide yourself with a real sense of place that is often missing in modern life. The area and community you pick to live in should be a place where you can feel the most comfortable and the most nourished, and where you can develop as a person.

If people aren't using the above as the all-important criteria for choosing a location to live, how are they choosing?

ACCESS TO THE JOB MARKET

A major motivator for Americans is going where the jobs are. I have heard people actually say, "Me and the family are thinking of moving to San Jose. They're really hiring down there." And that, literally, is the amount of thought that is put into it. They have failed to look into all other aspects of the lifestyle that living in San Jose would provide. "I'm in high tech. They're hiring high tech. Bingo! It's a match!" Of course, they'll hate the traffic congestion, and they've never liked stucco houses, and the weather will be hot and sticky, but "it's a hot job market."

INVESTMENT VALUE

When home buyers look through the real estate section in the newspaper, sometimes the primary criterion they use to pick a house is not whether it has a big yard or open-beamed ceilings or a fireplace in the living room. They figure out what its resale value will be. "We'd be paying four-fifty for it right now, but in five years that price will double. How can we go wrong?" A house is not a stock option. That's a piece of paper in your file cabinet. A house is a home. At the end of the day, this is the place that can determine whether you feel cozy or whether you feel exiled, whether you feel acclimated and established or whether you feel like a perpetual visitor. People who live in mansions can feel as homeless as the guy sleeping on a park bench with a newspaper over his face. The most important reason to buy a house is because you want to live in it, not because you want to sell it sometime in the future.

THE COMMUTE

Nowadays it is impossible to ignore commuting time when choosing a place to live since the amount of time spent in a car in traffic drastically affects quality of life. And yet it should not necessarily be the all-deciding factor. The real focus on choosing a residence should be "What is it like when I'm there," not "How do I get from there to work?" With some individuals and some families, a longer commute for husband or wife may be justified by the fact that the house is in a bucolic, safe, beautiful setting rather than being close to the office. Ask the people who work in New York City and commute from Connecticut if they wish they had a $4,000-a-month loft in SoHo with half a kitchen instead of their cozy farmhouse on five acres.

SCHOOLS

Parents place a great deal of stock in what school systems their children will be in. And well they should. However, parents should not ignore other aspects of community life just because of the schools. Beverly Hills has excellent schools, but do you want the stress of paying to live in such an exclusive community? And are other values being passed on in schools that may be famous for their scholastic excellence but are full of people who are spoiled and privileged and have too much money to throw around? A better choice might be an environment where the people have the same value system that you do, where the whole ambience is more to your liking, and then pay extra to send your children to private schools if you feel the public school system will place them at a disadvantage.

▼ There is nothing wrong with considering the obvious aspects of life described above when you are choosing an area to live in. What I am saying here is that it is important not to leave out the subtle and personal aspects of your living environment. Which environment will meet your deepest needs? To align your decision with your innate needs, the following are noteworthy factors.

URBAN V. SUBURBAN

The energy level of living in the middle of a bustling city is different from that of living in a quiet suburb on the outskirts of that city. Are you invigorated by the stimulation, the activities, and the resources that a large city provides? Do you need to be in the center of things and have art and entertainment events at hand? Do you thrive on cultural activities? Or do you function better in a small, intimate community where everyone knows your name? Do you prefer a less hectic environment? Would you rather spend your time on more solitary pursuits like reading rather than attending opening night at the opera? Perhaps you've been a city dweller all your life and you're ready for peace and quiet, or you're a country cousin who yearns for the big time.

RURAL

For many, the suburbs aren't far out enough. They need to live someplace where they can't see their neighbor's house. They yearn for a far more simple way of life where they are surrounded by natural beauty and serenity. Only then can they relax and really feel at home. While it may be slow death for chronic city dwellers, there is much to recommend this kind of life for those who want to spend a lot more time in the great outdoors either just sitting on the porch watching the sun dip below the horizon, or doing something more exciting like river rafting and hiking.

REGION

Region is an important consideration because different areas of America have their own flavors. I mean that literally in the food, but also culturally and environmentally. The deep South has a very different feel to it than Northern California. New England is an entirely different experience from the Midwest. Some people have vowed that they will never set up house more than twenty miles from the ocean, which commits them to coastal living. If you know you are a mountain person or a desert person or a prairie person, that will play heavily in what region of the country you choose to live because those environments express who you are. Temperament is another thing to factor in. I have a friend who loved being near the mountains and thought about moving to Montana. But after spending three weeks in Missoula without ever seeing the sun, she realized she would be depressed if she stayed on permanently. This is a woman who, temperamentally, had to have sunshine, and it is lucky for her that she knew that much about herself before committing to a move. I know people who crave the rainy, green climate of the Pacific Northwest and cannot understand why anyone would want to live in the desert, and I know people who live in Arizona who think they own a little slice of heaven.

OUTSIDE THE BORDERS

Many Americans recognize the merit of living abroad. Another culture appeals to something deep in their souls. Among the current favorites are Mexico, Costa Rica, Italy, Argentina, Greece, and Thailand. On a train from Madrid to Barcelona, I met a man named Jack Treadway. He was a most unusual Minnesotan who spends six months a year traveling the world selling seeds. For the other six months, he lives with his family in Thailand in a beautiful house with five servants. "I could never afford this lifestyle in Minneapolis," he told me. When you are thinking about choosing a lifestyle, it pays to expand your mind. You have a whole world to choose from, and if there is another country that has always held you fixated, perhaps you are being drawn to live there.

HOUSE V. APARTMENT V. BOAT

Straight off, how many of you automatically think about residing in a house when choosing a new place to live? But if you're adventurous and you love the water, perhaps a better choice would be selling your house and moving onto a boat. Anchors aweigh! If, on the other hand, your first choice is gardening or lounging in your own swimming pool, you will want a house with a good-sized plot of land. But if you're away a lot, an apartment will probably meet your needs. Come and go as you please and let someone else worry about the upkeep. Another option is a bungalow rather than a regular-sized house. Once again, there is less maintenance; in addition, a smaller abode is cozier and creates more of the feeling of a home. During an interview, the actor Michael Caine insightfully pointed out that children especially prefer a smaller home where they can be together with their parents and siblings, as opposed to feeling alone and alienated in a large house where they're lucky to pass by the other members of the family once a day.

FAMILY

For people with children, what can be most important is making sure their kids know their cousins and their aunts and uncles. They don't want their children to grow up never knowing their roots, never connecting with their own flesh and blood. Wherever their extended family is, that is home, and everything else about the location of their house matters very little to them. Perhaps you don't have children, but you have aging parents you want to stay close to. They only have a few years left and that connection is significant enough that you feel a strong need to live close by. And I have met many people who simply like living in the same place where they grew up. They love the memories associated with the area, knowing the place intimately, and revisiting the same old haunts. To them, the friends of high school are friends for life. For people like this, there is no place else in the world that holds any allure. John Mellencamp said that about living in a small town in the Midwest. He could have fallen for the trappings of Memphis or L.A., two places where the music community is centered, but he loved his home soil.

3. LEISURE TIME: BALANCING YOUR LIFE ▼

My definition of success revolves around how people spend their time. For most, time is divided up between four activities: work, sleep, maintenance, and leisure. Sleep is a given. You sleep as much as you need to. For work, you have to put in whatever time is necessary to finance your lifestyle, or more if you are absolutely passionate about it. The time one spends in maintenance activities—doing dishes, going to the dentist, getting the tires rotated, taking out the garbage, filling out your tax return—is somewhat negotiable. Some maintenance is always required (even if you have a maid, she cannot go to the dentist for you), but many people get roped into more maintenance than is healthy because their lives are too complicated, and they are trying to maintain too lavish a lifestyle. Some people are so inundated with the details of maintaining a princely existence that they have no time to just feel alive. Yet another lesson to be learned from small children: You can buy them a hundred dollars worth of baseball equipment if you want to, but they'll have just as much fun hitting an old ball with a stick. They know how to squeeze everything they can out of the moment—without paying for it.

After work, sleep, and maintenance, you're lucky if you have three to four hours a night for leisure activities and probably more time on the weekends. According to my dictionary, leisure is spare time that can be devoted to rest and recreation. Although free time has been a feature on the human landscape for thousands of years, people tend to think of it superficially and overlook its contribution to their quality of life. But leisure actually holds far more significance than we give it credit for. One important service it provides is as a balance to those activities that are centered around survival. For many, their leisure hours provide the only time in which they can indulge their true interests. If you love doing watercolors, for instance, and find that you don't have the knack for making a living at it, your off hours are the only time you have to add this important artistic activity to your life. Letting it fall by the wayside is tantamount to not adding salt to your food. You can live without the salt, but why would you want to? Half the point of eating is for it to be a pleasurable experience, not just an act of survival. One of the most exciting aspects of today's world is that work provides enough surplus of time and money that we can pursue other activities for their own sake.

Work and leisure represent the two poles of our lives. For people who are wildly passionate about their work, leisure does not have quite as much allure as it does for those who are just holding down a job. The former do not depend on their free time for pleasure because they derive so much pleasure from work. But many people enjoy their leisure time far more than their work, and I have been amazed to discover how many out there feel guilty about that. It is almost as if they cannot take themselves seriously unless work is the dominant feature on their landscape. This society's true attitude toward leisure is belied by the fact that it is a multibillion-dollar-a-year industry. We applaud it out of one side of our mouth, and dismiss it out of the other.

Once again, I think we have our history to thank for this. Our legacy is simple: Work is laudable, upstanding, and agreeable in the eyes of God, and free time is virtueless and godless. Too much of it will turn one into a reprobate. In the old way of thinking, *leisure* became synonymous with *lazy*. If work is so important to you that your identity is cemented to it, you are considered a solid citizen and worthy of respect. But if you dare to identify with your leisure pursuits (for instance, when people at parties ask "What do you do?" you answer "surfer" instead of "dental hygienist"), you are considered a dilettante, somebody who putters through life but isn't "getting anywhere." If you could see my friend's little son whirling around on the grass, you would realize that free time holds just as much purpose as work. When you are doing something that turns you on, the creative force of the universe can manifest in you as an individual without being hampered by the practicalities of making it "pay off" in some way. To paraphrase Oscar Wilde, whatever you decide to do in life, as long as there isn't any money in it, you'll probably be all right. If you are employing your free time wisely, you are using it to manifest that which is uniquely you. Is there no purpose to that? Is it less profitable to your life than spending time at the office? This is not meant to devalue work, but to bring its counterpart leisure up to par and give it its full due.

In terms of leisure, most people today fall into three camps:

LEISURE CAMP NUMBER ONE: *"I live and die for my work."*

Typically, Type-A individuals fall into this camp. They are so driven that they feel guilty if they are not working. Whenever they aren't actually on the job, they are thinking about it. These people are the ideological descendants of this country's founding fathers, and they are easy to spot. Just go to the beach and look for the guy clicking away on his laptop computer while his kids are swimming. "Hey Dad, watch this!" "Just a minute, Bobby. Daddy has to finish the quarterly report."

For such people work isn't just a necessity, it's an addiction. Their minds can't put it down. The unstructured nature of aimless leisure hours makes them antsy. Even if they don't love the work itself, they need it because it provides structure for their lives. For true workaholics, non-work weekends are regarded with dread because all they have to look forward to is feeling aimless and lost. Often these people fill their weekends and nights with endless tasks just to keep from being alone with themselves and still. They're like sharks; they have to keep moving or they think they'll drown. Some of them may actually be on target, in a way. An abuse-based person who doesn't like herself has good reason not to be still because it means she has to subject herself to an offensive and derisive inner dialogue. Keeping herself busy working redirects her attention and offers her much-needed esteem; it makes her feel like she's accomplishing something. The entire culture supports this avoidance technique by telling her what a fine person she is for never taking a minute for herself.

My concept of "farting around," which is just another way of saying "enjoying unstructured time," is unthinkable for these people. They just don't get it. "Fart around? But what would that accomplish?" If they do find some leisure activity that interests them, they attack it with the same intensity they do work. Of course, this defeats the whole idea of leisure, which implies at its core that it is relaxing. These people even outfit themselves for these after-hours activities as if they were gearing up to start a business. Have you ever met someone who decided to take up scuba diving, then went right out and bought $4,000 worth of gear?

LEISURE CAMP NUMBER TWO: *"I can't wait for the weekend."*

The flip side of the workaholic is the person who puts up with work because he hasn't found a way to avoid it. If he had his way, he would never work at all. Work is just a necessary nuisance that pays for all his toys. Frankly, I don't have a problem with people whose primary focus is leisure. I think leisure time is fantastic. However, if you fall in this camp, focusing all that time and interest on what you do *after* work means you are consigning yourself to eight-hour shifts of meaningless boredom because you've never paid enough attention to your career to make it worthwhile. You are condemning the largest block of time in your day to something you can barely tolerate. Just as the workaholic is using work to avoid something, the person in this camp is also avoiding something. He uses his other pursuits to avoid the sometimes formidable task of finding a meaningful career. Work is different from leisure. It uses your talents and skills to make a distinct contribution, and it rewards you for that with a paycheck. If you have to work, but you feel that your current job is wasting your time and your talents, then you need to do something about it.

LEISURE CAMP NUMBER THREE: *"For me, work and play are balanced."*

Those in the third group have found a way to make both parts of their life count. They are thoroughly involved in their work, which provides deep satisfaction, and they have enough pastimes after hours to keep themselves amused and enthusiastic. A small percentage of this group has managed to accomplish the ultimate: They find it difficult to distinguish between work and leisure because they derive the same amount of pleasure from both. Life is one continuum where it's difficult to tell where the job starts and where the fun ends. This is the best of both worlds—which doesn't mean that every single moment is enjoyable. Some aspects of even the most fulfilling job, such as filling out reports or returning phone calls, can be tedious. Some aspects of even the most delightful leisure activity can be dull, such as dragging around a ton of ski equipment. The important thing is that the core of the activity is fulfilling.

My view is that it doesn't matter which one you find most satisfying. If your job isn't everything to you, it's healthy to be able to say so. And this doesn't even imply that you're not good at your job. Andre Agassi, one of the top tennis players in the world, said that tennis was not the center of his life. It was just one aspect, and not necessarily more important than any other aspect. If you want to know how important your own job really is to you, ask yourself whether you would keep doing it if you won the lottery. A person with a strong sense of self can actualize her energy without having a career. She may find life's meaning where she least expects it.

4. RELATIONSHIPS: A WORK IN PROGRESS ▼

Human beings are social animals, and even for the most intro-verted person of all, the relationships in his life have played a large part in forming him. The family is our first school for learning how to be in a relationship. It is a big pot into which people who didn't choose each other (except perhaps for the Mom and Dad) are thrown together and expected to get along and thrive. The lessons we learn in this melting pot tell us how to read other people's emotions, how to draw personal boundaries, how to reach out and make connections, how to say no when it is imperative and when to say yes. They teach us empathy, wisdom, compassion, tolerance, self-control, and coopera-tion. Everything we absorbed from the family we grew up in will have a deep and lasting impact on all of the relationships we are able to form later in life, whether they are intimate or casual. Once we have learned to form bonds in which our own needs are met and the needs of others are also met, then we can call ourselves a success.

If you want to understand something about your own relationship patterns, a good place to start is to take a look at your parents. How did they get along with each other, and how did they get along with their parents? How did they treat you when you were hurt, when you needed something, when you made a mistake? However they treated you, it is a safe bet that that is how you learned to treat yourself. Since your primary relationship in life is with yourself, before concentrating on how to treat others, pay attention to whether you are as good to yourself as you would have wanted your parents to be. Happiness and satisfaction are key elements to a healthy lifestyle, but if we aren't good to ourselves, if we haven't yet learned to genuinely care about our own welfare, happiness will always be out of reach no matter where we live, what our hobbies are, or how great our job is. A direct extension of our relationship with ourselves is the one we have with others. If you have ever wondered why you were abrasive and impatient with others when you didn't mean to be, remember that it is impossible to generate empathy and compassion for a friend, a sister, a co-worker, or a son if you have not learned to first direct these qualities toward yourself. "Charity begins at home," then, can be taken literally. In turn, we often find that acts of kindness and generosity directed outward are returned to us. Think of it. If you spent your days directing good will in your own direction, and you acted in a way that encouraged others to treat you benevolently, how joyful could your life be? Make no mistake about it: Even if you think of yourself as a loner, you are in a world full of people, and relationships are central to a satisfying lifestyle.

We can, of course, go on to have healthy relationships ourselves even if our own parenting was hopelessly inept, but it is much easier if Mom and Dad gave us a foot up by providing love, support, intelligence, and attention when we were in our formative years. People whose early relationships were healthy are better prepared to take on some of life's challenges. They tend to do better in school with less struggle, and to become better learners in general, because they have the confidence to be more fearless in the face of risk. And because they're not particularly afraid of change, they are willing to explore and try new things. It is very difficult to form a creative and individualized lifestyle for yourself if you are not willing to be explorative. You cannot swim into new waters, after all, if you aren't willing to get your feet wet. Those who come from dysfunctional homes often overcome their early experiences through tremendous personal effort, and go on to create full and satisfying lives for themselves. They simply have to carry heavier emotional baggage while they are doing so.

Strong family support also helps people form stronger and more meaningful relationships later in life, and, interestingly enough, better relationships with their own bodies. People who weren't abandoned, abused, or belittled as children are more relaxed in their own skin. They are more in touch with their emotions, which is a central component to building a successful relationship. As Daniel Goleman says in *Emotional Intelligence*, "Seeing how the brain itself is shaped by [abuse]—or by love—suggests that childhood represents a special window of opportunity for emotional lessons."

But the lessons of childhood are not our destiny. We can go on to re-parent ourselves and make an effort to get along with others more than anyone ever made an effort to get along with us when we were young. And indeed we must heal the old wounds if we want to create a healthy and satisfying lifestyle for ourselves. Remember, you are responsible for your own happiness. Whatever hand you were dealt originally, you are continually being dealt new cards to play the game with. You form new relationships all the time, and each time you begin with a clean slate. You can decide whether to make this relationship one that will contribute to your happiness or detract from it. You can also decide whether your appearance in the lives of others will contribute to theirs.

One key part of the process of making relationships work for you is not just deciding when to enter and when to stay, but deciding when to leave. People who are genuinely toxic, or with whom you simply have no real affinity, are better off left in your past than included in your future. No enjoyable accoutrements can compensate for being surrounded by people who make you miserable. Picture a person with a vault full of money living in a luxurious, spacious house with someone she can barely stand to talk to. This couple needs a larger house—so they can stay out of each other's line of sight. My maternal grandparents' marriage was spent in bitter argument. They would both have gone on to some level of happiness if they had faced the music sooner and given each other a break by leaving. My paternal grandparents were married for more than fifty years, which they spent ignoring each other. What all four of these people failed to realize was that by making the less risky choice of staying in their marriages, they condemned themselves to a joyless lifestyle when they might each have gone on to find someone more suitable. Or they might have gone on to blaze their own trails and carve out completely individualized lives for themselves.

The important thing is that, whatever relationship you choose, it should nourish your inner self. If it doesn't fit in with some formalized picture of what others think it should be, so be it. Today we can be as creative with our relationships as we can be with our wardrobes. While society still puts pressure on its members to get married, it is becoming increasingly acceptable to make alternative arrangements that are more suitable to personal needs. Marriage really might not be for you, and even though you will catch hints suggesting that somehow you aren't complete without a mate, it is you, not society, that has to live with your choices. By knowing yourself well and understanding your real needs, you can determine whether you want a different-sex or same-sex partnership, or whether you want no partnership at all but to live in a community of friends, or whether to live with a host of animals surrounded by a garden and household plants. I know people for whom this last choice is bliss. They don't wake up in the morning to people, but are able to choose quality time with people when they need and want it.

5. HEALTH AND LONGEVITY ▼

Comedian Jack Benny had a classic routine based on his comic reputation for being stingy. He's walking down the street when a mugger approaches him, pulls out a gun, and says, "Your money or your life!" There is a long pause and no answer. "I said, your money or your life!" the mugger repeats. "Just a minute," Benny finally retorts, "I'm thinking it over!"

Chapter Eleven began with the story of an advertising executive in Japan who worked till he dropped. He was "held up" by the culture he lived in, and he actually chose to give up his life instead of his money. In this country, in addition to work, we eat, smoke, and drink till we drop. Many of us have developed habits that are hard on our bodies, and we know it. Yet until there's a health crisis that scares the hair off our head, we don't make any effort to change those habits. Until we actually *feel* something going wrong, we seem to think we're all right. There's an old joke about a man who says he can fly. To prove it, he jumps off a forty-story building. As he's falling, he passes someone leaning out of a twentieth-floor window, and he says, "So far, so good!" Just because he hasn't hit bottom yet, he deludes himself into thinking there is no bottom to hit.

People whose lavish lifestyle depends on long work hours (and the stress that goes with them) are particularly loathe to give up a six-figure income for something as "trifling" as health, even though the stress probably means they won't be around long enough to enjoy their wealth. "My kingdom for a horse!" said Shakespeare's Richard III. Standing alone on a battlefield waiting to be slaughtered, Richard knew that without a horse, and fast, he wouldn't live long enough to enjoy his kingdom. Today's equivalent of that is "My stock portfolio for my health!" All the perks—the summer home in the Hamptons, the country club with the world-class golf course and spa, the garage with three Mercedes and six motorcycles, the home entertainment center that rivals the command console at Kennedy Space Center—what good will they do you if you have high blood pressure, emphysema, a failing heart, a lung cavity that is as pitted as the surface of the moon, or a liver that is disintegrating?

Lifestyle is about *life*, and life cannot be experienced with any pleasure at all without a healthy body. Your body, after all, is the primary "kingdom" you live in. There is no "you" without your body. Your experience of all there is in the world comes through the body's five senses, so if that body is impaired, ailing, weak, or diseased, your whole quality of experience will deteriorate fast. All of a sudden, the illness becomes the headline, and everything else is shoved to the back of page 17. The most affection-based gift you can give yourself is a clean bill of health.

Happily, Americans are growing more health conscious. As our life expectancy grows, so does our awareness that physical fitness goes hand in hand with a rewarding lifestyle. When I was a boy, my friends and I used to ask each other, "Would you rather be like Errol Flynn and have a swashbuckling life burning the candle at both ends, or would you rather live longer and not have as much fun?" As kids, of course we couldn't really conceive of death no matter what adults said, so we couldn't help being attracted to the flashy lifestyle. It appealed to our sense of glamour and adventure. If, as our great-grandparents did, you anticipate using your body for only fifty years (give or take a few), then you might feel justified by the philosophy "Live fast, die young, leave a beautiful corpse." But life expectancy has practically doubled since those days. If this body you're occupying is going to be around for seventy-five to a hundred years, the issue of developing a healthy lifestyle takes on a whole new significance. It just makes sense to take better care of yourself. Here are three steps to a healthier life.

1. PREVENTIVE HEALTHCARE

Regular checkups with healthcare professionals help to ensure your continued survival. Many simple procedures such as mammograms, prostate and colorectal exams, EKG readings, and a check on your heart rate and blood pressure can literally save your life. If you do have a condition that poses a real risk, but as of yet shows no symptoms, early detection can reduce the level of treatment later. The more intense treatments for diseases and conditions that have progressed into later stages can result in more pain, suffering, and financial burdens for you. It pays to check yourself out.

Of all the arts and sciences, medicine has, throughout history, remained the most archaic. While great architectural achievements were being made all over Europe, as exemplified by the giant and complex cathedrals, "doctors" were still performing rudimentary surgery without anesthetics and with filthy hands. If the patient survived the operation, he was likely to die two days later of infection. The preferred method of treatment for most ailments was bleeding, which, in addition to doing no good whatsoever, left the patient anemic. But although we now have remarkably sophisticated resources at our disposal, many adults inexplicably fail to take advantage of them. Men tend to be worse in this area than women, who seem to take a more conscientious approach to seeking medical help. My father, who served in World War II, held an attitude that is typical of a macho approach to health. He was disdainful of the whole medical profession, and he boasted that from the end of his army service until just before he died, he had not once visited a physician. The implication seemed to be that only weak people had to check with their doctors. The strong ones made it on their own.

With the complexity of the human body and all that can go wrong with it, including a host of new and old diseases, it only makes sense to practice preventive medicine. Just like with tune-ups for a car, it keeps the engine humming. Once we feel better physically, we are free to go on to enjoy everything else. If, on the other hand, there is an acute pain in one tiny place in your body—like your back molar—the whole world turns into a tooth. You can be seated in a three-star restaurant in Paris, but if your tooth is killing you, you may as well stay home and eat Jello.

Another area in which preventive techniques have proven effective is in mental health. Once again, we are extremely fortunate to live in an era when immense efforts are being made to understand the mind and guide it on the healing path. In previous centuries we were bound to carry the traumas of the past to our graves. Yet how many people hold the same attitude toward seeing a therapist that my father held toward seeing a doctor? General health includes mental health because the well-being of mind and body are interrelated. People with serious emotional disturbances often find that, sooner or later, the problem manifests somewhere in their bodies. And even people who work out regularly and have attained beautiful bodies, and who in every other way have met their goals of success, will find that while they think they're finished with their past, the past isn't finished with them. The wounds inflicted on us when we were young have an enduring quality, and they tend to haunt us throughout our lives unless we revisit them. This point is a common theme in this book, but it can hardly be said enough. By enlisting the help and feedback of a trained psychotherapist, you are doing what is the equivalent of having your teeth cleaned. Would you let your teeth go the same way you let your emotional life go? Is your psyche less important? Dealing with psychological issues by enlisting professional assistance puts you in charge of your mental health, not the other way around.

2. HEALTHY HABITS

"You are what you eat" is one of my favorite expressions. In a way, it is literally true because elements of the food you take into your body soon become part of your body. One way to shower affection on ourselves is to be more discriminating about what we put in our mouths. Increased awareness of the dietary components of good health is reflected in society today by the fact that growing numbers of Americans are eating less red meat, less processed foods, more greens, and more organically grown foods. People are cooking from scratch instead of opening a can or defrosting a frozen dinner.

As a world traveler, I am acutely aware of how grossly overweight Americans are. You simply do not see substantial numbers of 300-pound individuals anywhere but here. If you want to live to be a hundred, and enjoy doing it, being obese is counterproductive. The major cause of all this obesity is a diet that converts straight into fat. I am not alone in marveling at how the French, with all their rich creamy foods, are able to remain so slender. From what I have observed, they eat foods that are fresh, without a lot of preservatives, and in amounts that are moderate by our standards. Seldom do you see someone being served a 14-ounce slab of steak for dinner. As Dr. Henry Bieler wrote in his nutrition classic, *Food Is Your Best Medicine*, "Your average American predilection for doughnuts and coffee, hot dogs with mustard, ice cream, fried meat, French-fried potatoes, pie à la mode, together with between-meal sweetened cola drinks, candy bars and coffee breaks, synthetic vitamins and aspirin cannot make for health."

When you consider the difference that a wholesome diet can have on the quality of life, a little discipline seems worth the effort. The same rule applies to other unsound habits: smoking, drinking, and taking drugs. Any of these, when practiced immoderately, is an affliction to the body. While moderate wine consumption is now thought to be beneficial in some ways, we cannot say that any amount of smoking is good for you. Tobacco kills more people in this country every year than automobile accidents, murder, and drug-related deaths combined. Yet millions continue to smoke. Have we truly lost our minds or is this a form of passive suicide?

3. WORKING OUT

One additional phenomenon that has occurred in the last twenty years is the rise of the health club. Given the overall sedentary nature of the lifestyles of people who work at a desk, this is a good sign. Sitting

around all day actually contributes to stress because you are not circulating the energy throughout your body. A surefire route to cutting out
this stress and pumping more energy into your life is to exercise regularly. Physical workouts get the adrenaline flowing and pump those all-
important endorphins, which create such a feeling of well-being,
throughout your system. Adults who work out regularly not only look
younger than their out-of-shape counterparts, they also remain both
physically vigorous and mentally acute. They retain these youthful
qualities far longer than people in previous generations. If you want to
enjoy the lifestyle you worked so hard to provide for yourself when you
are sixty-five, you have to start thinking about taking care of your
health when you're twenty-five.

A well-balanced workout plan focuses on three areas: wind,
strength, and flexibility. Wind involves cardiovascular activities like
running, swimming, basketball, handball, and aerobics. Aerobics
classes are designed to use all parts of your body and to increase your
endurance by working your heart, lungs, and general circulation. In
regard to the second area, strength, there is mounting evidence that as
we grow older, moderate weight training is beneficial in the maintenance of healthy muscle tone and the retention of bone mass. If you're
not used to this, it is wise to start out with very mild weights and work
your way up. The third of these is flexibility, and in my view it is the
most important of the three exercise goals. As human beings age, the
most significant loss seems to be in this area. Yoga, which consists of a
series of stretching exercises, is the antidote to old age. A prominent
massage therapist told me, "I can spot people over fifty who are doing
yoga because they stand up straight."

If, however, I had to pick one physical activity above all others, it
would be walking. Nothing is better for you, and poses fewer risks,
than taking a brisk forty-five-minute walk every day. Besides the benefits to your body, it gives you the opportunity to stop and smell the roses.

▼ The phrase "Don't forget to smell the roses," has become over-
used and hackneyed. That's too bad because it means something none
of us should forget. It means that in the course of remembering every-

thing we *have* to do just to get by, let's not forget what we *need* and *want* to do to feel alive. Smelling the roses is a metaphor for stopping at any moment in the day and remembering to be present and immediate to that moment. Real satisfaction can be experienced only in the now. Whatever so-called satisfaction we experience from reminiscing about things past or musing about things to come is highly limited because it is actually just a concept. Only the now is real. Are you content with the lifestyle you are living? Are you turned on to your own life? You owe it to yourself to create a lifestyle that is congruent with your values and that contributes to your well being. The alternative is too bleak to be contemplated because it means you are letting precious life slip by without maximizing its potential.

The choice is yours. The power is yours. All it takes is one step at a time.

Chapter 12

FOUR STEPS TO PERSONAL FULFILLMENT

A journey of a thousand miles begins with a single step.

CHINESE PROVERB

One winter evening, I was up late watching an old movie. One of the characters was an aging bookkeeper whose job it was to count, recount, and then recount once again on his adding machine column after column of figures. His secret love, however, was creating magical, imaginative toys that brought joy to children. When he was asked why he didn't quit his unfulfilling, monotonous job to concentrate on what he loved, he looked off into the distance and intoned, "Some day . . . when my ship comes in."

When my ship comes in. How many people whittle their lives away waiting for that elusive day? Well, guess what. Your ship docked a long time ago, and the cargo is still waiting to be unloaded. If getting our hands on that precious cargo—our heart's desire—were so easy, we would all have metamorphosed from that frog into Prince Charming by now, and we would have Prince Charming's life. Unfortunately, many, many things crop up to obstruct us: We're dying to bow out of a career we've been stuck in for twelve years, but we don't have the necessary background education to change to another field. We want to pick up and move to a warmer climate, but we're reluctant to look for a new family physician and plumber (I have to admit, that is hard!), not to mention all new friends. We've always wanted to play the piano, but we'd have to move the couch out of the living room to make room for it, and besides, where are we ever going to find the right teacher? Excuses, excuses. What are you going to do? You have identified what you need to create your ideal lifestyle. You know the kind of environment you would really like to live in, what your leisurely pleasures would be, how healthy and trim you'd like to be, an interesting line of work you would like to pursue, and the kind of person you'd like to meet and grow old with. And yet here you are in a puddle. How do you segue into making the necessary changes?

Wait a minute. Did somebody say changes? Let's not kid ourselves, for most people, making significant changes in their lives is about as appealing as going in for a tax audit. We know we have to, but does anyone really look forward to it? Not only do few people charge in to pick up their cargo, but many never even go near the docks. You, however, having bought this book and read it this far, may be the exception. Inside you, there must be the germ of an impulse to do more than kill time and wait to be hooked up to life support when you're eighty-four. The purpose of this chapter is to provide the support and information you will need to set realistic goals, identify obstacles, find techniques to overcome them successfully, and ultimately find out for yourself that your ship really has come in—you just need to show up at the dock.

THE FOUR-STEP PROGRAM ▼

Right from the outset, you have to create a map if you want to manifest change because, contrary to public opinion, it doesn't happen through hoping, wishing, praying, chanting, or sprinkling fairy dust on your pillow. These things may help, but you actually have to *do* something, and you have to do it purposefully and intelligently, if you want to effect change. At one time or another, most of us have entertained dreams of what we would like to do with ourselves given half a chance. I've heard many people say, "I've always thought I would make a good architect." Or "I've got a lot of great tales in me. I should write a book of short stories." Or "I've kept all my old clothes from when I was twenty-two because some day I'm going to lose enough weight to fit into them again." Or "I really want to meet a man, but I hate to put myself out there on the meat market." I don't need to spell this out for you. You can compose your own list in twenty minutes. If you know what will be on the list, why, then, are so many things left undone?

It's very hard to get to first base if all you're working with is a concept and years of talking about it to your friends. What you need is a plan. Without one, all you have is talk, and talk, as they say, is cheap. Nothing worthwhile is ever accomplished without an effective plan of action. A plan takes what seems like an insurmountable obstacle and reduces it to a series of comprehensible steps that can be followed one by one until, eventually, the desired goal is reached. It converts an impenetrable maze of problems that look like a jungle into an orderly grid of streets and avenues that can be traversed at will. In addition, a plan bestows the much-needed confidence that you really can attain your heart's desire no matter how far out of reach it may have seemed in the past.

The following is a four-step program that will head you in the right direction.

STEP ONE: *Identify those things in life that are meaningful to you.*

In one way or another, we have discussed this several times in the book. Now it is time to be concrete and do it for yourself. As I have said, a successful lifestyle reflects the real needs and wants of the individual. The only way, then, for you to realize the lifestyle you've always wanted is to be crystal clear about your needs. If you find yourself having difficulty being specific, refer to Chapters Four and Five. Those words will remind you that somewhere inside you, your body possesses the hidden knowledge your intellect may be missing. You cannot go through this first step hastily; without it, there are no other steps.

To assist your intuition you can brainstorm with your friends. Ask them what they see as the common themes in your life, what you always seem to be longing for but are unable to articulate. Sometimes others can read you more clearly than you can read yourself. You can also use the media to stir your imagination. Every major metropolitan newspaper now has weekly sections on career choices, health, travel, leisure, and relationships. Peruse these regularly to see if there are doors you haven't even thought to knock on, ideas you haven't thought to entertain. One additional source many people never think to check is an old diary or old letters you may have written when you were a teenager. They'll tell you a lot about early themes in your life. If you have neither one, reflect on what you used to daydream about when you were sixteen. Often, that was the period when we were most in touch with what we were meant to do with our lives because we had not yet outgrown the connection to our heart's desire. And we were not afraid to freely express it.

When I was young, I used to daydream about moving to a South Sea island. I spun a whole new world for myself in the confines of my little bedroom in our apartment house in Brooklyn. But I never took seriously the idea of moving to an idyllic place in a warmer climate because, as a "sophisticated" New Yorker, I was brainwashed into thinking of myself as a city dweller. This belief endured for years. In my twenties and thirties I actually did thrive on the high-wire energy of the Big Apple. In fact, between the power job and the night life, I considered myself the consummate New Yorker. Eventually, though, my real needs caught up with me. I realized that I craved a location with a slower, friendlier rhythm and a moderate temperature. The place I called home would have to give me access to nature—to the ocean, forests, and mountains. It had to be a more natural environment where I could think and meditate without the nonstop distractions of a metropolis. Until I identified all these requirements, I had no idea how to attain them. And considering my big-city background, they came as somewhat of a surprise to me.

STEP TWO: *Visualize a lifestyle that reflects your needs.*

Being aware of your needs is important, but it certainly isn't enough. Now you must relate those needs to the five elements of a successful lifestyle—work, location, leisure, relationships, and health. There may also be other aspects of your life that are meaningful to examine, but I have found that the above five pretty much cover all the bases.

To link up your needs with real-life choices, you have to imagine or visualize a potential future. This does not involve idly passing the time with wishful thinking, but engaging in a specific process. Visualization is a tool of the imagination that enables a person to observe the result of a change in his life before he actually makes a move forward. It forms the necessary link between recognizing one's needs and actually fulfilling them.

The human mind works with visual images much like a movie does. It has dialogue and sound, but mainly it has a way of "seeing" thoughts. A constant parade of movie-type images pass before our inner eye all the time. The images that are produced by the unconscious really do seem like full-length movies sometimes; they're called dreams. What people don't realize is that the conscious mind produces its own movie each time the person has a decision to make. It runs through scenarios, trying out possibilities for you to choose from without ever having to rise from your La-Z-Boy recliner. In fact, visualizing is essential to life. Without the ability to visualize, you would be unable to function. Most of the goals you have sought and the plans you've made, and the result of those goals and plans, began as a movie inside your head. Every single day you produce a new feature film with the main character—"me." The title of the movie? "What Am I Doing with My Day?"

Step Two of this process simply requires you to take the ordinary visualization process and make it more deliberate and more complete. Sit down and picture the kind of job you would jump out of bed to go to. Imagine yourself at the YMCA in an exercise class with tight abs and well-toned muscles; you radiate health. Create a photograph in your mind of your new home by a river with daffodils along the bank. Include all the important details and include everything you would like to happen, even if it seems out of reach. Visualizing your desires with clarity will help them seem within your reach. It will make them real.

As you generate these images, what kind of feedback are you receiving from your gut? Rely on your intuition to tell you if this is a lifestyle change that will deepen your life and be truly rewarding. Your gut will tell you if this is really your dream or something you saw in a magazine, an idealized picture of a successful life you were conditioned to believe in or the lifestyle that will authentically meet your essential needs.

STEP THREE: *Determine the changes you'll need to make.*

Merely visualizing an ideal lifestyle will not lead to results. The next step to take is to construct a business plan. Looking at the lifestyle your visualizations have created, work your way backward and determine exactly the changes you will need to make, the route you will need to take, to bring them to fruition. This is called your business plan.

A business plan is a trajectory of action. It comprises a series of practical steps that mobilizes one's energy so he or she can success-fully create a new enterprise. Along with it comes a timeframe that must be adhered to. The business plan that allows for each step to be carried out whenever you feel like it is basically a plan for disaster. You may never feel like it. The typical way of thinking for most people is "Well, maybe next week I'll check out Weight Watchers." Or "I'll send away for college brochures as soon as I've finished my spring cleaning." These amoeba-shaped timeframes have a way of spilling time until there is none left. Instead, decide on a specific target and give yourself an explicit and clear timeframe. People who are serious about making changes come up with a two-year plan or a five-year plan, and so on, whichever is appropriate to the goal. The important thing is to make the plan as precise as it is realistic to do, and to spell out individual steps that you can envision actually completing. Once you have the steps laid out before you, it is much easier to carry out the plan.

Returning to my case, I had been to the Monterey Peninsula in California many times on vacation. It finally dawned on me that there was a reason for my returning there year after year. That was where I truly wanted to set up the rest of my life. For seven or eight years, I thought about moving, but the idea seemed too impractical and the obstacles too great. How would I adapt to living in a small community when I still thought of myself as Mr. Big City? Would I go stark raving mad out of sheer boredom in a little bedroom community? How could someone like me transplant his business to a small town that didn't even have a major airport? Without a plan to at least answer my concerns, I would never make this dream come true.

What finally motivated me to do something? The death of a friend. She was a young woman who seemed as healthy as I was. But she wasn't. She found out she had a heart condition, and after an unsuccessful heart transplant, she died. As if I needed one more reminder—life was short. That very week I created a plan for extracting myself from Los Angeles, where I had recently relocated, and moving into a new home up north.

STEP FOUR: *Take action.*

The most difficult part of this entire process is not the previous three steps, but this one: setting it into motion. The whole program is academic until you commit by taking action. There are cogent reasons why this step is essential:

1. Action breaks the ice and takes you from the passive to the active mode. You are no longer just talking about doing something with your life, which costs you nothing and involves no risks, but you are putting your money where your mouth is.
2. Once you launch yourself on your new path, the whole project feels more doable. Instead of being focused on the obstacles that appear dominant in the thinking stage, you refocus on the possibilities.

The point is that once you commit yourself to the first step of the journey, no matter how small that is, you are then on your way. I cannot overemphasize the importance of actually making the first move toward your goal. Once I began writing this book, I began hearing about how many people around me had always wanted to be writers themselves. It seemed as if everybody I knew had an idea for a novel, a screenplay, or a play. Ideas came from the most unlikely places: my masseuse, my attorney, my plumber, and so on. Some of the ideas I heard were pretty imaginative and viable, and yet nothing ever got written. Why? Because the concept stayed in the talk stage. None of these people ever simply picked up a pen and began to do it. They didn't sit down and just write page one. It doesn't matter if it's good or not. (My editor tells me that writing is just like cooking pancakes—you always ruin the first ones.) Of course, sitting down to write page one means you have to overcome a great deal of anxiety and inertia, and most people are not willing to face that. Making any significant change in your life is just as difficult as writing a book, if not more so, but the rewards are great. They are well worth the effort.

When my friend died, it triggered a thought: If I sat around talking about moving to Monterey and never lifted a finger to make it happen, I just wouldn't do it. With this sudden incentive, I finally actualized my plan. I picked up the telephone, dialed a realtor in Monterey, and said, "Paul, I'll be up there next Saturday. Let's find a house." That was it! After eight years of saying, "Some day, some day I'm going to move," I had finally committed myself to action simply by doing this one tiny thing—I picked up the telephone.

APPLYING THE FOUR STEPS ▼

These, then, are the steps you need to take in the order you need to take them. Now you will have to be specific about how to actuate these steps.

FOR STEP ONE: *Make a list of your strengths and interests so you can identify what, in life, is meaningful to you.*

It is important to include not only the "known," but the unknown. Don't just write down leisure activities you've already tried, but write down the ones you've always *wanted* to try. Don't just note that you want a relationship, but include what kind you're really interested in. If you want a new job, by all means do not limit yourself to those listed in the want ads. This is your chance to think freely. If you feel stuck, consult your gut for genuine answers to these questions. Ask yourself practical questions like the following:

- How do I really enjoy spending my time?
- What am I good at?
- Do I want to date someone who has the same interests that I do or someone who has the same temperament?
- Do I want the structure of a health club or am I more comfortable finding an exercise regime I can do in my home?
- What leisure activities have I seen other people engage in that I always thought I would enjoy but was afraid to try?
- Do I really care about accumulating wealth or do I prefer to pursue an activity for its own sake?
- What do I expect from a primary relationship? Do I want someone who is looking for a commitment or someone who just wants to have fun and do things together?
- Would I prefer my new job to be in an office, at home, or outdoors; in one place or on the run?
- Do I want to go to a mainstream health practitioner or an alternative one?
- Am I a team player or am I better off working on my own?
- Is it absolutely necessary that I make my home in this country or would I be more happy abroad?
- Do I want to spend my leisure time goofing off or being useful?

- Do I want to have children of my own or is it more fun to be Aunt or Uncle?
- Would it be better for me to have two very different part-time jobs rather than one full-time job? Would that keep my interest level up?

FOR STEP TWO: *Match up your list of preferences with potential lifestyle choices through visualization.*

Once you have identified the areas of your life where you have real aspirations, and once you have concretized those desires and goals in a list, you are ready to think about how to make them show up in your life. To begin this process, you cannot be in a noisy, distracting environment, so find a nice quiet place where you feel comfortable—your own den, the beach, a forest path, the library. Then search your soul and your brain for ways that you can actualize your deepest desires. Let loose your intuitive powers and be creative. Remember, this is between you and you. Nobody else is privy to this, so you can cut loose and be as imaginative as you want. Not every idea that comes to you will be usable, but it is important that you entertain them all the same. Sometimes an idea we ultimately reject leads to another one we *can* use. But if we edit ourselves too severely in the beginning and require ourselves to be too "sensible," we rein in our creative selves unnecessarily. Remember, the imagination is like a wild horse; it needs a large field to run free in.

One way to proceed with a lifestyle preference is to see yourself performing activities that will support it, activities you take real pleasure in. Visualizations should not just be practical, plodding exercises in seeing a goal attained. They are meant to make the attainment of the goal, the process toward it, desirable. Even for work—which people tend to think of as a necessity rather than a luxury—to find a job that contributes to your lifestyle (instead of just financing it) visualize the skills you possess that energize you and see yourself bringing home a paycheck with them. When I decided to leave show business, for example, and wasn't sure what to do next, I reviewed what I had done before and took the best of the lot. I had acquired business skills from selling computers and presentation skills from being a performer. I enjoyed exercising both and realized I could work them into my new career as a professional speaker to corporate audiences.

To help you visualize new lifestyle choices, here are some ideas:

- For a new career, take the Myers-Briggs personality test, which will help you articulate what is unique about your temperament and preferences and how they play on each other.
- This may seem businesslike to some, but if you are looking for a mate, picture precisely what characteristics would make you happy: He'll be interested in nature, she'll like art and music, he'll be funny and playful, she'll be mature and serious, he will be dependable, she will be a thoughtful person and a good listener. And so on.
- Consult travel magazines and literature for other locations to live. They will contain photographs that will help your visualizations come alive, as well as important information to help you ascertain if your image of the place matches reality.
- When you go on vacation, observe what those around you do for fun. Even if at first you think "That's not me," don't be too quick to dismiss it if it looks like it might be fun. Close your eyes and see yourself engaged in the activity—water skiing, mountain biking, exotic cooking, crafts, quilting, and so on.
- If your desire is to become vigorous and healthy, imagine eating fresh salads with flavorful ingredients, taking brisk walks in majestic settings, and swimming in a mountain lake.
- Think about someone you've liked for a long time who is available and imagine yourself going out with the person. Make the details real in your head. What is the setting, the mood, the conversation? How can you make the evening a success?
- Take stock of all the elements you need to be surrounded by and then try to picture a place in this country that would satisfy those needs. Do you thrive on country air or sea air? Do you need to step outside to crowded, busy streets? Have you always wanted to live in a high-rise and look down on the city below? Is the house you live in just fine, but it needs changes like a flower garden or a swimming pool to be your perfect environment?

- What ways can you find to network with people who have exactly the kind of career you want for yourself?
- What kind of exercise club would make you want to go three times a week? Would it have to be jazzy and glamorous or low-key but plush?
- Almost every major city offers free or low-cost night classes in a wide variety of subjects. Think about taking a class in something you never would have considered before. It will expand your horizons and make you receptive to new ideas.

FOR STEP THREE: *Create a business plan that actualizes the changes.*

Whatever aspect of your life needs changing, a business plan will help, even if the area you're looking into is a leisure activity. For instance, suppose you've always wanted to take up watercolor painting. If you just go out and buy a cheap set of watercolors, brushes, and paper, take no instruction, and flounce around on your own, you will most assuredly be dissatisfied with the result. Even if you keep at it, you won't see any marked improvement. The quality of the paints and paper, how you hold your brush, the amount of water you use, all make a great deal of difference. If you take your steps in the right order, though—find out what the best materials are and read a simple book for beginners—you will be launching your new hobby in a more sure-footed way. Business plans are sometimes no more complex than that. With many hobbies, the right materials and a little know-how are all you need. For any new endeavor, however, you can bet that the more planning you put into it, the more success and satisfaction you can expect.

No area of lifestyle change requires more planning than a switch in careers. Most well-paying jobs require education, experience, and training, which takes money, time, and effort. After all, why pour your resources into an enterprise unintelligently? A good business plan ensures that you've thought things through and you're doing the right thing at the right time.

Let's say you are a legal secretary but you've always wanted to learn and teach physics. You know that you like the sciences and you've always loved working with young people. Many times in your adult life you've almost been able to see yourself in front of a lively classroom conducting experiments, but actually *doing* it has always remained an elusive dream. What changes would you have to begin making for this dream to come true? What other issues would you need to take under consideration? Since you will have to go to graduate school and obtain a teaching credential, will your family's standard of living be reduced while you're there? Will your tuition fees wipe out the annual European vacation? Are there problems with terminating the job you now have? The first part of the plan is anticipating the initial problems you will encounter and then finding ways to solve them.

Next, you must take on the practical realities of actualizing your dream. Without taking these on with focus, purpose, and practicality, you can almost guarantee that you will fail. As I said earlier, first and foremost, business plans require time structuring. Your timing may have to be adjusted as you go along since you can never predict all eventualities, but as near as you can, make an informed decision about how long each step will take. For example:

Week One: Spend quality time with your family discussing your goals and explaining why you need to do this and how you will make it work.

Week Two: Send away for brochures and run an investigation of grad schools.

Week Three: Set about lowering your monthly expenses by looking into moving into a lower-priced house or apartment, cutting back on frivolities, or refinancing your credit card debt at a lower rate.

Week Four: Wake your mind up by cracking the books. Begin studying for entrance exams.

Month Two: Take entrance exams.

Month Three: Apply to the grad schools that look most promising.

September of next year: Begin grad school.

Year Two: Investigate high schools in your area that are looking for
physics teachers.

Year Three: Begin your interesting new career as a physics teacher.

FOR STEP FOUR: *Make the first move.*

This may sound simple, especially if it looks like a relatively easy step,
but you could come across unexpected resistance. If the challenge you
have set for yourself is meeting and dating new women, then you could
start by attending a singles function. If you've decided to move to a cat-
tle ranch in rural Idaho, you have to sell your house and shop at Sierra
Designs for a heap of winter clothing. Perhaps the first choice here
sounds easier than the second, but that doesn't mean it will create any
less resistance. Taking the first step is difficult for most people. But difficult or not, you must take it. As Yogi Berra said, "When you come to
a fork in the road, take it." Berra's famous quip implies that the hard
part is not really deciding which road to take, but actually acting on the
decision—any decision.

When I stopped ruminating about whether to move to Monterey
and finally made my decision, I thought I was home free. Then I
noticed that although I had made a decision, time was passing and I
still wasn't actually living in Monterey. How come? What I came to
realize was that I was focused on the obstacles instead of the possibilities, and it was holding me back. Here, then, is the real question for
anyone who wants to make a meaningful life change: How do I stop
obsessing about the obstacles and start looking at the possibilities? If
you're an abuse-based thinker, you don't. Abuse-based thinkers are forever mired in the hindrances, forever falling over the stumbling blocks,
tangled up in all the reasons for not taking action. For years, the fellow
whose locker was next to mine at the health club would go through the
same little ritual whenever we were at our lockers at the same time. He
was an overweight, middle-aged physician who was utterly dissatisfied
with his health and weight. "You know," he would say, "I wish I was as
slim as you are." I knew what his diet was, so naturally I responded
with "Why don't you cut down on your food intake?" His comeback

was "Ed, it's not just the food. I like those martinis when I get home and you know how many calories are in martinis. I sure wish I could change my ways." One day after the ritual had been repeated almost word-for-word for the umpteenth time, I realized I was fed up. "This is all an excuse," I said. "You don't really want to change. If you did, you would do it. So please don't tell me this anymore. Don't say you want to lose weight because I don't believe you." The man never spoke to me again. He even moved his locker. He could not come to grips with his abuse-based thinking that revolved around "I can't because."

Once you commit to Step Four, you simply must recognize all the bad habits of your mind that have kept you mired in dissatisfaction so far in your life. If you look for a common theme, you will probably find that the focus is on "I can't" and not on "I can."

CHANGING CAREERS IS GOOD FOR YOU ▼

Career seems to be a linchpin in people's lives. It is what we train and educate ourselves for. It is where our identities are caught. It is what we spend the most hours a week engaged in. We're either at work or on our way to work or thinking about it or complaining about it. In addition, the career is the most difficult arena in which to make fundamental changes. Work equals survival, and before all else, we have to meet our survival needs. Once a person is able to effect change in this essential area, it's easier to make it in other areas. For these reasons, I believe that the whole subject of changing careers deserves its own section in this chapter.

Changing careers is good for you. Let me say that again. *Changing careers is good for you.* Does this fly in the face of how you've been conditioned? Because the generations before you did not have the same opportunities as you have to change careers once, twice, or three times within a lifetime, are you still burdened with archaic thinking on the subject? Years ago when I quit my first sales job, my friend's father was shocked and disappointed in me. He chewed me out for even thinking about leaving such a fine company, which I had been with for only two years. He had held only one job his entire life—working for the post office—and he was proud of it. I'm certain he didn't love his job, but it did give him security, and it was part of his value system to stick with it. While being stuck in one work situation primarily holds weight for older generations in this culture, Europeans of all ages face the same problem today. Sitting at a café in Paris near the Sorbonne one fine afternoon, I overheard two French university students bemoaning the lack of mobility and choice in the French job market. One of them said, "I'm going to America. You can do anything over there."

Not only can we change jobs here, but we can also change the entire course of our career, which is unheard of in some cultures. Thanks to the women's liberation movement, women now have more career choices than ever, and men have been liberated from having the sole responsibility for supporting the family. This means that when they do want to make a significant change, they can more easily cut down on their expenses during the transition.

Why, then, don't more people take advantage of this unprecedented mobility? The fact is, there is no good reason to chain yourself to one career. Most people don't want that, and they certainly don't need it. According to the Gallup Organization in *Now, Discover Your Strengths*, the vast majority of people do not enjoy the careers they currently have, yet they do nothing about it. "Globally, only twenty percent of employees working in the large organizations we surveyed feel that their strengths are in play every day." In other words, eight out of ten employees feel miscast in their current roles. And here comes the really strange part: "Most bizarre of all, the longer an employee stays with an organization and the higher he climbs the traditional career ladder, the less likely he is to strongly agree that he is playing to his strengths." What does this spell out? That the people who should be feeling the most successful—those who have climbed the traditional career ladder—are actually the least likely to be following their bliss. More than eight out of ten who appear to be succeeding probably do not feel successful. If you are one of those people who are not experiencing fulfillment from their careers, it is time to start looking around for another one.

One significant reason that people are reluctant to change careers is that, unfortunately, they are so identified with the work they do. Identity is a big thing to shift. The Gallup Organization validates this in *Now, Discover Your Strengths* by saying that if we define ourselves by our achievements and the knowledge we have already acquired, "we become reluctant to change careers or learn new ways of doing things because then, in the new career, we would be forced to jettison our precious haul of expertise and achievement. We would have to jettison our identity." Too much to ask of some people, it would seem, even though they would be happier if they just held their breath and took the leap. If you want to make the jump, you must first pry yourself away from your one-note identity and broaden your image of yourself. You are not what you do. You are what you are.

Many people are terrified of finding themselves thrashing around in a whole new field where they feel completely underqualified. One way to work with this fear is to take stock of the strengths and skills that have gotten you this far in your current line of work. If they have held up so far, chances are they are transferable to a new environment. All of your abilities, talents, and capacity can be leveraged into an interesting new career.

The conclusion of the Gallup people is that a successful transition to a new career can be made as long as you pay attention to your strengths. "This self-awareness [of your strengths] will give you the self-confidence to break free from the tyranny of the 'shoulds': You 'should' become a lawyer or a doctor or a banker because your family expects you to. You 'should' accept that next promotion into management because your organization and society at large expect you to." They could not have made my point better if they had read this book. It falls on your shoulders to decide what success really means to you.

A perfect example of this principle is one of my oldest friends, Don Seger. From the time he was a teenager, he knew he wanted to be a physician. He was so adept at his studies that he catapulted through college in three years, finished his medical studies specializing in orthopedics, taught at Harvard, and then went into private practice. After twenty years of this, he realized that his priorities were changing.

What had once made him happy no longer did; it simply wasn't a challenge anymore. A sideline he had always been interested in was books. He loved them. At midlife he decided to quit his high-paying career as a physician and open a bookstore specializing in rare books. I can honestly say it is a match made in heaven. The man is thriving, even though in many people's eyes his move was a "step down." Certainly his new adventure is a drastic departure from the old. When I raised the question to him, Don quickly identified three factors common to both careers: first, the attention to detail and the need for quality; second, the personal-service aspect; and third, the intellectual connection to the subject (both careers require a large store of knowledge). At this point in his life, he knew that the bookstore would simply make better use of his skills, and he wasn't afraid to take the risk. The change has introduced a new vitality into his life.

THE VIRTUE OF SIMPLICITY ▼

Throughout this entire chapter I have been talking about making significant changes in your lifestyle. I don't want to finish discussing this subject without addressing an important point. It is very difficult to even consider making changes, let alone find the wisdom to make the right ones, if your days are so complex you don't have time to think. "Things" have a way of keeping you busy, of keeping you tied up in the details of living so that you don't have time to think about life itself. Once you simplify your life, however, the whole idea of making changes is easier to approach. It doesn't feel like one more thing to add to an already hectic schedule.

The media makes high living and lavish spending seem like the norm, or at least something to aspire to. We are encouraged to complicate our lives with gadgets and appliances and grown-up toys and extravagances. Photographs of the outlandishly large and Byzantine compound that Bill Gates calls home have been splashed across the newspapers. This type of financial indulgence, which is far out of range for ordinary mortals, is nevertheless touted as a desirable lifestyle choice, as a sign that you have "arrived." I look at his house and I think of everything he has crammed inside—clothes, jewelry, electronic gadgetry, antique furniture, and so on—and it seems too complicated to keep up with. How do you dust all that furniture? You hire maids. How do you keep track of all those maids? You hire someone to keep track of the maids who dust the furniture.

We are encouraged to complicate our lives with more and more and more. More, by definition, is supposed to be better. If we follow in this tradition of overconsumption, we simply become slaves to our possessions and to whatever we have to do to keep a roof over their heads. The more you acquire, the more mired down you get, the harder it is to work your way out of the trap. Imagine how difficult it would be for Bill Gates to say to himself one day, "I'm sick of owning all this crap. The responsibility of keeping this house up and running a multibillion-dollar-a-year business is too stressful. I think I'll give it all up and teach a computer class to high school students in the inner city." It's possible that Bill Gates has hidden desires just like this, but how could he ever let them into his consciousness?

According to Thomas Stanley and William Danko, the authors of *The Millionaire Next Door*, the typical person with above-average wealth is actually "frugal" with her expenditures. She doesn't flash her money around. Frugal, in this case, is defined as behavior "reflecting economy in the use of resources." Frugality is in contrast with wastefulness, which is defined as "a lifestyle marked by lavish spending and hyperconsumption." The opposite of being tied up in these golden handcuffs is a lifestyle characterized by simplicity and economy—no matter how much money you have in the bank. Sam Walton, founder of Wal-Mart, is a perfect example. Despite his personal fortune, he continued for his whole life to live in a modest home that met his needs, and he drove around town in an old pick-up truck. He loved being a successful businessman, but he didn't need to prove his success to anyone by flashing his wealth around. It would have been infinitely easier for Sam Walton to uproot himself and change his lifestyle than it would be for Bill Gates today.

For those of us with ordinary jobs and ordinary expenses, there is another reason to keep life simple and eliminate the excess baggage. The person who spends less and saves more has more resources to make important alterations in his life if he wants to. He is in a better position to experiment with lifestyle changes, to invest in his dreams, than someone who has squandered his paycheck every week on baubles. If you have accrued massive credit card debt and you can barely cover your expenses at the end of the month, how are you going to afford moving to a new location, joining a health club, or retraining yourself for a new career? If your overhead is low, you are in a much better position to do all these things.

The benefits of simplicity extend to the ability to deal with stress. The complexity of our lives is probably the single most potent factor contributing to stress. One statistic I came across alleged that the average person today has to juggle more information in a single day than the average nineteenth-century citizen had to deal with in a lifetime. Even if that is not literally true, it certainly points to the fact that contemporary life presents us all with an ongoing challenge to our sanity. Anyone who has tried to program a VCR, set up a personal computer, or even install a new answering machine can appreciate how frustrating modern living can be. Every new invention that is designed to make our lives "easier" represents some new body of knowledge we are expected to acquire.

I strongly believe that a return to moderation and simplicity would soothe our harassed nervous systems and provide sanity to our overworked minds, making it easier for us to make wise decisions. These two qualities offer a kind of successful lifestyle that is ultimately more satisfying than what most of us experience today.

Chapter 13

THE COURAGE TO SUCCEED

The will to be oneself is heroism.

ORTEGA Y GASSET

After a speech I gave one evening, a young woman approached me by the side of the stage. She had a job in the marketing department of a large corporation, but she wanted to quit and become a freelance management consultant. She'd been nursing this dream for several years, but so far she had not made her move. When I asked how come, she answered, "My mother thinks I'm better off in a big corporation."

"Is that what *you* want?" I asked.

"No."

How else could I answer? "Then let your mother work for a large corporation, and you do what you want to do."

Her response was one I had encountered many times before: She was afraid to take the risk and buck the opinion of others. With some innocence, she finally asked me what happens to all those people who never manage to risk doing what they are afraid of.

"They usually start drinking their scotch and soda before lunch," I said, "or they eat compulsively, or they have affairs to escape a life they're bored with, or they shoot themselves, or . . . they shoot people at the post office."

As she walked away, I wondered if this intelligent young woman had the fortitude to go against her mother's wishes, society's brainwashing, the possible disdain of her peers in the corporate world, and all the other obstacles discussed in previous chapters. If it were easy to do what you want with your own life, everyone would be doing it and I wouldn't have to write this book. In fact, it takes great courage to strike out on your own path.

RULES FOR LIONS AND LAMBS ▼

One of the most endearing themes in *The Wizard of Oz* is the Cowardly Lion's quest for courage. He roars to intimidate. He grimaces and postures to scare. But he is the one who is scared. His mistaken impression, very common in our culture, is that courage and bravery are synonymous with braggadocio. When I was in the Marine Corps, I learned better. The larger-than-life John Wayne characters who jump out of their foxholes and rush into a blaze of enemy machine-gun fire are not heroes; they are fools. A famous general once said that he didn't want his soldiers to die for their country, he wanted them to live for their country. That means to fight wisely and live to fight another day. Truly brave people who have nothing to prove know that. They simply do what is required of them in challenging situations. At the end of *The Wizard of Oz*, that is the lesson the Cowardly Lion finally learns. Dorothy needs his help, and without thinking he risks himself to save her from the Wicked Witch.

This chapter is devoted to the struggle of ordinary lions and lambs like you and me who have courage sometimes and not at other times. We want to face life's challenges and emerge with the feeling that we have done our best and have been true to ourselves. To accomplish such a thing in our culture, an ordinary person needs extraordinary courage because society will not be waving flags and cheering her on. It may even try to exact retribution from her for daring to be different.

Honoring the "courage of one's convictions" is synonymous with doing what is right. Coincidentally, this happens to be my personal definition of integrity. Only a person with integrity can reject a culturally dictated path of action in favor of what she knows to be right for herself. This is not to say that those who don't live from this kind of integrity aren't in possession of many other fine qualities. People who stay in jobs they dislike year after year certainly show forbearance and perseverance. Perhaps even a sense of duty. However, the courage to follow your own path is more difficult because the culture will offer considerable resistance; and it is more rewarding because doing what is right for you is what nature intended.

The whole concept of integrity includes wholeness and soundness of character. This implies a responsibility not only to meet your own needs, but to give back the best of yourself to the society that spawned you. Your impact on the world, however, will have more value if you follow your uniqueness than if you blend in and act like a termite in its mound.

FEAR AND ITS NEMESIS—COURAGE

I will discuss ways to overcome your fears and find the courage to succeed, but they will have little effect if I do not first discuss the twin subjects of fear and fearlessness in some depth. It is a difficult subject for many because fear is an inherently painful state, and there is a natural tendency to avoid it. People who experience excessive fear (sometimes to the point of paralysis) have trouble believing in their own strength and their ability to meet life's challenges. Even if they don't admit it to themselves, they secretly think the slightest breeze could toss them overboard. Almost always, these people received very little support when they were young, and now they do not have faith that the universe will support them in their endeavors. (We tend to project *onto* the wide world that which we were exposed to in the small world of our nuclear family.) The domino effect here is that because the person doesn't perceive that anyone will be there for him, he cannot be there for himself. This means that the person perceives neither outer nor inner support, and this breeds fundamental distrust when he contemplates initiating any major changes in life. To say it briefly, there is a distinct lack of optimism. In everything the person tries, he torments himself that he will make a mistake, that he is courting disaster, that others will show disdain for him when he fails—which he surely believes he will. There is, then, a real absence of faith. You could say that that is what fear boils down to: no faith in your own inner capacities or in the world's willingness to support you.

If you have a basically fearful attitude toward life, you will end up a slave to it, perhaps without even knowing it. Whenever acceptable risks present themselves, ones that could open up your life, that hold the possibility of freedom from old restrictions, you will not act on them. People who live in fear over long periods of time, and who cannot find a way to break away from it, end up turning in on themselves. They become brittle, resentful, and small-minded. Show me a person who acts like a victim, who is petulant, bitter, and perpetually disappointed, and I will show you someone with a core of fear.

Paradoxically, the only way to deal with that fear is to reach in and touch it. I call this a paradox because it takes courage to let yourself be vulnerable enough to do that; we must employ courage if we want to face our lack of courage and the fearfulness that lies beneath it. Unfortunately, that is the paradox we are all faced with. The steps in the next section are designed to help you over this hurdle.

As those who have come before you have found, though, courage alone isn't enough. It's too hard to face your fear of taking the kind of risks that will change your whole life with that alone. You must find a way to make friends with your deepest fears. That has become a New Age cliché, but it doesn't make it less true. Wild fear is like an untamed animal. If you attack it, it strikes back. If, however, you surround it with patience and compassion, it will respond. You need patience because fears don't just go away with a snap of the fingers; it takes a certain amount of equanimity and forbearance to stay with your fears until you work them through. And you need compassion for yourself when you are afraid because compassion is the quality that allows you to tolerate deep and painful feelings.

A wise therapist once told me that his clients, whenever they were face to face with emotions that were so fundamental as to threaten their identity and stability, would always say to him, "I don't know what to do." The great secret, he said, was "Don't do anything. Just leave it alone." There is real talent involved in just learning to apply simple attention to a strong emotion; not to wade around in it in circles, not to struggle with it, not to fight it, not to hide from it, not to run away. Just be there. But in that "just being" there is great strength because in that "being" we realize that what we call "I" is merely a space in which experience occurs. "Oh look, there's anger. Oh look, now there's fear. Now my toe itches. Now I wonder if I paid the phone bill on time. Now I'm bored. Now I wish I had a big, cold lemonade." It goes on like that all day, just an endless parade of thoughts and feelings marching past your inner field of vision. And "you" are the stage, that big open space where all the players can do their thing. In any given 24-hour period, an extraordinary variety of thoughts and emotions will pass through—fear is only one of them. Try to remember that the next time you are ensnared by it.

If you are able to pay attention to it for long enough, you will begin to see how impersonal the emotion really is. It isn't *your* fear. It's just fear. With sustained objective attention, you lose the notion that you "own" the fear, that it is "your" problem and the burden is on you to figure out a way to solve it. It's just there when it's there, and as with all other mind content, it's gone when it's gone. Fear is just another phenomenon of life. The magnificence of this impersonalness is that it allows you to examine and understand your fear, as well as its roots, in a way you never could if you "owned" it. You are perfectly free to investigate what it looks like, what seems to make it raise its little head once in a while, under what circumstances it appears to quiet down, where you experience it in your body, how it influences your decisions, and the multitude of ways in which it holds you back in life. Strong emotions, when stripped of the label "MINE," can no longer fill you with shame, self-loathing, or even a dread of the emotion itself. Feelings come to be seen as "just feelings."

OVERCOMING YOUR FEARS ▼

If you can truly commit to living your own idea of what life should be, the courage you need will find you. Here are three techniques to help you overcome all those fears that will try to sabotage your efforts.

1. Let Your Gut Have a Majority Vote

As discussed in Chapters Four and Five, the most reliable source of information available to you, and your wisest guide, is your intuition. Your rational mind can be flooded with superfluous information, can be unduly influenced by the opinions of others, and can be swayed by a harsh inner critic that doesn't believe you have a right to look out for your own best interest. Your intuition is subject to none of these factors. It is a surprisingly pure place in you that can be used to make some of the most important decisions of your life. And that is why this step reduces your fear. Most of our anxiety over making a decision comes from second-guessing ourselves, from the doubt that surfaces when we wonder about our ability to assess the choices in front of us and make a decision. Our gut, however, is implacable because it is capable of direct knowing. That means there is no guesswork. When you are really able to tune in to your intuition, you are not trusting in *something about yourself* like your intelligence or your strength or your willpower. You are trusting *in* yourself. It is basic and fundamental, and it cannot be shaken.

The key, then, is to stick with the instructions you receive from your gut. Others will offer you advice (it is harder to stop people from giving unsolicited advice than it is to stem a leak in the Hoover Dam), and you should consider it carefully, especially when it comes from people you respect when they genuinely mean well. There are many steps to making an important decision, and the input of others is as valid as anything else, so go ahead and weigh what others have told you. But once you have received your instructions from your gut, don't be swayed. When it's time to make your decision, every piece of advice and every snippet of information from other sources should have no more than 49 percent of the vote. Your gut should always have 51 percent. In other words, never give away your shares in the company and lose control of its direction. Your intuition should always have a clear majority that overrides everything else.

The reasons for this are simple. One, other people never really know you inside out the way you know yourself. Even if you aren't shy about sharing your hopes, dreams, and aspirations with others, they can never perceive the nuances as well as you can. Only you are aware of the volume of personal history that feeds into a decision, and the complexity of your own personality. So the amount of information you possess far outweighs any other source. Two, no matter how much the people around you love you, everybody's prime directive is self-interest. That means that they can never embrace your best interests as well as you can. Your intuition knows exactly what your best interests are, so let it be the chairman of the board.

2. To Overcome Your Fears, Determine What You Fear Most

I heard of a therapy group leader who was extremely demanding of his clients. If they wanted to stay in his group, they had to face the defense systems they had carefully rigged over the years, and they couldn't hide from reality. After a period of time, one participant said to him, "You know, I'm really afraid of you." The leader answered, "Good. I want you to be more afraid of me than you are of anything inside yourself. If you can stick it out with me, you can handle anything."

That is part of the dynamic behind this point. Within reason, try to face that which you fear most. This builds your emotional muscles, so to speak. If you're afraid of speaking up in a crowd, for instance, and you can make the decision one time to speak in front of an auditorium-size audience, next week using your full voice to a group of five people will seem like child's play. If you're afraid of saying no to people, and you can muster up the courage to deny the request of the most demanding person you know, then saying no to every other person in your life will be much easier.

Another approach to this point is to place your fears in proper perspective by determining the exact element in an upcoming situation that you fear most, and then comparing it to what will happen if you don't face it. People who are terrified of inoculations, for example, are often most afraid of the image that is wedged in their minds of the glistening point of a needle piercing their bare skin. But the ones who hyperventilate, yet go ahead and endure the experience anyway, can do so because they are able to look ahead to the consequences of *not* getting the shot—they'll contract polio, malaria, or some other heinous disease. They put their immediate fear in perspective by comparing it to the real dangers they face if they avoid what has to be done.

Can you do this with your life? Can you take a hard look at your fear of making significant changes to your lifestyle and then contrast this fear with what it will be like to go through life unfulfilled? Which one, honestly, is the most disastrous and tragic course? To me, nothing stacks up in importance to a life unlived. Once you face up to this level of loss and recognize that it is the worst-case scenario, your fear of change will melt away. When fear melts away, that is what we call courage.

3. Don't Give Up

The only reason to give up a course of action you have sincerely committed to is if unexpected information comes your way that shows you that if you continue, you will harm either yourself or others. That can happen. Other than that, though, it is of critical importance to be fully committed to the task of changing your life—whatever that may mean—and to your personal growth and fulfillment.

If this were easy, more people would be doing it every day. The first obstacle is lack of faith in ourselves. Since the people who make great strides in the world tend to grab the headlines, it is tempting to believe that only special people are capable of this kind of commitment. Only people who have reached CEO status, or who have won the Nobel Prize, or who have a chestful of war medals for bravery, appear to possess the right amount of fortitude to succeed in a quest despite all the difficulties. The rest of us fear that we will buckle under the strain. The reason is that most of us have witnessed ourselves time and again decide upon a plan of action and then abandon it, either because it proves difficult or because we simply lose interest. Unfortunately, this has created an internal picture of ourselves as weak-willed and irresolute, and that identity determines the kind of risk we will take and how much we will commit to carrying it out. But although buckling under might have been true of us in the past, it does not have to hold true for our future. It doesn't take a special kind of person to make a commitment to the realization of his own dreams. It merely takes a recognition of how genuinely important it is to do so. Once you sincerely and heartily acknowledge the significance of the change, you may find that it is hard *not* to do it. To paraphrase a line from a movie I saw recently, "It's not hard to do the right thing. It's hard to know what the right thing is. Once you know it, it's hard not to do it."

A second obstacle is the frustration and anxiety we have to endure when our objectives either are not reached immediately or are not on schedule. Some people think that if they were really meant to achieve a certain goal, it would come easily. Nothing could be further from the truth. Much of what is worthwhile in life has to be fought for, and the battles can be long and difficult. Of course, this doesn't mean you should trap yourself in chasing a dream that is utterly elusive and that you don't have the capacity to achieve. Someone may want desperately to be an opera singer, for example, but simply not have the God-given voice. (Some people will actually choose an impossible goal so that they can rationalize their failure.) As a good friend in the publishing business says: Keep your hopes high and your expectations realistic. If you are enduring too much failure in your quest, it will bear stopping and evaluating whether you're on the right track. Perhaps there is a better and more approachable way to pursue your dream. Perhaps there is another dream that should be pursued. You might also consider the fact that when you first began your quest, you were possibly much younger. You might have had different needs then, a different idea of what made life worthwhile. As we mature, our dreams mature with us. That is another reason for stopping from time to time to re-evaluate which goals are worth pursuing.

A third obstacle to staying the course has been mentioned many times in this book, but it bears repeating. External influences will sometimes work against you. Your own internal resolve must stand up to these if you want to succeed.

THE FEAR OF FOLLY ▼

Some people are paralyzed by the thought, "What if I make my dream a reality and it was the wrong dream?" This is an almost unthinkable scenario. The person has overcome all these challenges, taken the big risks, uprooted herself in significant ways and created an entirely new lifestyle, which then fails to provide the satisfaction upon which she has pinned her hopes. She finally works up the courage to bail out of a loveless marriage and then finds a new set of problems to cope with in single life. She moves to a small town in Minnesota, but she doesn't feel at home there after all. He quits his job with an international conglomerate to work for a small start-up and it goes belly-up the first year.

If any of these things happened to you, would you feel like a fool? Would you think you should have stayed put and never made any changes at all? If so, you would be wrong. Many people refuse to pursue their dream on the chance that they may be wrong about what they want, or because they might not be able to make the new lifestyle work. So they do nothing. They tread water and try not to drown in the sameness of daily life. Realistically, things could go wrong, not once but several times. It did to me. I had to stab around for a while before I found my successful lifestyle. But I am living proof that the operative word is *perseverance*. I just kept going until I was happy with what I found.

Whenever you take a risk, nobody can guarantee that it will work out according to your predictions and specifications. (But of course, even if you stay where you are, no one can guarantee that life will work out either.) You may have to try out numerous scenarios and variations on scenarios before you strike gold. Failure, however, does not mean you should stop trying. Quite the contrary, it means you should learn from your mistake and try again, this time armed with better information. Failure, as I've said, is a catalyst for success.

When and if you do fail, it is one of those times when you must resist the advice of all those people who play it safe and who did not support your endeavors to follow your dream in the first place. They will use the fact that things didn't work out as an opportunity to say, "I told you so." Don't listen to them. It is difficult, but you must keep your own counsel and continue to trust your gut. If you don't succeed at first, do not lose faith in the process. Change, especially significant change, doesn't necessarily come easily. The important thing is to trust in the notion that you have a right to fight for your own happiness, to stick your neck out and make your own mistakes, to fall on your face and get back up again, to take charge of your own life. You are not a failure for failing; you are brave to have tried.

Having said that, for certain kinds of changes there are ways to minimize the risk of failure. You can put your big toe in the water without diving in. First of all, make sure that the goal you are pursuing is real and deep, not just a whim. To accomplish this, you need to do some soul-searching. How does this goal sit with your gut? Is this change something that will bring lasting fulfillment or is it a temporary fix? Let's face it, not everything we crave speaks to our heart's true desire.

Next, measure your decisions carefully. How can you take small and sensible steps to achieve your goal? How can you check out ahead of time what the consequences of your choices are likely to be? Before you quit your old job and give up your paycheck for a new career, talk to people ensconced in that career and pick their minds for details. If you want to be a criminal lawyer, sit in on a few trials first. If you want to take up an expensive new pastime like scuba diving, don't buy equipment, rent it. You can avoid a costly investment that may or may not pay off. If you have a burning desire to move to Kenya, visit the place first. Go on a safari, look at farms, take in the local color. If you think you're in love with someone you've just met, don't give up your highly desirable rent-controlled apartment and move into his place within the first month. There is something to be said for dating.

In other words, there are ways to take risks without being reckless. Only you can decide what the best course is for you.

THE EXISTENTIAL ORGASM ▼

What does it feel like to "arrive," to finally know that your life is where it should be?

Recently, as I was on my way to give a speech to a large group of executives about the meaning of success, my consciousness was suddenly overwhelmed by an incredible rush of emotions. They stemmed from the realization that I was about to be paid handsomely for speaking on a subject I was passionate about. How could I be so lucky? I can articulate my sum total of feelings in that moment with one statement: "It feels good to be alive!"

This peak experience, which descends upon me from time to time, I call an *existential orgasm*. I never know when I will be blessed by it because it occurs in the most unanticipated of places. One glorious afternoon I was sipping a glass of wine at an outdoor café in Paris. For no apparent reason, I suddenly had an urge to climb up on the table and begin jumping for joy. During a game of handball at a gym near my home, my body unexpectedly took over the match. I could do no wrong. There was an indescribably pleasant sensation in my chest, and I had the sense that I could go so far as to take off and fly if I put my mind to it. The qualities of expansiveness, limitlessness, euphoria, and fearlessness were all rolled into one. Professional athletes call that being "in the zone." Joseph Campbell recalled a similar peak experience that he enjoyed once when he was competing in a college track meet. He simply knew that he could not lose the race, and he later described it as a moment of rapture. It was, he said, the closest he ever came to the experience of being a saint.

These existential orgasms, these few moments of rapture, are windows into the essence of life. Along my way, they have made all the struggles and pain I have gone through seem worthwhile. But great moments are not won by the faint of heart. If you can summon the courage and fortitude to honor your own uniqueness, the prize is waiting for you. You have then earned the right to say, "I have lived my life consciously." Existential orgasms are the payoff for mustering up the courage to be a success on your own terms. That brief moment of rapture, which is the acknowledgment from your body that you have followed your bliss, completes the circle that began when you created your own definition of success and stuck with it.

BIBLIOGRAPHY

CHAPTER 1: IF I'M SO SUCCESSFUL, WHY AM I TAKING PROZAC?

Campbell, Joseph. *The Hero with a Thousand Faces.* Princeton: Princeton University Press, 1972.
———. *The Power of Myth.* New York: Doubleday, 1988.
Faludi, Susan. *Stiffed.* New York: HarperPerennial, 2000.
Freudenberger, Herbert. *Burn Out.* New York: Bantam, 1981.
Hill, Napoleon. *Think and Grow Rich.* New York: Fawcett Books, 1990.
Miller, Arthur. *Death of a Salesman.* New York: Penguin, 1998.
Terhorst, Paul. *Cashing In on the American Dream.* New York: Bantam, 1988.

CHAPTER 3: LESSONS FROM AN UNSEDUCED MAVERICK

Brodow, Ed. *Negotiate with Confidence.* West Des Moines: American Media, 1996.
Dalai Lama. *The Art of Happiness.* New York: Riverhead Books, 1998.
Terhorst, Paul. *Cashing In on the American Dream.* New York: Bantam, 1988.
Vonnegut, Kurt. *Timequake.* New York: Berkley Books, 1998.
Wilson, Sloan. *The Man in the Gray Flannel Suit.* New York: Dell, 1966.

CHAPTER 4: DISCOVERING THE *YOU* IN YOU

Charles, C. Leslie. *Why Is Everyone So Cranky?* New York: Hyperion, 1999.
De Becker, Gavin. *The Gift of Fear*. New York: Dell, 1997.
Goleman, Daniel. *Emotional Intelligence*. New York: Bantam, 1995.
Ishac, Allan. *New York's 50 Best Places to Find Peace & Quiet*. New York: Universe Books, 2003.
Miller, Alice. *The Drama of the Gifted Child*. New York: Basic Books, 1981.
Miller, Arthur. *Death of a Salesman*. New York: Penguin, 1998.
Peck, M. Scott. *The Road Less Traveled*. New York: Touchstone, 1978.

CHAPTER 5: TAPPING INTO YOUR GUT

Charles, C. Leslie. *Why Is Everyone So Cranky?* New York: Hyperion, 1999.
Peck, M. Scott. *The Road Less Traveled*. New York: Touchstone, 1978.
Taylor, Jeremy. *Where People Fly and Water Runs Uphill*. New York: Warner Books, 1992.

CHAPTER 6: ABUSE WILL NOT MAKE YOU SUCCESSFUL

Bradshaw, John. *Healing the Shame that Binds You*. Deerfield Beach: Health Communications, 1988.
Golding, William. *Lord of the Flies*. New York: Perigee, 1959.
Miller, Alice. *Banished Knowledge*. New York: Anchor Books, 1990.
———. *For Your Own Good*. New York: Noonday Press, 1990.
Miller, Arthur. *Death of a Salesman*. New York: Penguin, 1998.

CHAPTER 7: A NEW PERSPECTIVE ON FAILURE

Campbell, Joseph. *The Hero's Journey*. Boston: Element Books, 1999.

CHAPTER 9: THE VICTIM MENTALITY

Bradshaw, John. *Healing the Shame that Binds You*. Deerfield Beach: Health Communications, 1988.

Cousins, Norman. *Anatomy of an Illness*. New York: Bantam, 1991.

Frankl, Viktor E. *Man's Search for Meaning*. New York: Washington Square Press, 1985.

Miller, Alice. *For Your Own Good*. New York: Noonday Press, 1990.

CHAPTER 10: THE CONFIDENCE MYSTIQUE

Covey, Stephen. *The Seven Habits of Highly Effective People*. New York: Fireside, 1990.

CHAPTER 11: YOUR MONEY OR YOUR LIFESTYLE?

Bieler, Henry. *Food Is Your Best Medicine*. New York: Ballantine, 1987.

Brando, Marlon. *Brando*. New York: Random House, 1994.

Buckingham, Marcus and Donald Clifton. *Now, Discover Your Strengths*. New York: Free Press, 2001.

Campbell, Joseph. *The Power of Myth*. New York: Doubleday, 1988.

Goleman, Daniel. *Emotional Intelligence*. New York: Bantam, 1995.

Harrison, Jim. *Legends of the Fall: The Man Who Gave Up His Name*. New York: Dell, 1981.

Miller, Arthur. *Death of a Salesman*. New York: Penguin, 1998.

Stone, Irving. *Lust for Life*. New York: New American Library, 1989.

Terhorst, Paul. *Cashing In on the American Dream*. New York: Bantam, 1988.

CHAPTER 12: FOUR STEPS TO PERSONAL FULFILLMENT

Buckingham, Marcus and Donald Clifton. *Now, Discover Your Strengths*. New York: Free Press, 2001.

Stanley, Thomas and William Danko. *The Millionaire Next Door*. New York: Pocket Books, 1998.

RECOMMENDED READING

Bieler, Henry. *Food Is Your Best Medicine*. New York: Ballantine, 1987.

Bradshaw, John. *Bradshaw on the Family*. Deerfield Beach: Health Communications, 1988.

———. *Healing the Shame that Binds You*. Deerfield Beach: Health Communications, 1988.

Brodow, Ed. *Negotiate with Confidence*. West Des Moines: American Media, 1996.

Bronowski, J. *The Ascent of Man*. Boston: Back Bay Books, 1973.

Buckingham, Marcus and Donald Clifton. *Now, Discover Your Strengths*. New York: Free Press, 2001.

Campbell, Joseph. *The Hero with a Thousand Faces*. Princeton: Princeton University Press, 1972.

———. *The Hero's Journey*. Boston: Element Books, 1999.

———. *The Power of Myth*. New York: Doubleday, 1988.

Charles, C. Leslie. *Why Is Everyone So Cranky?* New York: Hyperion, 1999.

Cousins, Norman. *Anatomy of an Illness*. New York: Bantam, 1991.

Covey, Stephen. *The Seven Habits of Highly Effective People*. New York: Fireside, 1990.

Frankl, Viktor E. *Man's Search for Meaning*. New York: Washington Square Press, 1985.

Freudenberger, Herbert. *Burn Out*. New York: Bantam, 1981.

Goleman, Daniel. *Emotional Intelligence*. New York: Bantam, 1995.

Harrison, Jim. *Legends of the Fall: The Man Who Gave Up His Name*. New York: Dell, 1981.

Miller, Alice. *Banished Knowledge*. New York: Anchor Books, 1990.

———. *The Drama of the Gifted Child*. New York: Basic Books, 1981.

———. *For Your Own Good*. New York: Noonday Press, 1990.

Miller, Arthur. *Death of a Salesman*. New York: Penguin, 1998.

Peck, M. Scott. *The Road Less Traveled*. New York: Touchstone, 1978.

Siebert, Al. *The Survivor Personality*. New York: Perigee, 1996.

Stanley, Thomas and William Danko. *The Millionaire Next Door*. New York: Pocket Books, 1998.

Taylor, Jeremy. *Where People Fly and Water Runs Uphill*. New York: Warner Books, 1992.

Terhorst, Paul. *Cashing In on the American Dream*. New York: Bantam, 1988.

Vonnegut, Kurt. *Timequake*. New York: Berkley Books, 1998.

Wilson, Sloan. *The Man in the Gray Flannel Suit*. New York: Dell, 1966.

ACKNOWLEDGMENTS

My incomparable agent and fellow Brooklyn College alumnus, Ellen Levine, has been everything a literary agent ought to be: passionate about my project, supportive when I needed support, and a master of the intricate doings of the publishing world. They don't come any better. After twelve years in show business, it is refreshing to feel this way about an agent!

At HarperCollins: Cosmic gratitude to Diane Reverand for believing in my book and to Megan Newman for catching the pass and following through. My charming editor, Kelli Martin, has my gratitude for her keen eye and for solving the structural problem that almost got away.

Susan Page, author of seven books including *The Shortest Distance Between You and a Published Book*, is my literary mentor. Her advice and encouragement have been invaluable. A truly generous, affection-based person, Susan also introduced me to Amanita.

Amanita Rosenbush (bookdok@earthlink.net) is my secret weapon. As "book doctor," she walked me step by step through the entire process and transformed an overwhelming monster into a manageable project. She was a genius at squeezing the material out of me. Working with her was like getting an advanced degree in writing.

My professional-speaker support group—Mark Oman, Alan Ovson, and Gary Purece—encouraged me to incorporate more personal experiences into my speaking and writing. I remember their reaction when I told them some of my life stories: "You've got to share that material!" Thanks to these generous, talented guys, the book I thought I was writing about business negotiation skills turned out to be something much more meaningful.

Robert Luthardt, Ph.D., my business and personal adviser for close to twenty years, had an enormous influence on many of the ideas in this book. Dr. Bob's concepts of abuse-based and affection-based thinking have played an important role not only in the book but also in my life.

Thanks to Lynn Goldberg of Goldberg, McDuffie, an old friend who popped up at a propitious moment, for her advice and encouragement. Ditto to Marty Feinberg Katz, my producer at PBS The Business Channel, and to generous friends and colleagues: Fred Berke, Marjorie Brody, Leslie Charles, Ed Collins, Godfrey Daniel, Jeffrey Gitomer, Ivy Helstein, Sam Hessel, Sam Horn, Gregg Stebben, Cara Wilson, and Barry Wishner.

And finally, to my valiant buddies in green for whom the run of the play was prematurely cut short in Southeast Asia, thanks for inspiring one lucky survivor's personal journey. See you in Valhalla. *Semper fi!*

ABOUT THE AUTHOR ▼

Author photograph ©2003 Gregg Wutke

Ed Brodow was raised in Brooklyn by well-meaning parents who expected him to realize the American Dream by becoming a successful attorney. Showing much better judgment, he succeeded instead in getting himself thrown out of law school and enlisted in the Marine Corps, where, despite his overtly insubordinate nature, he was commissioned as a lieutenant during the height of the Vietnam War. Miraculously avoiding harm's way, Ed landed back in New York City, where he sold computers for IBM and Litton Industries.

Throwing away a promising career in the corporate world (it promised to drive him crazy), Ed decided at the age of thirty to become a professional actor. Within a year, although he had never set foot on a stage before, he won the lead in a European feature film (*Jackpot*). He spent the next decade appearing in movies and television opposite Jessica Lange (*Frances*), Ron Howard (*Fire on the Mountain*), Christopher Reeve (*Love of Life*), and other Hollywood luminaries.

Tiring of the show business rat race, Ed leveraged his business and acting talents to become a motivational speaker and author specializing in the art of negotiation. Today, he is CEO of Ed Brodow Seminars, Inc., and author of *Negotiate with Confidence*. His Negotiation Boot Camp™ Seminars and Success Keynotes have attracted an impressive client list that includes American Express, Baker Hughes, Cisco Systems, The Gap, Goldman Sachs, The Hartford, Hyatt Hotels, IBM, Kimberly-Clark, Learjet,

Microsoft, Mobil Oil, the Pentagon, Philip Morris, Raytheon, Sun Microsystems, TRW, and Zurich Insurance.

As a television personality, Ed hosted his own two-hour special on PBS The Business Channel and has been featured as negotiation guru on Fox News, *Inside Edition*, and KRON-TV4 in San Francisco. His ideas on negotiation and success have been showcased in the *Washington Post*, *Entrepreneur* magazine, *Smart Money*, *Men's Health*, *Professional Speaker*, and *Selling Power*.

Ed lives on the Monterey Peninsula in Northern California with his giant-bird-of-paradise plant, Bubba. An accomplished baritone, he performs occasional vocal recitals, loves traveling in Europe, and manages to play a little handball now and then.

To book Ed Brodow as the speaker at your meeting or convention:
ed@brodow.com
www.brodow.com